This is an excellent book and a must-read for researchers interested in understanding and enhancing the new discipline of biodiversity valuation. The author provides a conceptual framework which re-organises current thinking and knowledge from economics and ecology to promote a renewed endeavour to reveal and measure the true value of biodiversity in a changing and uncertain world.

Douglas C. MacMillan, *Professor of Environmental and Ecosystem Economics at the School of Anthropology & Conservation, University of Kent, UK*

For those wishing to 'value biodiversity', this book gives an excellent review of the feasibility and appropriateness of monetary valuation. Bartkowski challenges conventional economic theory, provides alternative perspectives on valuation and rationality, and highlights that valuation processes must recognise the abstract, uncertain links between biodiversity and wellbeing.

Marije Schaafsma, *Senior Research Fellow in Geography and Environment, University of Southampton, UK*

In this timely and thought-provoking contribution, Bartkowski explores the complexity of the economic, ecological and philosophical dimensions of a ubiquitous but under-theorized topic: the economic valuation of biodiversity. This book is bound to become a must-read and to launch debates in the three disciplines that it contributes to renew.

Yves Meinard, *Researcher at Université Paris-Dauphine, PSL Research University, CNRS, UMR [7243], LAMSADE, France*

Economic Valuation of Biodiversity

While biodiversity loss is an ecological phenomenon, it also has further dimensions – political, social and, last but not least, economic. From the economic perspective, the rapid loss of biological diversity can be viewed in two ways. First, the consequence of this deterioration process is a loss of options and an increase in scarcity of the environmental 'good', biodiversity. Second, economic activity and the structure of global and local economic institutions have frequently been identified as the major drivers of biodiversity loss. In economic terms, this constitutes a market failure – market-based economic activities lead to processes which undermine the long-term stability of these very activities.

This book provides an ecological economic perspective on the value of diversity in ecosystems. Combining insights from various sub-disciplines of ecology and environmental/ecological economics, the author constructs a conceptual framework which identifies the ways in which biodiversity influences human well-being and offers a novel, unifying perspective on the economic value of biodiversity.

This framework demonstrates that biodiversity's economic value mainly results from uncertainty about the future, regarding both supply of and demand for ecosystem services, and interconnections between ecosystems. The book goes on to identify suitable methods for economic valuation of biodiversity and discusses the currently underdeveloped and underused approach of deliberative monetary valuation.

Combining a strong theoretical framework with practical examples, this book will be of great interest to students and researchers of ecological economics, ecosystem services, environmental values and environmental and resource economics.

Bartosz Bartkowski works at the Department of Economics of the Helmholtz Centre for Environmental Research (UFZ) in Leipzig, Germany. He has a PhD in economics from Martin Luther University Halle-Wittenberg in Germany. His research interests span environmental and agricultural economics, environmental ethics and sustainability science.

Routledge Studies in Biodiversity Politics and Management

Economic Valuation of Biodiversity

An Interdisciplinary Conceptual Perspective

Bartosz Bartkowski

Routledge
Taylor & Francis Group

LONDON AND NEW YORK

from Routledge

First published 2017
by Routledge

2 Park Square, Milton Park, Abingdon, Oxfordshire OX14 4RN
52 Vanderbilt Avenue, New York, NY 10017

Routledge is an imprint of the Taylor & Francis Group, an informa business

First issued in paperback 2018

British Library Cataloguing in Publication Data
A catalogue record for this book is available from the British Library

Library of Congress Cataloging in Publication Data
A catalog record for this book has been requested

ISBN: 978-1-138-03936-0 (hbk)
ISBN: 978-0-367-15238-3 (pbk)

Typeset in Times New Roman
by Wearset Ltd, Boldon, Tyne and Wear

Contents

Acknowledgements

The book you are holding in your hands is the effect of some three years' intensive work (2013–2016). It is based on my PhD thesis, submitted in July 2016 at the Martin Luther University Halle-Wittenberg, Germany. I had the great opportunity to work on both the thesis and the resulting book at the Department of Economics of the Helmholtz Centre for Environmental Research (UFZ) in Leipzig, Germany, as a fellow of the Helmholtz Research School ESCALATE (Ecosystem Services under Changing Land-Use and Climate). Looking at the front cover you see my name only – but the creation of such a fully fledged contribution does not happen in an intellectual or social vacuum. So while this contribution is mine and I am responsible for all the good and (especially) bad things about it, I owe a lot to a lot of people. Their help, support and encouragement were essential to make this book happen; they deserve to be acknowledged for this.

For starters, I was very lucky when it comes to supervisors. Professor Bernd Hansjürgens, the primary supervisor of my thesis, had already supervised my Master's dissertation and in 2013 gave me the opportunity to try out real scientific work, which I am extremely thankful for; I also very much appreciate the freedom and trust he offered me. Nele Lienhoop, my de facto primary supervisor, a great colleague and collaborator on numerous papers, deserves an even more emphatic 'thank you!' She has been a mentor to me, but at the same time we have been equals; our relationship has been founded upon mutual respect. I could hardly imagine a better supervisor and colleague.

A number of people have read and commented on various parts of this book at various stages of the writing process. In addition to my above-mentioned supervisors, these include (in chronological order): Professors Ralf Seppelt, Helge Bruelheide and Kurt Jax, Nils Droste, Marc Völker and Professor Marlies Ahlert. I am particularly thankful to them because they had no obligation whatsoever to read my then still half-baked work. Their comments helped significantly improve some parts of what has become the book you are holding in your hands. Similarly, the four anonymous reviewers Routledge asked to take a look at my book proposal made some very helpful remarks which led to changes in focus as compared to my PhD thesis. Other people didn't read anything that has become part of this book, but still they discussed with me ideas directly or indirectly related to its topics. Among those, Yves Meinard, Keith Farnsworth, Katie McShane and Jess Goddard deserve being explicitly mentioned. Also, multiple colloquia at the UFZ's Department of Economics provided me with a number of opportunities to test my ideas 'in the battleground'. I learned a lot from these discussions, which forced me, among other things, to make my ideas clearer and more concise. I would like especially to acknowledge comments I got from Professors Erik Gawel and Bernd Klauer as well as from Johannes Schiller – they made me (intellectually) sweat most, in a very productive way.

Sometimes it is much easier to ask someone experienced in a field instead of digging into it yourself. I did this many times and thus benefited from the expertise of others. Nele Lienhoop, Marc Völker and Elisabeth Kindler were particularly helpful on numerous occasions.

But working in science is not only about working in science. Thus, a few rather personal thank yous are in order. In the three years I spent in the dungeons of the UFZ (before moving only recently into a light-filled office above ground), I had two loyal and cheerful companions, Sophie and Christine. Special thanks go to Sophie, who has become a friend for life (I hope) and, on top of that, supported me logistically and psychologically when I conducted my challenging case study (reported in Chapter 5). Also, she introduced me (inadvertently) to the dehesas, which have become my favourite example of biodiversity's spillover value. I also would like to thank Marc Völker, Sebastian Strunz, Harry Schindler, Nils Droste, Nadine Pannicke, Wolfgang Bretschneider and many other colleagues from the Social Sciences Division of the UFZ, with whom I have had innumerable discussions on topics as diverse as *Game of Thrones*, jazz, the NBA and degrowth.

Last but not least, I would like to thank my family, whom I owe everything not mentioned yet and much more.

1   Introduction

Biodiversity is difficult to define. It is likewise difficult to succinctly describe its
role in supporting human activities, but its importance is nonetheless real.

(Heal, 2000, p. 87)

Ecologists and ecological economists have stressed that biodiversity has an
important value in so far as it is instrumental for ecosystem functioning and ecosystems' capability of providing essential life-supporting ecosystem services for
humankind.

(Baumgärtner et al., 2006, p. 492)

Biodiversity loss and economic valuation

Hardly any term, besides possibly *sustainability*, has become so popular in
environmental discourses in so short a time as did *biodiversity*. Coined in 1985
and presented to the general public three years later (Wilson, 1988), already by
1994 it was identified as having experienced a 'dramatic' and 'explosive' growth
in popularity (Harper and Hawksworth, 1994). Indeed, as early as 1992 the Convention on Biological Diversity (CBD) was a major result of the Rio Earth
Summit. One consequence of the CBD is the periodic publication of the highly
influential Global Biodiversity Outlooks. In recent years, the Millennium Ecosystem Assessment (MEA), published in 2005,[1] the launch of the TEEB (The
Economics of Ecosystems and Biodiversity) process in 2008 and IPBES (Inter-
governmental Science-Policy Platform on Biodiversity and Ecosystem Services)
in 2012 have been signs that the growth in interest and popularity of the biodiversity concept is not decreasing. One reason for this is that this concept helps
to frame some of the most important environmental problems of today (Meinard
et al., 2014; Meinard and Quétier, 2014). Consequently, since its introduction
the biodiversity concept has engaged scholars from numerous disciplines and the
number of related publications has skyrocketed (Figure 1.1).

Different disciplines focus on different aspects of biodiversity. Yet most of them
are interested in assessing the causes, rapidity and consequences of biodiversity

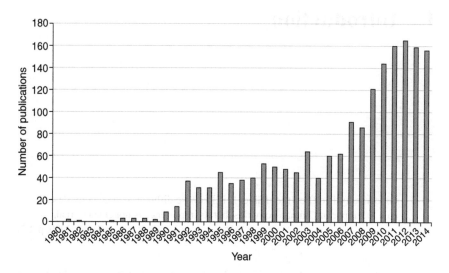

Figure 1.1 Growth in the number of biodiversity publications.

Note
Based on a title search for 'biodiversity' or 'biological diversity' in the Web of Science database on 20 March 2015; bars indicate the number of matching publications in a given year.

loss. In 2009 a multidisciplinary group of experts led by Johan Rockström of the Stockholm Resilience Centre published an influential report in which they presented the concept of 'planetary boundaries' (Rockström et al., 2009; Steffen et al., 2015). They identified key ecological processes at the global level which humanity is highly dependent on, and made an attempt at quantifying and assessing them against a 'safe operating space', a set of limits whose transgression is considered dangerous for the long-term survival of humanity. They came to the conclusion that three out of the nine planetary boundaries identified have already been trespassed, the most severe trespass being that of the biodiversity boundary, as indicated by the current rates of biodiversity loss, which are estimated to be 100–1,000 times as high as the fossil record (Barnosky et al., 2011; Cafaro, 2015; McCallum, 2015).[2] In fact, the unprecedented rates of biodiversity loss are one reason why many commentators speak of a new 'geological era', the *Anthropocene* (Crutzen, 2002; Lewis and Maslin, 2015; Steffen et al., 2011), characterised by the heavy influence of humanity on many essential Earth processes. Accordingly, it was observed that 'The context in which biodiversity conservation strategies are currently being developed is not, of course, the time behaviour of untouched natural systems, it is the time behaviour of jointly determined ecological-economic systems' (Perrings et al., 1995, p. 72). Thus, while biodiversity loss certainly is an ecological phenomenon, it also has further dimensions – political, social and, last but not least, economic. From the economic perspective, the rapid loss of biological diversity can be viewed in two ways. First, the consequence of this deterioration process is a loss of options and an increase in scarcity of the environmental good biodiversity. It has been argued that 'future losses of biodiversity and ecosystems may significantly reduce the productivity of our economic systems' (Helm and Hepburn, 2014, p. 7). Second, economic activity and the structure of global and local economic institutions have frequently been identified as the major drivers of biodiversity loss (Dasgupta and Ehrlich, 2013; Pereira et al., 2012). In economic terms, this constitutes a market failure – market-based economic activities lead to processes which undermine the long-term stability of these very activities.

For this massive market failure to be corrected, many approaches are possible. The classic environmentalist movement and scientists associated with it have used mainly moral arguments to convince the public that by destroying the environment we are effectively harming ourselves (McCauley, 2006). Also, it is often thought that the sustainability[3] goal can only be achieved through a dramatic institutional and cultural transformation of modern societies (cf. Kallis et al., 2012). However, appeals to morals and attempts to radically transform society have not been successful so far and are unlikely to be so in the near future (Jakob and Edenhofer, 2014; van den Bergh, 2011). Also, it has been repeatedly recognised that there exist trade-offs between (short-term) human well-being and the preservation of natural ecosystems (McShane et al., 2011; Raudsepp-Hearne et al., 2010).

Until another 'Great Transformation' can be initiated, society should be able to deal with environmental problems within the institutional framework of today, shaping it gradually. For instance, it appears essential to make clear the meaning of ecosystem change for human well-being in such a way that it would influence individual and collective decision-making. Also, trade-offs implicit in the relationship between modern societies and the ecosphere have to be made explicit to facilitate rational decision-making and at least correct the market failure referred to above. This can be done by means of economic valuation, which allows one to demonstrate the scarcity of ecosystems and the goods and services they provide as well as 'to unravel the complexities of socio-ecological relationships, make explicit how human decisions would affect ecosystem service values, and to express these value changes in units (e.g. monetary) that allow their incorporation in public decision-making processes' (Pascual et al., 2010, p. 190). Above all, it is a potentially highly potent source of information. Despite being quite controversial (some of the controversies will be discussed in the present book) and even though it exhibits limitations (e.g. Hansjürgens and Lienhoop, 2015; Wegner and Pascual, 2011), when applied properly, economic valuation has the potential to play 'a major role [...] in stemming the rising tide of degradation of ecosystems and the loss of biodiversity' (Sukhdev et al., 2014, p. 136).

This book is concerned with the economic value of biodiversity.

Motivation and structure of the book

As this is supposed to be a scientific book, the reader can expect a number of things: first, there should be a clear research gap that is supposed to be closed;

second, the approach and methods to be used in closing it should be transparent; third, the book should have a clear and concise structure that allows the closing of the research gap. In what follows, these issues will be briefly discussed.

Research gap

In the introductory section above, a link was identified between biodiversity and economic valuation: biodiversity can be and often is viewed as an environmental good. Like most environmental goods, however, it is not traded in markets and therefore has no price. Yet prices are important providers of information about the relative scarcity of goods. This insight is the main motivation for economic valuation of environmental goods – it is hoped that *shadow prices*[4] of these goods can be used to inform decision-making at various levels.

The problem and starting point of the present book is that 'there is certainly not yet an established framework for valuing biological variety' (Nijkamp et al., 2008, p. 218), a conclusion which, almost 10 years later, still seems to be an adequate description of reality. In fact, in Chapter 4 it will be shown that the situation in the field of the economic valuation of biodiversity is almost as precarious as it was when Nijkamp and colleagues reached their above-quoted conclusion.

But why is this a problem? Obviously, as will be shown in Chapter 4, the lack of a biodiversity-specific valuation framework has not prevented economists from making attempts at estimating the economic value of biodiversity. However, the lack of a consistent, established framework has two negative consequences: first, many approaches chosen by those wanting to estimate biodiversity's economic value are deficient: they do not really provide the information they are supposed to provide. If we want to know the price of bread, it is unhelpful if the number we find under this heading is actually the price of rye flour or the running costs of the bakery shop. The same holds analogously for biodiversity. But while it is relatively straightforward to estimate the price of bread, it is anything but simple to estimate the shadow price of biodiversity. Second, and this is even more problematic from the perspective of information provision, the approaches chosen to date in biodiversity valuation studies are inconsistent and incomparable. Which estimate, which study should one choose if the goal is to inform a decision-making process? The overarching aim of this book, as indicated in its title, is thus to develop an interdisciplinary conceptual perspective on the economic valuation of biodiversity.

An important preliminary question that should be asked to clearly identify the research gap that is to be closed by the present book is: what is already there and what is missing? Many approaches, arguments and ideas regarding the economic value of biodiversity and its estimation are available. There is no need to reinvent the wheel here. What is needed, though, is conceptual clarity, consistency and comprehensiveness. Which of these many approaches and ideas do actually hit the target, i.e. capture (parts of) biodiversity? In other words, which are relevant? And how do they interact, do they overlap or are there gaps between them? How do they fit together? What is missing is a consistent, unifying conceptual framework which would filter, adapt, extend (where necessary) and pull together the scattered approaches, arguments and ideas developed to date in the context of the economic valuation of biodiversity. Such a framework will be offered in this book.

One of the main reasons for the currently precarious state of biodiversity valuation research is probably the fact that biodiversity is a highly abstract, complex concept, which has ensued a *terminological chaos* of sorts. While biodiversity has been analysed from many different vantage points, including many related to the topic of economic valuation and relevant to it, there have been very few attempts to consistently connect the insights from these analyses. Thus, one aim of the present book is to clarify what biodiversity is and what it 'does'. It is essential to have a clear view about what the valuation object is before one can identify why it is valuable and how its value can be estimated properly. This is, in fact, a major problem of biodiversity valuation studies to date: as criticised by Pearce (2001, p. 27), and confirmed by the literature review reported in Chapter 4, '[i]f we look at the literature on the economic valuation of "biodiversity" much of it is actually about the value of biological resources and is linked only tenuously to the value of diversity'.

The lack of a coherent conceptual framework for the economic valuation of biodiversity has serious repercussions for valuation practice. First, it is not clear why biodiversity is actually valuable. What useful properties or functions does it have that influence human well-being (positively or negatively)? Also, there are many different valuation methods which are variously useful in different contexts. The question is then: is there a method or a class of methods that is particularly well-suited for the estimation of the economic value of biodiversity? As this question cannot be answered without first clarifying (i) what biodiversity is and (ii) why and how it is valuable, it constitutes an essential part of the research gap that is to be closed in this book.

Prima facie, it would seem that there are already publications which fill the gap(s) identified here. Two of them should be especially mentioned to show how they are different from the present volume. Nunes et al. (2003; see also Nunes and van den Bergh, 2001) offer an ecological economics perspective on biodiversity, a large part of which focuses on valuation. However, while very informative in many respects, their overview suffers (against the background of the research questions listed above) from a very broad understanding of 'biodiversity', which allows them to discuss its economic value in terms of the provision of ecosystem services, habitats etc. It will be argued here that these are not parts of biodiversity. Nonetheless, those aspects of their book that are really biodiversity-specific will be considered in the discussion in Chapter 4. The other important overview is the first report of the international TEEB initiative on *Ecological and Economic Foundations* (Kumar, 2010). Here, however, the focus is even broader and while many of the threads discussed in the present book can be found there, they are scattered and lack a consistent unifying perspective. Such a perspective will be unfolded in this book.

To sum up, the research gap which has motivated the development of the present book consists in the lack of a consistent conceptual framework for the economic valuation of biodiversity. Such a framework is necessary if economic valuation studies of biodiversity are to provide relevant and meaningful information.

Approach and methods

As the title of the book suggests, its starting point is economic theory. This has much to do with the author's education. However, the idea is to enrich the economic perspective by insights from other disciplines, particularly ecology and environmental ethics. Thus, if one would want to pigeonhole the book's approach, ecological economics would be the most obvious tag. Nonetheless, the book is certainly exposed to criticism for not fundamentally questioning the more-or-less conventional economic approach to value and valuation. While the author is aware that there are serious points of criticism (some of them are mentioned in various parts of the book), the working assumption from which the book's argument unfolds is that economic valuation has, on the whole, more advantages than downsides. This should be kept in mind by the reader.

To answer all the questions suggested above, a number of steps have to be made, many of them iteratively. First of all, it is necessary to investigate the relevant bodies of literature. As this book is about the *economic valuation* of *biodiversity*, there are two large bodies of literature to be critically reviewed. First, the economics literature: welfare economic foundations of economic valuation, the relevant concepts of total economic value (TEV) and ecosystem services (ESS) and valuation methodology. Second, the ecological literature: definition(s) of biodiversity, its ecological importance (particularly, the so-called biodiversity–ecosystem functioning (BEF) literature). In addition, as already suggested above, it is important to analyse environmental ethics' answers to questions regarding biodiversity value. When an overview about the issue is achieved, it is time to look at how economists deal with the valuation object biodiversity, both from a theoretical perspective and in valuation studies. Based on the insights gained from the three large bodies of literature surveyed beforehand, it will be possible to assess the merits and limitations of the various approaches advanced by economists in the context of the economic valuation of biodiversity.

Provided that the extensive literature survey(s) will reveal that Nijkamp et al. (2008) were right in complaining that biodiversity as an object of economic valuation is understudied and underdeveloped, the next logical step will be to develop a framework for economic valuation of this special environmental good. Such a framework is necessary as a basis for future biodiversity valuation studies for three interrelated reasons: first, economic valuation is a means of providing information about environmental goods; to be meaningful, this information must 'hit the target', i.e. be clearly related to this specific environmental good. This also ensures, second, that the results of different valuation studies of biodiversity are comparable and consistent with each other. Third, such a demanding environmental good as biodiversity might necessitate the application of specific valuation methods and approaches, which can only be identified on the basis of an encompassing conceptual framework.

The core of the framework will be conceptual, but methodological orientation will also be given, because biodiversity seems to necessitate the application of specific valuation approaches (see above). Since their application must be thoroughly justified, there will be a need for another review of literature, this time on particular valuation approaches and methods. Furthermore, to test the framework's compatibility with the preferences of stakeholders in a real-world context, a focus groups-based case study will be presented. This instance of qualitative social research has proven useful in the preparation of many economic valuation studies, and so it appears a sensible approach to verify the conceptual ideas developed in this book. The idea is to show that (i) the sources of the economic value of biodiversity have been properly identified, and (ii) the conceptual arguments can be translated into a language understandable for laypeople, of whom it cannot be expected to read the 180 or so pages that follow.

Structure of the book

The overall structure of the book has already been implicitly suggested in the discussion of the research gap and aims. The book consists of six chapters and an Excursus (including the Introduction). Each chapter begins with a short introduction and ends with a brief summary of the findings. Therefore, it is not necessary to go into the details of the book's structure here. The general outline is as follows:

Chapter 2 is a brief presentation of current approaches, theories and concepts on which economic valuation of environmental goods is based. These include: the welfare economic concepts that underlie economic valuation as well as clarification of some common misunderstandings regarding the latter's scope; the ecosystem services and the total economic value frameworks commonly used for environmental valuation; and an overview about economic valuation methods.

In Chapter 3, the ecological concept of biodiversity is introduced. The many different approaches to its definition are first analysed; biodiversity measuring is briefly discussed; last but not least, biodiversity's ecological value, namely, its influence on ecosystem functioning, is introduced and discussed in some more detail.

The Excursus takes a different perspective and gives a brief overview of the environmental ethics literature related to biodiversity and its value, with a special focus on the question of whether biodiversity can have 'value on its own'.

In Chapter 4, the state of the art in the area of economic valuation of biodiversity is presented. First, a systematic critical review of biodiversity valuation studies is offered. It includes a classification of biodiversity proxies found in the applied literature and a critical assessment of their use. Second, the theoretical and conceptual literature on biodiversity's economic value is analysed. Three issues are particularly in focus: the so-called Noah's Ark problem, the various sources of biodiversity's economic value suggested in the literature, and the relationship between uncertainty and biodiversity value.

The insights provided by Chapter 4 feed into the core part of the present book – the conceptual framework for the economic valuation of biodiversity[5] (Chapter 5). This chapter is divided into two large parts: a conceptual and a methodological one. In the first part, a conceptual framework of biodiversity's economic value is developed. On the basis of an explicitly discussed understanding of biodiversity, it offers a taxonomy of the sources of biodiversity's economic value, which are combined so as to form a coherent conceptual framework. Based on that, the framework's implications for the TEV and ESS frameworks are briefly discussed. Furthermore, to verify the compatibility of the conceptual reasoning developed in Chapter 5 with the preferences of stakeholders in a real-world setting, the results of a focus groups case study are reported.

The methodological part of Chapter 5 first identifies biodiversity-specific challenges facing any application of the previously presented conceptual framework. Starting from this, available valuation methods are analysed so as to identify those that are particularly well-suited for valuing biodiversity. Since deliberative choice experiments, which are identified as particularly promising, are a relatively novel and still developing method, they are discussed in more detail with a focus on their potential to handle the valuation object biodiversity. Also, some suggestions regarding the coupling of the conceptual framework with quantitative data are offered in this chapter.

Chapter 6 summarises the main arguments and results of the book; it discusses the limitations of the book's approach and identifies open questions which it could not answer and which constitute material for future research. It closes with brief final remarks.

Throughout the book, a number of objects are used to make the text more comprehensible and readable. Small side-remarks are put into endnotes. Larger expositions which, however, are rather of secondary importance for the main arguments advanced in the book (for instance, because they are more detailed than absolutely necessary) can be found in boxes. Furthermore, some information, especially quantitative and structuring, is put into figures and tables, for which sources are indicated in the captions. If no source is indicated, the figure/table was created by the author of this book himself.

Notes

1 Already in 1995 the much less influential, even though very similar, Global Biodiversity Assessment was published by the United Nations Environment Programme (UNEP).
2 Since estimates of global species richness remain highly uncertain (Schuldt et al., 2015), there is much debate about the exact extinction rate. This uncertainty does not, however, change the general message regarding the order of magnitude of biodiversity loss.
3 Sustainability or sustainable development is commonly defined in line with the definition by the so-called Brundtland Commission: 'Sustainable development is development that meets the needs of the present without compromising the ability of future generations to meet their own needs' (World Commission on Environment and Development, 1987). For a more recent perspective, see Klauer et al. (2013, under review).

4 A shadow price is the price that a good *would* have if it were traded in a perfect market, i.e. with all externalities internalised and given comprehensive property rights. Another, formally equivalent interpretation is that the shadow price of a good reflects its marginal contribution to social welfare (i.e. a function of individual utilities).

5 As will be argued in the main body of the book, since biodiversity is a property of eco-systems, it is more sensible to speak of its contribution to the economic value of an ecosystem, rather than its economic value as such. Nonetheless, to make the arguments more readable, the phrase 'economic value of biodiversity' will often be used as a surrogate.

References

Barnosky, A.D., Matzke, N., Tomiya, S., Wogan, G.O.U., Swartz, B., Quental, T.B., Marshall, C., McGuire, J.L., Lindsey, E.L., Maguire, K.C., Mersey, B., Ferrer, E.A., 2011. Has the Earth's sixth mass extinction already arrived? Nature 471, 51–57.

Baumgärtner, S., Becker, C., Faber, M., Manstetten, R., 2006. Relative and absolute scarcity of nature: Assessing the roles of economics and ecology for biodiversity conservation. Ecol. Econ. 59, 487–498.

Cafaro, P., 2015. Three ways to think about the sixth mass extinction. Biol. Conserv. 192, 387–393.

Crutzen, P.J., 2002. Geology of mankind. Nature 415, 23.

Dasgupta, P.S., Ehrlich, P.R., 2013. Pervasive externalities at the population, consumption, and environment nexus. Science 340, 324–328.

Hansjürgens, B., Lienhoop, N., 2015. Was uns die Natur wert ist: Potenziale ökonomischer Bewertung. Metropolis, Marburg.

Harper, J.L., Hawksworth, D.L., 1994. Biodiversity: Measurement and estimation. Philos. Trans. R. Soc. Lond. B. Biol. Sci. 345, 5–12.

Heal, G.M., 2000. Nature and the marketplace: Capturing the value of ecosystem services. Island Press, Washington, DC.

Helm, D., Hepburn, C., 2014. The economic analysis of biodiversity. In: Helm, D., Hepburn, C. (Eds), Nature in the balance: The economics of biodiversity. Oxford University Press, New York, pp. 7–32.

Jakob, M., Edenhofer, O., 2014. Green growth, degrowth, and the commons. Oxf. Rev. Econ. Policy 30, 447–468.

Kallis, G., Kerschner, C., Martínez-Alier, J., 2012. The economics of degrowth. Ecol. Econ., The Economics of Degrowth 84, 172–180.

Klauer, B., Bartkowski, B., Manstetten, R., Petersen, T., under review. Sustainability as a fair bequest: An evaluation challenge. Ecol. Econ.

Klauer, B., Manstetten, R., Petersen, T., Schiller, J., 2013. The art of long-term thinking: A bridge between sustainability science and politics. Ecol. Econ. 93, 79–84.

Kumar, P. (Ed.), 2010. The economics of ecosystems and biodiversity: Ecological and economic foundations. Routledge, London; New York.

Lewis, S.L., Maslin, M.A., 2015. Defining the Anthropocene. Nature 519, 171–180.

McCallum, M.L., 2015. Vertebrate biodiversity losses point to a sixth mass extinction. Biodivers. Conserv. 24, 2497–2519.

McCauley, D.J., 2006. Selling out on nature. Nature 443, 27–28.

McShane, T.O., Hirsch, P.D., Trung, T.C., Songorwa, A.N., Kinzig, A., Monteferri, B., Mutekanga, D., Thang, H.V., Dammert, J.L., Pulgar-Vidal, M., Welch-Devine, M.,

Peter Brosius, J., Coppolillo, P., O'Connor, S., 2011. Hard choices: Making trade-offs between biodiversity conservation and human well-being. Biol. Conserv. 144, 966–972.

Meinard, Y., Quétier, F., 2014. Experiencing biodiversity as a bridge over the science–society communication gap. Conserv. Biol. 28, 705–712.

Meinard, Y., Coq, S., Schmid, B., 2014. A constructivist approach toward a general definition of biodiversity. Ethics Policy Environ. 17, 88–104.

Nijkamp, P., Vindigni, G., Nunes, P.A.L.D., 2008. Economic valuation of biodiversity: A comparative study. Ecol. Econ. 67, 217–231.

Nunes, P.A.L.D., van den Bergh, J.C.J.M., 2001. Economic valuation of biodiversity: Sense or nonsense? Ecol. Econ. 39, 203–222.

Nunes, P.A.L.D., van den Bergh, J.C.J.M., Nijkamp, P., 2003. The ecological economics of biodiversity: Methods and applications. Edward Elgar, Cheltenham; Northampton, MA.

Pascual, U., Muradian, R., Brander, L., Gómez-Baggethun, E., Martín-López, B., Verma, M., 2010. The economics of valuing ecosystem services and biodiversity. In: Kumar, P. (Ed.), The economics of ecosystems and biodiversity: Ecological and economic foundations. Routledge, London; New York, pp. 183–256.

Pearce, D.W., 2001. Valuing biological diversity: Issues and overview. In: OECD (Ed.), Valuation of biodiversity benefits: Selected studies. OECD, Paris, pp. 27–44.

Pereira, H.M., Navarro, L.M., Martins, I.S., 2012. Global biodiversity change: The bad, the good, and the unknown. Annu. Rev. Environ. Resour. 37, 25–50.

Perrings, C., Mäler, K.-G., Folke, C., Holling, C.S., Jansson, B.-O. (Eds), 1995. Biodiversity loss: Economic and ecological issues. Cambridge University Press, Cambridge.

Raudsepp-Hearne, C., Peterson, G.D., Tengö, M., Bennett, E.M., Holland, T., Benessaiah, K., MacDonald, G.K., Pfeifer, L., 2010. Untangling the environmentalist's paradox: Why is human well-being increasing as ecosystem services degrade? BioScience 60, 576–589.

Rockström, J., Steffen, W., Noone, K., Persson, Å., Chapin, F.S., Lambin, E.F., Lenton, T.M., Scheffer, M., Folke, C., Schellnhuber, H.J., Nykvist, B., de Wit, C.A., Hughes, T., van der Leeuw, S., Rodhe, H., Sörlin, S., Snyder, P.K., Costanza, R., Svedin, U., Falkenmark, M., Karlberg, L., Corell, R.W., Fabry, V.J., Hansen, J., Walker, B., Liverman, D., Richardson, K., Crutzen, P., Foley, J.A., 2009. A safe operating space for humanity. Nature 461, 472–475.

Schuldt, A., Wubet, T., Buscot, F., Staab, M., Assmann, T., Böhnke-Kammerlander, M., Both, S., Erfmeier, A., Klein, A.-M., Ma, K., Pietsch, K., Schultze, S., Wirth, C., Zhang, J., Zumstein, P., Bruelheide, H., 2015. Multitrophic diversity in a biodiverse forest is highly nonlinear across spatial scales. Nat. Commun. 6, 10169.

Steffen, W., Grinevald, J., Crutzen, P., McNeill, J., 2011. The Anthropocene: Conceptual and historical perspectives. Philos. Trans. R. Soc. Math. Phys. Eng. Sci. 369, 842–867.

Steffen, W., Richardson, K., Rockström, J., Cornell, S.E., Fetzer, I., Bennett, E.M., Biggs, R., Carpenter, S.R., Vries, W. de, Wit, C.A. de, Folke, C., Gerten, D., Heinke, J., Mace, G.M., Persson, L.M., Ramanathan, V., Reyers, B., Sörlin, S., 2015. Planetary boundaries: Guiding human development on a changing planet. Science 347, 6223.

Sukhdev, P., Wittmer, H., Miller, D., 2014. The Economics of Ecosystems and Biodiversity (TEEB): Challenges and responses. In: Helm, D., Hepburn, C. (Eds), Nature in the balance: The economics of biodiversity. Oxford University Press, New York, pp. 135–150.

van den Bergh, J.C.J.M., 2011. Environment versus growth: A criticism of 'degrowth' and a plea for 'a-growth'. Ecol. Econ. 70, 881–890.

Wegner, G., Pascual, U., 2011. Cost–benefit analysis in the context of ecosystem services for human well-being: A multidisciplinary critique. Glob. Environ. Change 21, 492–504.

Wilson, E.O. (Ed.), 1988. Biodiversity. National Academy Press, Washington, DC.

World Commission on Environment and Development, 1987. Our common future. Oxford University Press, Oxford; New York.

2 Theory and concepts of economic valuation

In this introductory chapter the theoretical, conceptual and methodological foundations of economic valuation of nature are presented. With small exceptions, the body of knowledge recapitulated here is standard environmental and resource economics. However, these foundations will be needed for the development of the conceptual framework that is the main goal of the present book: since it is a valuation framework, it must be ensured that it is consistent with economic valuation theory. This chapter is meant to give an overview about selected topics, all of which are important for the arguments developed further on in the book.

In the first section of this chapter the scope of economic valuation is clarified. First, the welfare economics of valuation is sketched; given that basis, a number of arguments are made about what economic valuation is (not) to clarify the approach of the book. After this, two particularly popular and widespread conceptual frameworks are introduced on which many valuation studies are based: the ecosystem services (ESS) and total economic value (TEV) frameworks. This discussion will later be taken up in Chapter 5, in which it will be shown how these frameworks can be extended or modified to better account for biodiversity and its value. The last section of this chapter gives a very brief overview about economic valuation methods, their relative merits and limitations. The links of these introductory considerations to later parts of the book are made more explicit in the text.

What is economic valuation?

The goal of the present book is to develop a conceptual framework for the economic valuation of biodiversity. Especially because this framework is necessarily founded in ecological considerations (regarding the function of biodiversity in ecosystems), it is essential to be clear about what economic valuation is, what its theoretical basis is, so as to draw a line between admissible and non-admissible theoretical arguments. This section is devoted to clarifying the theoretical scope of economic valuation: its first subsection gives a brief overview about welfare economic foundations of valuation; the second subsection offers a conceptual delimitation by responding to some common misunderstandings regarding the scope and function of economic valuation.

Welfare economic foundations

As already mentioned in the Introduction, economic valuation is rooted in neo-classical welfare economic theory. The concept of economic value is based on a number of critical (and frequently criticised) assumptions. It will be argued further on that some of them can and should be relaxed or modified, but it is important to be clear about the starting point for potential modifications. First, economic value is the result of human preferences under the assumption of *consumer sovereignty* – i.e. the assumption that people know best what is good for themselves and act accordingly. This is an essential part of the so-called *preference utilitarianism*, which equates the satisfaction of subjective preferences with welfare. Second, to translate preferences, which cannot be observed directly, into values, one has to study the actual or hypothetical choices people make. The theoretical basis for this is, most fundamentally, the Revealed Preference Theory introduced by Samuelson (1938). However, as Pearce (2001, p. 30) rightly noted, 'especially if we adopt stated preference techniques [...] [w]e learn what people care about, what their motives are for conservation, what their reactions would be to different management objectives'. Thus, in some contexts economic valuation can provide information over and beyond simple observation of choices made by people. Third, as it is assumed that economic value results from *human* preferences, the theory of economic valuation is inherently anthropocentric, i.e. only humans are assumed to have intrinsic value. Everything else can only be instrumentally valuable. However, because of the assumption of consumer sovereignty, the underlying preferences of economic subjects need not be anthropocentric (nor utilitarian, for that matter). In fact, there is no restriction regarding the ethical source of preferences.[1] Empirical investigations found that participants in economic valuation studies are motivated by very different ethical considerations (Spash et al., 2009). Fourth, economics in general and welfare theory in particular are based on the premise of *methodological individualism* (cf. Elster, 1989), which means that economic values are to be sought in individual preferences, not in 'social/collective preferences' (but see Kenter et al., 2015; Kenter, 2016; Hansjürgens et al., 2017). Fifth, economic value is the result of trade-offs individuals (have to) make between substitutable goods – these trade-offs are usually expressed in a common numeraire, mostly money, but in some studies also energy (cf. Faucheux and Pillet, 1994), life satisfaction (e.g. Ambrey et al., 2014) and other metrics.

As most environmental goods are either public goods/commons or, if they are private, are traded in rather distorted markets, market prices for them are either non-existent or they are poor approximations of these goods' actual economic value. Thus, shadow prices have to be estimated, i.e. hypothetical prices which would exist in perfect markets, in which all externalities are internalised and no further distortions exist.

Turning to technicalities, the basic model[2] on which economic valuation is based starts with the assumption that any individual maximises her utility subject to a budget constraint:

$$\max U = U(X) s.t. P'X \leq M \tag{2.1}$$

U being the individual's utility, X a vector of n goods and services, P the corresponding price vector and M income. For each element of the vector X, x_i, a so-called Marshallian demand function can be derived:

$$x_i = x_i(P,M), i = 1,\ldots,n \tag{2.2}$$

Environmental quality (Q) can be introduced into that problem threefold: directly as an argument in the utility function; indirectly via its influence on the production of a household good ($Z(Q)$) such as health; or indirectly via the production function of goods purchased by the individual/household in the marketplace. Independent of that, the marginal welfare change triggered by a change in environmental quality Q can be expressed as:

$$-\frac{dM}{dQ} = \frac{\dfrac{\partial V}{\partial Q}}{\dfrac{\partial V}{\partial M}} \tag{2.3}$$

with V being indirect utility, defined as $U = V(P, M)$.

The Marshallian welfare measure, while quite common in practical applications, is problematic because of its assumptions regarding income elasticity of demand: 'the ordinary (Marshallian) demand curve does not hold the level of utility [...] constant, but rather holds income constant' (Mitchell and Carson, 1989, p. 23), which limits its applicability in analyses of price or quantity changes (Freeman, 1993, pp. 50–52). Thus, the Hicksian welfare measures compensating and equivalent variation/surplus can alternatively be used.[3] Compensating variation (*CV*) is the change in income necessary to make the individual as well off after the (marginal) environmental change as she was before:

$$V(P^1,Q^1,M^1 - CV) = V(P^0,Q^0,M^0) \tag{2.4}$$

The superscripts are used to denote parameter levels before (0) and after the change (1).

Equivalent variation (*EV*), on the other hand, is the change in income before the (marginal) environmental change necessary to make the individual as well off as she would be if the change were to take place:

$$V(P^1,Q^1,M^1) = V(P^0,Q^0,M^0 + EV) \tag{2.5}$$

These basic concepts can then be applied to changes in both prices and quantity/quality of (environmental) goods and services.

The magnitudes actually measured in most economic valuation studies are called (marginal) willingness to pay (WTP) or (marginal) willingness to accept compensation (WTA). Table 2.1 presents the correspondence of these two with the Hicksian welfare measures, depending on the sign of the environmental change.

As already mentioned, in many applications the goal of economic valuation is to compute *shadow prices* (e.g. Arrow et al., 2004). Shadow prices are the marginal contributions of goods to human welfare:

$$p_i = \frac{\partial u(x)}{\partial x_i},$$ (2.6)

where $u(\cdot)$ is the utility function, x a vector of consumption goods $x = (x_1, x_2, ..., x_i)$, and p_i the shadow price of i-th good. Shadow prices signal the relative scarcity of goods and allow for comparisons between them (i.e. their absolute values have no meaning). They can have various numeraires, but typically money is chosen for practical reasons. A special case is the rate of discount, which is an intertemporal shadow price. However, as discounting is not relevant for the present book, the reader is referred to Arrow et al. (2014) and Gollier (2013), who summarise the state of the art in this research area nicely.

Scope and function

In the last section, the welfare economic foundations of economic valuation were presented. It is important to understand what economic valuation is before developing any framework for economic valuation of anything (in the case of the present book: biodiversity). In this book, it is *assumed* that economic valuation is a sensible and useful enterprise. In public debates, this view is often challenged. Much of the criticism is based on misunderstandings regarding what the scope and function of economic valuation is. Since a common ground regarding the meaning, reach and limitations of economic valuation is important for the arguments developed in this book, this section gives a tentative response to the question of what economic valuation is (not), thus also responding to some common criticisms. It thus offers a conceptual delimitation and provides context for interpreting the conceptual framework presented in Chapter 5 and its future applications in valuation studies as well as the consequences to be drawn from these studies. A more comprehensive and multi-faceted treatment of this subject can be found in Pascual et al. (2010).

Economic valuation of environmental (public) goods has been a controversial issue almost from the approach's beginnings. There are several points of critique,

Table 2.1 Correspondence of CV and EV with WTP and WTA

	Compensating variation	*Equivalent variation*
Positive environmental change	WTP	WTA
Negative environmental change	WTA	WTP

including objections against the marginalist approach in the face of complexities and discontinuities in ecosystems (Dasgupta and Mäler, 2003; Norgaard, 2010; Wegner and Pascual, 2011); fears of commodification of nature (Gómez-Bagget-hun and Ruiz Pérez, 2011; Kallis et al., 2013; McCauley, 2006; Silvertown, 2015); opposition to the perceived dominance of monetary values and emphasis on the importance of other value categories (Chan et al., 2012; Martínez-Alier, 2002; Sagoff, 1988); and concerns for justice and equity-related side effects of economic valuation exercises (Kallis et al., 2013; Matulis, 2014).

The basic justification of economic valuation of environmental goods and services (and of their framing as such) can be phrased as follows: 'Conservation policy often appears to take place in an analytical vacuum. Frequently, it is not clear what we are supposed to be conserving or what are the relevant trade-offs' (Weitzman, 1993, p. 157). In the most basic sense, the goal of economic valuation is to make trade-offs explicit. However, its role and scope are often misunderstood, so it might be in order to list a few main points of what economic valuation is and what it is not (see also Bockstael et al., 2000; Hansjürgens, 2004; Sukhdev et al., 2014). They mirror the understanding of economic valuation that underlies the arguments developed in the present book.

• Economic valuation certainly is an inherently anthropocentric approach. All ecosystem values are viewed as instrumental in satisfying human preferences. Also, economics is consequentialist – it generally does not ask where these preferences come from (preference utilitarianism). This is often criticised because economic valuation supposedly excludes considerations going beyond anthropocentrism and because it does not exclude 'bad' or 'immoral' preferences. This criticism should be acknowledged by environmental economists, but it does not follow that economic valuation cannot be useful. Anthropocentrism can be viewed as a kind of minimum standard, because all common ethical theories agree that human well-being is important. They disagree as to whether and what other entities should be granted moral status (see the Excursus). Furthermore, ethical frameworks going beyond anthropocentrism are all but uncontroversial in environmental ethics (cf. Eser et al., 2014; Spangenberg and Settele, 2016). Utilitarianism, while shown to be highly problematic in many respects, can be argued to be *democratic* or *liberal* in the sense of paying attention to people's preferences (cf. Bartkowski and Lienhoop, 2017). Economic values should not be viewed as definitive, since they may indeed be based on 'immoral' preferences, and public debates may well correct these preferences. But this correction is not the job of economists:

> Of course, in a more fundamental sense focusing attention on changes in income and consumption to the exclusion of other aspects of well-being, such as social relationships and sense of self-worth, involves a kind of value judgment. But this judgment is implicit in the division of labor between economists and others.
>
> (Freeman, 1993, p. 41, fn. 2)

In this sense, economic valuation provides information about the preferences of stakeholders, which are *one* factor in public decision-making.

- Economics is commonly defined as the analysis of the human pursuit of goals given limited or scarce means (Robbins, 1932). Biodiversity and other aspects of ecosystems are both scarce and potential contributors to human well-being. Therefore, they are a 'natural' object of interest for economists. Specific uses of economic valuation of ecosystems include: project appraisal and regulation (through cost–benefit analysis, cost-effectiveness analysis, multi-criteria analysis etc.), definition of command-and-control measures and taxes in environmental policy, identification of emerging conservation markets (e.g. ecotourism), correction of prices and incentives and inclusion of natural capital into national accounting systems (Costanza et al., 2014; Kontoleon et al., 2007; Pearce, 2001). In more general terms, the goal of economic valuation is to make trade-offs explicit. Sometimes economics is criticised for its preoccupation with trade-offs (e.g. Aldred, 2006; Holland, 2002; Vatn and Bromley, 1994). Yet it was rightly remarked that it is 'tempting to occupy the aesthetic high ground and to say that tragic choices cannot be evaluated. But decisions have to be made, and thinking in terms of numerical indices makes decision-makers face trade-offs explicitly' (Dasgupta, 2001, p. 23).[4]
- Economic valuation can only be applied to *changes* in the supply of environmental goods and/or services. Even though the most widely cited economic valuation study (Costanza et al., 1997) chose a different approach and estimated the total economic value of the world's biosphere, this is not consistent with welfare economics and, which is more important, not really sensible (Bockstael et al., 2000). Economic valuation can only be sensibly used to assess trade-offs between goods that are *substitutable*. Total valuation amounts to estimating the WTP for the existence (vs non-existence) of a given good, which in most cases does not appear a sensible thing to do. As will be argued further on in this book, this has important consequences for the conceptualisation of the economic value of biodiversity.
- In contrast to what is often suggested (Dempsey and Robertson, 2012; Gómez-Baggethun and Ruiz Pérez, 2011; McAfee, 1999; McCauley, 2006; Monbiot, 2014), economic valuation is not the same as commodification/ privatisation of natural environment. Also, the latter is not a logical consequence of valuation. Quite the contrary, most environmental goods are public goods or commons, which cannot be well handled by markets and require other institutional approaches to management (Costanza, 2006). So, from the economic point of view, monetisation does not imply commodification. However, it should be acknowledged that an exclusive framing of (the value of) ecosystems in economic, especially monetary, terms can be very problematic and lead to a suppression of other considerations in public debates (Aldred, 2010, chap. 7; Kallis et al., 2013).

It is often emphasised that the economic value is only a part of the overall value of any ecosystem (Kumar, 2010) and that economic valuation is not 'a panacea;

rather, such valuation is one piece of helpful information in the complex task of sustainably managing our natural assets' (Costanza, 2006, p. 749). Furthermore, there is a pragmatic reason for embracing the ecosystem services and economic valuation approaches: paraphrasing Winston Churchill, they are the worst means to facilitate the preservation of an intact biosphere except all those other means that have been tried from time to time.[5] Or else, in the words of Harvey (1997, p. 156):

> At this point, the critic of money valuations, who is nevertheless deeply concerned about environmental degradation, is faced with a dilemma: eschew the language of daily economic practice and political power and speak in the wilderness, or articulate deeply-held nonmonetizable values in a language (i.e. that of money) believed to be inappropriate and fundamentally alien.

In this and the previous section we clarified what economic valuation is, from a theoretical and conceptual perspective. In the next section, the focus will be, more specifically, on common frameworks used in economic valuation studies.

Common frameworks

When it comes to application, economic valuation of environmental goods and services is mostly based on two conceptual frameworks: the ecosystem service (ESS) framework and the total economic value (TEV) framework. In what follows, these conceptual foundations of most economic valuation studies are briefly presented. The reason for doing this is that biodiversity's role in these frameworks is unclear and should be clarified, and that many elements of the conceptual framework developed in this book are inspired by the insights provided by ESS and TEV as well as their limitations. More specifically, since biodiversity is more or less absent from these frameworks (or, at least, it is not explicitly included) but they are highly influential and frequently used, it will be shown in Chapter 5 how they can be modified/extended so as to explicitly include biodiversity and its value.

The ecosystem service framework

The ecosystem service (ESS) framework has become the dominant conceptual foundation of much research in the areas of conservation biology, ecology and economic valuation, among others. Most valuation studies use the concept of ESS and choose ecosystem services as valuation objects (de Groot et al., 2012). To give an overview of the ESS approach, in this section the underlying cascade model is presented, followed by a brief presentation of the most common classifications. Furthermore, biodiversity's unclear role in the ESS framework is briefly discussed here. Later on, in Chapter 5, we will identify consequences of the conceptual framework developed here for the ESS framework.

A common way of depicting the idea behind the ESS concept is the so-called *cascade model* (see Figure 2.1). In different sources, the exact structure and nomenclature varies, but the basic idea remains the same: ecosystems (and biodiversity) are the stage for biophysical processes that shape biophysical structures. Some ecosystem processes are then interpreted as functions (e.g. nutrient cycling), which generate services (e.g. provision of clean water), which create benefits (e.g. contribution to health), benefits being the source of (economic) value. The cascade model was originally developed by Roy Haines-Young and included in TEEB's interim report (TEEB, 2008, fig. 3.1) and then explicitly proposed and discussed by Haines-Young and Potschin (2010a; Potschin and Haines-Young, 2011), but there exist a number of modified and extended versions of it. Note that in the TEEB version of the cascade (de Groot et al., 2010, fig. 1.4), the structures and functions boxes are embedded in a box headed 'Ecosystems & Biodiversity'. In the original cascade by Haines-Young and Potschin (2010a) the larger box is missing. In other versions of the cascade, the first box is 'biodiversity', instead of 'structure' (e.g. Martín-López et al., 2014, fig. 2). This unclear role of biodiversity in the cascade and the ESS framework in general will be discussed in more detail below.

The cascade authors themselves have stressed, however, that the definition of and distinction between *benefits*, *goods* and *services* is anything but straightforward (Potschin and Haines-Young, 2011), a point reinforced by Chan et al. (2012), among others (see below).

Conventionally, the cascade is interpreted in the direction as presented above, from structures to values. However, it has been proposed that a more reasonable way of utilising the concept might be the other way around (Jax et al., 2013), whereby a definition of well-being helps to predefine which services are of importance from the human perspective, which then leads to the identification

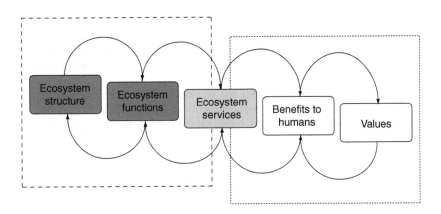

Figure 2.1 Cascade model.

Note
Based on Haines-Young and Potschin (2010a) and Jax (2010, fig. 4.4).

of the functions and processes behind them and thus, to the definition of areas worth protection. This interpretation makes it especially clear that the ESS concept is inherently anthropocentric, as already indicated by the chosen wording. A similar perspective can be found in Spangenberg et al. (2014a), where it is argued that it is primarily human agency that determines what eco-system services are derived from ecosystems.

The central part of the cascade model is the ecosystem services 'module', which can be seen as the interface between eco- and human systems. The most widely quoted definition of ecosystem services was provided by the Millennium Ecosystem Assessment (MEA, 2005, p. 40): 'Ecosystem services are the benefits people obtain from ecosystems.' There exist, however, many different, more specific definitions of ecosystem services (Box 2.1).[6] They differ mainly in terms of the localisation of ecosystem services within the cascade framework, as well as in the definition of important sub-concepts, such as benefits or functions. For an overview, see Lamarque et al. (2011) and Häyhä and Franzese (2014). Of course, the definition of ecosystem services determines their classification, the relation to biodiversity etc. For instance, it has been criticised that MEA wrongly equates ecosystem services and benefits, while these are actually causally linked yet separate things (Boyd and Banzhaf, 2007). Sometimes, the literature distinguishes between ecosystem goods and ecosystem services (e.g. Costanza et al., 1997). In what follows, when the term 'ecosystem services' is used, both tangible ecosystem goods and less tangible ecosystem services are meant, in accordance with the definition by TEEB (Kumar, 2010, p. xxxiv).

Box 2.1 Influential definitions of ecosystem services

Numerous definitions of 'ecosystem services' have been proposed in the literature. The most influential and widely cited include (in chronological order):

> **Ecosystem services** are the conditions and processes through which natural ecosystems, and the species that make them up, sustain and fulfil human life.
>
> (Daily, 1997)

> **Ecosystem goods** (such as food) and **services** (such as waste assimilation) represent the benefits human populations derive, directly or indirectly, from ecosystem functions [the habitat, biological or system properties or processes of ecosystems].
>
> (Costanza et al., 1997)

> **Ecosystem services** are the benefits people obtain from ecosystems.
>
> (MEA, 2005)

> Final **ecosystem services** are components of nature, directly enjoyed, consumed, or used to yield human well-being.
>
> (Boyd and Banzhaf, 2007)

[E]cosystem services are the aspects of ecosystems utilized (actively or passively) to produce human well-being.

(Fisher et al., 2009)

Ecosystem services: The direct and indirect contributions of ecosystems to human well-being. The concept of 'ecosystem goods and services' is synonymous with ecosystem services.

(Kumar, 2010)

It should be noted that the definitions have not come into existence in a vacuum – each definition was influenced by the previous ones, implicitly or explicitly. For instance, Fisher et al. explicitly acknowledge that their definition is based on the one proposed by Boyd and Banzhaf. In the literature, however, each of the definitions is used, including recent publications. There is no obvious trend to adopting the most recent of these influential definitions.

The classic yet contested approach to classification is to refer to the categorisation proposed in the Millennium Ecosystem Assessment (MEA, 2005). Four broad categories of ecosystem services have been identified there: provisioning, regulating, cultural and supporting services. Another influential classification is the TEEB classification (de Groot et al., 2010), in which the category of supporting services was dropped and replaced by habitat services, which cover only part of the supporting services domain.

Still, many problems related to the classification of ecosystem services have been identified. It has been discussed, for example, whether the parallel quantification of supporting, on the one hand, and other services, on the other hand, may result in double-counting (Boyd and Banzhaf, 2007; Jax et al., 2013). Martín-López et al. (2014) pointed out that provisioning services are the easiest to quantify and value (and, therefore, the most frequently valued), but their appreciation by stakeholders is on average significantly lower than for regulating and cultural services (see also de Groot et al., 2012).

The state-of-the-art classification to date is the CICES (Common International Classification of Ecosystem Services). It is closer to the TEEB than the MEA classification in that it explicitly excludes supporting services, focusing solely on 'final products of ecosystems' (Haines-Young and Potschin, 2010b, p. 8). Its current version is presented in Table 2.2.

Nevertheless, there appears to be no unequivocally agreed upon standard available yet (Lamarque et al., 2011; Nahlik et al., 2012). Indeed, some maintain that a single, 'one-size-fits-all' classification is neither feasible nor sensible (Fisher et al., 2009).

Overall, the ESS framework has spurred a huge amount of research on the interrelations between socio-economic and ecological systems. It is helpful in recognising and demonstrating the reliance of human well-being on intact ecosystems (Kumar, 2010; Norgaard, 2010). However, it exhibits numerous limitations and is constantly being developed further (Cord et al., under review). As

Table 2.2 CICES classification of ecosystem services

Section	Division
Provisioning	Nutrition Materials Energy
Regulation and maintenance	Mediation of waste, toxics and other nuisance Mediation of flows Maintenance of physical, chemical, biological conditions
Cultuaral	Physical and intellectual interactions with ecosystems and land-/seascapes [environmental settings] Spiritual, symbolic and other interactions with ecosystems and land-/seascapes [environmental settings]

Source: http://cices.eu (retrieved on 26 June 2016).

will be discussed presently, the role of biodiversity within the ESS framework is among the still unsolved issues. The present book will provide some hints in this regard in Chapter 5, especially by showing that biodiversity does not really fit the ESS cascade and suggesting that the cascade be complemented by the framework developed here.

The common approach is to view the role of biodiversity within the ESS framework entirely in terms of its contribution to and supporting role for the provision of final ecosystem services (Cardinale et al., 2012; Elmqvist et al., 2010; MEA, 2005). Indeed, it was pointed out that in many ESS classifications biodiversity appears to have no explicit place (Atkinson et al., 2012). For instance, biodiversity is not even mentioned in the CICES classification, while in the TEEB classification only some of its aspects are included within the 'habitat services' category. Schröter et al. (2014, p. 3) assert that

> other components of biodiversity [than those captured within the habitat/supporting services categories] are included in the cultural and amenity service category of TEEB and MA, through the components' roles in the ES cultural heritage, spiritual and artistic inspiration, and aesthetic appreciation.

Furthermore, as already mentioned above, there exist many versions of the ESS framework, including many versions of the cascade model (e.g. Haines-Young and Potschin, 2010a; Jax et al., 2013; Spangenberg et al., 2014b), each of which interprets biodiversity in a different way (see also above).

Cardinale et al. (2012) note that the literature on the links between biodiversity and ecosystem services is rather inconclusive, identifying strong positive relationship for some services (e.g. agricultural yields), mixed effects for others (e.g. long-term carbon sequestration), negative effects for a small group of services (e.g. biocontrol) and data gaps for many others (e.g. flood protection). Another influential synthesis of empirical data suggests that there may exist trade-offs between biodiversity and some provisioning ecosystem services (Maes et al., 2012). Also, cross-spatial conflicts may emerge between the maintenance of biological diversity and the provision of some ecosystem services, since ecosystems are interconnected and '[i]ncreasing the biodiversity [in one ecosystem] may lead to an overall loss of biodiversity and other sources of ecosystem values [across ecosystems]' (King and Wainger, 2001, p. 122). The specific relationship between biodiversity and ecosystem services is highly dependent on the perspective adopted and the research purpose involved (Jax and Heink, 2015).

Similarly, Mace et al. (2012) argue that two different perspectives on the relationship between biodiversity and ecosystem services can be distinguished: under the *ecosystem services perspective* the two are essentially synonyms. Under the *conservation perspective* biodiversity is interpreted as an ecosystem service. The latter approach seems to be exemplified by the inclusion in valuation studies of 'biodiversity preservation' as a distinct ecosystem service, as discussed in Chapter 4. Mace and colleagues interpret this as an acknowledgement of the intrinsic value of biodiversity (on this, see Excursus). They criticise both perspectives:

> Under the 'ecosystem services perspective' a functional role is implicit but in practice it is not represented other than by some simple measurement of ecosystem service flows. Also, this perspective does not reflect the values of biodiversity that are not based on its functional role in ecosystem processes. The 'conservation perspective' ignores the role of biodiversity in underpinning ecosystem processes, and usually focuses on a subset of biodiversity that includes charismatic species and those on threatened species lists.
>
> (Mace et al., 2012, p. 21)

Instead, they propose a 'multi-layered' perspective on biodiversity as: regulator of ecosystem services, a final ecosystem service and a good. In Chapter 5 we will take another look at their interpretation of the relationship between biodiversity and ecosystem services.

The total economic value framework

The ESS framework, discussed in the previous section, while inspired by economic thinking (Gómez-Baggethun et al., 2010), is a multidisciplinary concept, used in various fields from ecology and geography to economics. The other framework frequently used in the area of economic valuation, total economic value (TEV), is more genuinely economic (although, it should be noted, the area of economic valuation is generally rather interdisciplinary and cannot be sensibly pigeonholed as purely 'economic'). In what follows, first the framework itself is briefly presented. Then, the question is tentatively answered whether TEV captures all economic value there is. This provides a basis for thinking, in Chapter 5, about how biodiversity fits the TEV framework and how it can be modified and extended to better accommodate biodiversity.

The TEV framework was first proposed by Alan Randall and John R. Stoll in the 1980s (Randall, 1987; Randall and Stoll, 1983); however, the basic distinction between use value and non-use value of an ecosystem goes back to Krutilla's (1967) seminal paper, in which he argued that environmental public goods have values which are not derived from their use, but from their sole existence and availability to future generations.

The TEV framework is depicted in Figure 2.2. The TEV of an ecosystem is divided into use and non-use values, which themselves consist of further subcategories of values, and the option value (see also Box 2.2). Exemplary carriers of the individual value categories are (Pascual et al., 2010):

- direct-use values: wood, game, fruits, tourism;
- indirect-use values: pest control, water regulation, soil fertility;
- bequest value: ecosystems enjoyed by future generations;
- altruistic value: ecosystems enjoyed by other people;
- existence value: ecosystems for their own sake.

It is important to note that, despite the word 'total' in '*total* economic value', TEV does not encompass the total value of the ecosystem in question (Turner et al., 2003), but only the values resulting from benefits people draw from ecosystems (Boyd and Banzhaf, 2007). Furthermore, as a consequence of the fundamental axioms of economic theory, economic valuation deals only with changes in the state of the ecosystem, not with its static totality.

Not all components of TEV can be estimated equally easily (see also next section). Particularly, stated preference methods, which are the only ones that offer a possibility of eliciting non-use values, have been quite controversial

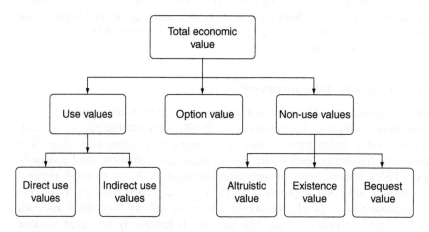

Figure 2.2 Total economic value (TEV) framework.

Note
Adapted from fig. 5.3 in Pascual et al. (2010).

(Diamond and Hausman, 1994; Sen, 1995; but see Interis, 2014). This has led some scholars to a pragmatic rejection of non-use values and to calls for estimating use values only (Cannon and Surjadi, 2004; see also Barkmann et al., 2008). The problem with the latter proposal is, however, that non-use values can make up a large part of the TEV of many ecosystems and environmental public goods.

Box 2.2 Option and quasi-option value

Originally formulated by Weisbrod (1964), **option value** results from risk-aversion and uncertainty about the future. It can be seen 'to arise when an individual [is] uncertain as to whether he would demand a good in some future period and [is] faced with uncertainty about the availability of that good' (Freeman, 1993, p. 261). It is similar to an insurance premium resulting from the fact that an ecosystem might contain useful properties or components of whose existence we are not aware or which we might need in the future (*demand* uncertainty), even though some interpreted it as related to supply uncertainty, too (e.g. Bishop, 1982). Formally, option value can be defined as

> the difference between the option price, the largest sure payment that an individual will pay for a policy before uncertainty is resolved, and the expected consumer surplus, which is the probability-weighted sum of consumer surpluses over all potential states of the world.
>
> (Pascual et al., 2010, p. 224)

Some authors argue that since it is largely an 'algebraic difference' between two measures, 'it is time to expunge option value from the list of possible benefits associated with environmental protection' (Freeman, 1993, pp. 263–264). In a more general sense, however, option value can be understood as 'a way of framing TEV under conditions of uncertainty, as an insurance premium' (Pascual et al., 2010, p. 196), which is highly relevant for conceptualising the economic value of biodiversity (see Chapter 5).

Sometimes, the term 'option value' is also used to describe what is properly called quasi-option value (Fisher and Hanemann, 1990); the concept of **quasi-option value** was originally formulated by Arrow and Fisher (1974). Contrary to option value, it does not depend on human risk attitudes, but is the result of the irreversibility of changes in an ecosystem: knowledge acquired in the future may reverse the original analysis of costs and benefits of a development project that would result in an irreversible transformation of an ecosystem. Quasi-option value is then 'the value of waiting for the resolution of uncertainty' (Pascual et al., 2010, p. 196). Thus, the ecosystem has an (unknown) value component called quasi-option value. The notion of quasi-option value was introduced into the economic theory of diversity (value) by Weikard (2003). However, it was noted that the concept is actually not a value category, but rather a decision-making rule (Freeman, 1993). Therefore, quasi-option value does not play a role in the context of the present work.

From most economic valuation literature one might get the impression that economic value is identical with TEV. This interpretation, however, is not entirely correct. As was pointed out in the influential first TEEB report on *Ecological and Economic Foundations*, TEV can be interpreted as the 'output value' of an ecosystem (Pascual et al., 2010). Yet it also has *insurance value*, which normally is not captured within the TEV. It is the value of those eco-system properties and/or components which make the ecosystem resilient and stable in the face of external disturbances. In the TEEB report it was suggested that insurance value is not preference-based (i.e. economic in the conventional sense) but a 'biophysical' value category (Pascual et al., 2010, fig. 5.1; see also Gómez-Baggethun and de Groot, 2010). This is debatable, and in this book it will be argued that insurance value is an economic value category just as those included in the TEV.

In a more recent contribution on the economic value of soil biodiversity, Pascual et al. (2015) extend the TEV framework to include insurance value by adding an additional level to it: instead of dividing TEV into use and non-use values, they start by distinguishing *total output value* (TOV) and *natural insur-ance value* (NIV) as the two main components of TEV (see Figure 2.3). TOV is then further subdivided according to the usual TEV (use, non-use values and option value).

In Chapter 5, a similar extension of the TEV framework will be proposed.

It should be noted that while the ESS and TEV frameworks are often com-bined in valuation studies, they are not perfectly overlapping. In particular, non-use values and option value from TEV can hardly be attached to any specific ecosystem services; rather, they can be related to entire ecosystems or their spe-cific components (e.g. particular species).

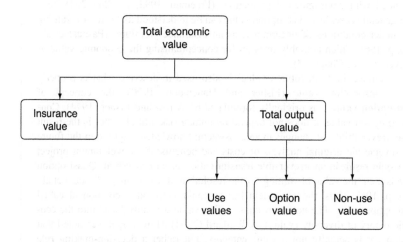

Figure 2.3 TEV with insurance value.

Note
Simplified version of fig. 3 from Pascual et al. (2015).

Valuation methods

To assess the TEV of an ecosystem, one may apply numerous different valuation methods. Some of the common economic valuation methods are better suited for the assessment of use values, others are more sensible when dealing with non-use values. Many environmental goods and services are not traded in markets. For those, 'values are often imputed (a) by looking at behavior that reveals consumer valuation of the commodities, (b) by unbundling the commodities and valuing component parts, or (c) by using surveys' (Nordhaus, 2006, p. 150). Methods corresponding to (a) and (b) are called revealed preference methods (where an example of (a) is the travel cost method, while hedonic pricing is an instance of (b)), those that correspond to (c) are stated preference methods. Both method classes are briefly presented below. In addition to these demand-/preference-oriented methods, the group of supply-side methods is discussed shortly.[7]

Note that economic valuation methods can also be classified as differently interpreting the inclusion of environmental goods in the utility function: if an environmental good is directly included as argument in the utility function, its value can be estimated by means of stated preference methods and possibly (depending on exact interpretation) revealed preference methods; the same holds for the inclusion via the production of a household good; only environmental goods which influence utility via the production function of marketed goods can be valued by means of methods such as the production function method.

The purpose of this brief exposition is to provide an overview about the relative strengths and weaknesses of available economic valuation methods – this will then feed into the arguments about which methods are best suited for the economic valuation of biodiversity. Specifically, this section reviews the general applicability of various valuation methods in different contexts. In Chapter 5 a biodiversity-specific layer of criteria will be added so as to identify methods that are particularly well-suited for handling this valuation object.

Supply-side methods

The most basic, one may say crude, class of economic valuation methods are the so-called cost-based methods. They include the replacement cost, avoidance cost and restoration cost methods; the idea behind them is to use the costs of some actions related to the environmental good or service in question as a proxy for its value. However, as was pointed out repeatedly in the literature (e.g. Bockstael et al., 2000; Heal and Kriström, 2005; Pearce, 1998), this approach is inconsistent with welfare economic theory: economic value is inherently grounded in human preferences. Cost-based methods can only provide information about the technical possibility of some action, not about its social desirability in terms of preferences. Their use as value proxies is only admissible under restrictive circumstances (Heal and Kriström, 2005, pp. 1185–1186).

Another method that is based on the analysis of the *supply* of ecosystem goods and services is the production function method: it is based on models which include ecosystem services and goods as factors of production of market goods. The economic value of ecosystems can be inferred from their contribution to the market value of those goods. This method has the important limitation that it is restricted to ecosystem goods and services that can be related to production processes. Furthermore, it is rather demanding in terms of data (McConnell and Bockstael, 2005). Both cost-based methods and production function approaches are based on market prices, which are often distorted due to market imperfections, such as subsidies, market power and various externalities.

Revealed preference methods

Some values of ecosystems can be derived from those consumer choices which can somehow be linked to non-market environmental goods. This idea is related to that behind production function and similar methods, but the focus is on the demand side of markets. Revealed preference methods are used to estimate them. There are basically two valuation methods in this category: the hedonic pricing method and the travel cost method.

The *hedonic pricing method*, also called hedonic valuation, builds upon the observation that differences in the prices of otherwise equal real estate which is located in areas with differing environmental characteristics can be used to estimate the incremental value that emerges from these differences (theoretically, many factors can be valued independently by using large samples of real estate data).

The *travel cost method*, first suggested by famous economist Harold Hotelling in 1947, is based on the assumption that people's willingness-to-pay for amenities they travel to, such as national parks, reflects their valuation of services provided by the underlying ecosystems (e.g. the value of recreation). Alternatively, different recreation destinations can be compared in a way similar to hedonic pricing.

There are at least two major problems of revealed preference methods. First, as with all methods based on actual (market) behaviour, they cannot provide any information about non-use values. Second, their reliability largely depends on the availability of high-quality data for the investigated markets. They can only be used for ecosystems which can be related to markets.

Stated preference methods

The third broad category of economic methods used for the valuation of ecosystem services is called stated preference methods. This group of methods is often considered crucial because they are the only ones that enable economists to estimate non-use values (Arrow et al., 1993; Bockstael and Freeman, 2005; Pascual et al., 2010). This happens via construction of hypothetical 'markets' in questionnaire-based surveys, where people are asked how much they would be willing to pay (or to accept as compensation) for an increase (or decrease) in the quality or quantity of a given ecosystem (service) as compared with a status quo scenario. Thus, welfare measures can be directly estimated.

The most common methods within this category are contingent valuation (CV) and discrete choice experiments (CE). There is some confusion regarding their names: in a proposal of a consistent nomenclature, the term *contingent valuation* was used as encompassing all stated preference methods that deal with public goods (Carson and Louviere, 2011). More usual, however, is the distinction between CV (where willingness-to-pay is elicited directly) and CE (where it is derived from choices among scenarios). The differences between CV and CE are related mainly to the preferences elicitation format and, to some extent, their vulnerability to some common problems of stated preference methods. They have in common that they are survey-based, elicit hypothetical preferences and make possible the estimation of non-use values.

Stated preference methods are potentially very useful as they are the only ones allowing for estimation of non-use values and do not rely on potentially distorted market data. At the same time, they are controversial because of their hypothetical nature and apparent proneness to a number of psychological biases (cf. Diamond and Hausman, 1994; Interis, 2014; Schläpfer, 2016). Nonetheless, they are very widespread (cf. de Groot et al., 2012) and constantly developed to account for many points of criticism. One increasingly popular area of development is deliberative monetary valuation (DMV), i.e. the combination of conventional stated preference elicitation approaches with group discussions supporting the formation of preferences for unfamiliar environmental goods. In Chapter 5, more will be said about DMV in the context of biodiversity valuation, including some reflection on its limitations.

Summary

The aim of this theoretical chapter was to set the economic ground for the rest of book (the ecological and environmental ethics perspective follow in Chapter 3 and the Excursus, respectively). Since our aim is to develop a conceptual framework for the economic valuation of biodiversity, it was necessary to clarify (i) what economic valuation is, (ii) what other frameworks are available and (iii) how economic valuation works in practice. Because most of the content of this chapter is more or less standard textbook knowledge in environmental economics, the overview was kept brief. Nonetheless, this overview is essential for the rest of the book: the theoretical understanding of the essence and scope of economic valuation is crucial to determine what the economic value of biodiversity may be; knowledge about common valuation frameworks (TEV and ESS) is necessary because the conceptual framework developed here is meant to close a gap left by them; a brief overview about the applicability of available valuation methods in different contexts helps as a basis for the discussion in Chapter 5, where an additional layer of biodiversity-specific criteria will be added so as to identify valuation methods particularly well-suited for biodiversity valuation. Thus, the arguments developed further on in this book will be based, implicitly or explicitly, on what was written in this chapter.

After we have considered what economic valuation is and how it usually works in practice, we now turn to the valuation object: biodiversity. On this basis, the conceptual framework for the economic valuation of biodiversity will then be developed in Chapter 5.

Notes

1 Actually, conventional welfare economics assumes, following Samuelson (1938), that people's sovereign choices reflect their individual welfare. This interpretation leads to problems, including circular reasoning (Sen, 1977), and has led some economists to theoretical arguments for considering 'ideal', 'well-informed' or 'rational' preferences instead of actual ones (which may contradict individual welfare) (e.g. Harsanyi, 1977; Mirrlees, 1982). In the context of economic valuation, it has been argued that the link from choices/preferences to individual welfare is unnecessary (Aldred, 1994). The understanding that underlies the present book's arguments does not assume this link to be present.
2 The following exposition is based on Bockstael and Freeman (2005). For a more exhaustive presentation of the theory of economic valuation of the environment, see Freeman (1993).
3 Bockstael and Freeman (2005) argue that it is not sensible to distinguish between variation measures (where quantities adjust to price changes) and surplus measures (where quantities are fixed). For simplicity, we follow their dictum and restrict the presentation to two measures, compensating variation and equivalent variation.
4 Nonetheless, in some contexts, trade-offs have to be made, but they are arguably of such a nature that monetisation is not appropriate. See, e.g., the issues of sacredness (Temper and Martínez-Alier, 2013) or taboo trade-offs (Daw et al., 2015; Stikvoort et al., 2016).
5 On 11 November 1947, Churchill delivered a speech before the British House of Commons, in which he said, 'No one pretends that democracy is perfect or all-wise. Indeed, it has been said that democracy is the worst form of government except for all those other forms that have been tried from time to time.'
6 To make matters even more complicated, the concept of *landscape services* has been proposed as an alternative to ESS (Bastian et al., 2014). In the context of soils, *soil functions* are a common term; the relevance of the ESS framework in this context is subject to debate (Baveye et al., 2016).
7 We ignore here the benefit transfer method, which transfers values estimated in one location to other locations, and focus on primary valuation methods. On benefit transfer, see, e.g., Spash and Vatn (2006) and Schmidt et al. (2016).

References

Aldred, J., 1994. Existence value, welfare and altruism. Environ. Values 3, 381–402. doi:10.3197/096327194776679665.
Aldred, J., 2006. Incommensurability and monetary valuation. Land Econ. 82, 141–161. doi:10.3368/le.82.2.141.
Aldred, J., 2010. The skeptical economist: Revealing the ethics inside economics. Earthscan, London; Washington, DC.
Ambrey, C.L., Fleming, C.M., Chan, A.Y.-C., 2014. Estimating the cost of air pollution in South East Queensland: An application of the life satisfaction non-market valuation approach. Ecol. Econ. 97, 172–181. doi:10.1016/j.ecolecon.2013.11.007.
Arrow, K.J., Fisher, A.C., 1974. Environmental preservation, uncertainty, and irreversibility. Q. J. Econ. 88, 312–319.

Arrow, K.J., Cropper, M.L., Gollier, C., Groom, B., Heal, G.M., Newell, R.G., Nordhaus, W.D., Pindyck, R.S., Pizer, W.A., Portney, P.R., Sterner, T., Tol, R.S.J., Weitzman, M.L., 2014. Should governments use a declining discount rate in project analysis? Rev. Environ. Econ. Policy 8, 145–163. doi:10.1093/reep/reu008.

Arrow, K.J., Dasgupta, P., Goulder, L., Daily, G.C., Ehrlich, P.R., Heal, G.M., Levin, S., Mäler, K.-G., Schneider, S., Starrett, D., Walker, B.W., 2004. Are we consuming too much? J. Econ. Perspect. 18, 147–172.

Arrow, K.J., Solow, R., Portney, P.R., Leamer, E.E., Radner, R., Schuman, H., 1993. Report of the NOAA Panel on Contingent Valuation. NOAA.

Atkinson, G., Bateman, I., Mourato, S., 2012. Recent advances in the valuation of ecosystem services and biodiversity. Oxf. Rev. Econ. Policy 28, 22–47. doi:10.1093/oxrep/grs007.

Barkmann, J., Glenk, K., Keil, A., Leemhuis, C., Dietrich, N., Gerold, G., Marggraf, R., 2008. Confronting unfamiliarity with ecosystem functions: The case for an ecosystem service approach to environmental valuation with stated preference methods. Ecol. Econ. 65, 48–62. doi:10.1016/j.ecolecon.2007.12.002.

Bartkowski, B., Lienhoop, N., 2017. Democracy and valuation: A reply to Schläpfer (2016). Ecol. Econ. 131, 557–560. doi:10.1016/j.ecolecon.2016.05.011.

Bastian, O., Grunewald, K., Syrbe, R.-U., Walz, U., Wende, W., 2014. Landscape services: The concept and its practical relevance. Landsc. Ecol. 29, 1463–1479. doi:10.1007/s10980-014-0064-5.

Baveye, P.C., Baveye, J., Gowdy, J., 2016. Soil 'ecosystem' services and natural capital: Critical appraisal of research on uncertain ground. Front. Environ. Sci. 4. doi:10.3389/fenvs.2016.00041.

Bishop, R.C., 1982. Option value: An exposition and extension. Land Econ. 58, 1–15.

Bockstael, N.E., Freeman, A.M., 2005. Welfare theory and valuation. In: Mäler, K.-G., Vincent, J.R. (Eds), Handbook of environmental economics: Valuing environmental changes. North Holland, Amsterdam, pp. 517–570.

Bockstael, N.E., Freeman, A.M., Kopp, R.J., Portney, P.R., Smith, V.K., 2000. On measuring economic values for nature. Environ. Sci. Technol. 34, 1384–1389. doi:10.1021/es990673l.

Boyd, J., Banzhaf, S., 2007. What are ecosystem services? The need for standardized environmental accounting units. Ecol. Econ. 63, 616–626. doi:10.1016/j.ecolecon.2007.01.002.

Cannon, J., Surjadi, P., 2004. Informing natural resources policy making using participatory rapid economic valuation (PREV): The case of the Togean Islands, Indonesia. Agric. Ecosyst. Environ. 104, 99–111. doi:10.1016/j.agee.2004.01.010.

Cardinale, B.J., Duffy, J.E., Gonzalez, A., Hooper, D.U., Perrings, C., Venail, P., Narwani, A., Mace, G.M., Tilman, D., Wardle, D.A., Kinzig, A.P., Daily, G.C., Loreau, M., Grace, J.B., Larigauderie, A., Srivastava, D.S., Naeem, S., 2012. Biodiversity loss and its impact on humanity. Nature 486, 59–67. doi:10.1038/nature11148.

Carson, R.T., Louviere, J.J., 2011. A common nomenclature for stated preference elicitation approaches. Environ. Resour. Econ. 49, 539–559. doi:10.1007/s10640-010-9450-x.

Chan, K.M.A., Satterfield, T., Goldstein, J., 2012. Rethinking ecosystem services to better address and navigate cultural values. Ecol. Econ. 74, 8–18. doi:10.1016/j.ecolecon.2011.11.011.

Cord, A., Bartkowski, B., Beckmann, M., Dittrich, A., Hermans, K., Kaim, A., Lienhoop, N., Locher-Krause, K., Priess, J., Schröter-Schlaack, C., Schwarz, N., Seppelt, R., Strauch, M., Vaclavik, T., Volk, M., under review. Towards systematic analyses of ecosystem services trade-offs and synergies: Current concepts, methods and research gaps. Ecosyst. Serv.

Costanza, R., 2006. Nature: Ecosystems without commodifying them. Nature 443, 749.

Costanza, R., d'Arge, R., de Groot, R., Farber, S., Grasso, M., Hannon, B., Limburg, K., Naeem, S., O'Neill, R.V., Paruelo, J., Raskin, R.G., Sutton, P., van den Belt, M., 1997. The value of the world's ecosystem services and natural capital. Nature 387, 253–260. doi:10.1038/387253a0.

Costanza, R., de Groot, R., Sutton, P., van der Ploeg, S., Anderson, S.J., Kubiszewski, I., Farber, S., Turner, R.K., 2014. Changes in the global value of ecosystem services. Glob. Environ. Change 26, 152–158. doi:10.1016/j.gloenvcha.2014.04.002.

Daily, G.C., 1997. Introduction: What are ecosystem services? In: Daily, G.C. (Ed.), Nature's services: Societal dependence on natural ecosystems. Island Press, Washington, DC, pp. 1–10.

Dasgupta, P., 2001. Human well-being and the natural environment. Oxford University Press, Oxford; New York.

Dasgupta, P., Mäler, K.-G., 2003. The economics of non-convex ecosystems: Introduction. Environ. Resour. Econ. 26, 499–525. doi:10.1023/B:EARE.0000007347.37345.55.

Daw, T.M., Coulthard, S., Cheung, W.W.L., Brown, K., Abunge, C., Galafassi, D., Peterson, G.D., McClanahan, T.R., Omukoto, J.O., Munyi, L., 2015. Evaluating taboo trade-offs in ecosystems services and human well-being. Proc. Natl. Acad. Sci. 112, 6949–6954. doi:10.1073/pnas.1414900112.

de Groot, R., Brander, L., van der Ploeg, S., Costanza, R., Bernard, F., Braat, L., Christie, M., Crossman, N., Ghermandi, A., Hein, L., Hussain, S., Kumar, P., McVittie, A., Portela, R., Rodriguez, L.C., ten Brink, P., van Beukering, P., 2012. Global estimates of the value of ecosystems and their services in monetary units. Ecosyst. Serv. 1, 50–61. doi:10.1016/j.ecoser.2012.07.005.

de Groot, R.S., Fisher, B., Christie, M., 2010. Integrating the ecological and economic dimensions in biodiversity and ecosystem service valuation. In: Kumar, P. (Ed.), The economics of ecosystems and biodiversity: Ecological and economic foundations. Routledge, London; New York, pp. 9–40.

Dempsey, J., Robertson, M.M., 2012. Ecosystem services: Tensions, impurities, and points of engagement within neoliberalism. Prog. Hum. Geogr. 36, 758–779. doi:10.1177/0309132512437076.

Diamond, P.A., Hausman, J.A., 1994. Contingent valuation: Is some number better than no number? J. Econ. Perspect. 8, 45–64.

Elmqvist, T., Maltby, E., Barker, T., Mortimer, M., Perrings, C., 2010. Biodiversity, ecosystems and ecosystem services. In: Kumar, P. (Ed.), The economics of ecosystems and biodiversity: Ecological and economic foundations. Routledge, London; New York, pp. 41–111.

Elster, J., 1989. Nuts and bolts for the social sciences. Cambridge University Press, Cambridge; New York.

Eser, U., Neureuther, A.-K., Seyfang, H., Müller, A., 2014. Prudence, justice and the good life: A typology of ethical reasoning in selected European national biodiversity strategies. Bundesamt für Naturschutz, Bonn.

Faucheux, S., Pillet, G., 1994. Energy metrics: On various valuation properties of energy. In: Pethig, R. (Ed.), Valuing the environment: Methodological and measurement issues. Springer Netherlands, Dordrecht, pp. 273–309.

Fisher, A.C., Hanemann, W.M., 1990. Option value: Theory and measurement. Eur. Rev. Agric. Econ. 17, 167–180.

Fisher, B., Turner, R.K., Morling, P., 2009. Defining and classifying ecosystem services for decision making. Ecol. Econ. 68, 643–653. doi:10.1016/j.ecolecon.2008.09.014.

Freeman, A.M., 1993. The measurement of environmental and resource values: Theory and methods. Resources for the Future, Washington, DC.

Gollier, C., 2013. Pricing the planet's future: The economics of discounting in an uncertain world. Princeton University Press, Princeton.

Gómez-Baggethun, E., de Groot, R.S., 2010. Natural capital and ecosystem services: The ecological foundation of human society. In: Hester, R.E., Harrison, R.M. (Eds), Ecosystem services. RSC Publishing, Cambridge, pp. 105–121.

Gómez-Baggethun, E., Ruiz Pérez, M., 2011. Economic valuation and the commodification of ecosystem services. Prog. Phys. Geogr. 35, 613–628. doi:10.1177/03091333 11421708.

Gómez-Baggethun, E., de Groot, R., Lomas, P.L., Montes, C., 2010. The history of ecosystem services in economic theory and practice: From early notions to markets and payment schemes. Ecol. Econ. 69, 1209–1218. doi:10.1016/j.ecolecon.2009.11.007.

Haines-Young, R., Potschin, M., 2010a. The links between biodiversity, ecosystem services and human well-being. In: Raffaelli, D.G., Frid, C. (Eds), Ecosystem ecology: A new synthesis. Cambridge University Press, Cambridge; New York, pp. 110–139.

Haines-Young, R., Potschin, M., 2010b. Proposal for a Common International Classification of Ecosystem Goods and Services (CICES) for integrated environmental and economic accounting (Report to the European Environment Agency). University of Nottingham, Nottingham.

Hansjürgens, B., 2004. Economic valuation through cost–benefit analysis: Possibilities and limitations. Toxicology 205, 241–252. doi:10.1016/j.tox.2004.06.054.

Hansjürgens, B., Schröter-Schlaack, C., Berghöfer, A., Lienhoop, N., 2017. Justifying social values of nature: Economic reasoning beyond self-interested preferences. Ecosyst. Serv. 23, 9–17. doi:10.1016/j.ecoser.2016.11.003.

Harsanyi, J.C., 1977. Morality and the theory of rational behavior. Soc. Res. 44, 623–656.

Harvey, D., 1997. Justice, nature and the geography of difference. Wiley, Oxford.

Häyhä, T., Franzese, P.P., 2014. Ecosystem services assessment: A review under an ecological-economic and systems perspective. Ecol. Model. 289, 124–132. doi:10.1016/ j.ecolmodel.2014.07.002.

Heal, G.M., Kriström, B., 2005. National income and the environment. In: Mäler, K.-G., Vincent, J.R. (Eds), Handbook of environmental economics: Economywide and international environmental issues. North Holland, Amsterdam, pp. 1147–1217.

Holland, A., 2002. Are choices tradeoffs?. In: Bromley, D.W., Paavola, J. (Eds), Economics, ethics, and environmental policy: Contested choices. Blackwell Publishers, Malden, pp. 17–34.

Interis, M.G., 2014. A challange to three widely held ideas in environmental valuation. J. Agric. Appl. Econ. 46, 347–356.

Jax, K., Heink, U., 2015. Searching for the place of biodiversity in the ecosystem services discourse. Biol. Conserv. 191, 198–205. doi:10.1016/j.biocon.2015.06.032.

Jax, K., Barton, D.N., Chan, K.M.A., de Groot, R., Doyle, U., Eser, U., Görg, C., Gómez-Baggethun, E., Griewald, Y., Haber, W., Haines-Young, R., Heink, U., Jahn, T., Joosten, H., Kerschbaumer, L., Korn, H., Luck, G.W., Matzdorf, B., Muraca, B., Neßhöver, C., Norton, B., Ott, K., Potschin, M., Rauschmayer, F., von Haaren, C., Wichmann, S., 2013. Ecosystem services and ethics. Ecol. Econ. 93, 260–268. doi:10.1016/j.ecolecon. 2013.06.008.

Kallis, G., Gómez-Baggethun, E., Zografos, C., 2013. To value or not to value? That is not the question. Ecol. Econ. 94, 97–105. doi:10.1016/j.ecolecon.2013.07.002.

Kenter, J.O., 2016. Editorial: Shared, plural and cultural values. Ecosyst. Serv. doi:10.1016/j.ecoser.2016.10.010.

Kenter, J.O., O'Brien, L., Hockley, N., Ravenscroft, N., Fazey, I., Irvine, K.N., Reed, M.S., Christie, M., Brady, E., Bryce, R., Church, A., Cooper, N., Davies, A., Evely, A., Everard, M., Fish, R., Fisher, J.A., Jobstvogt, N., Molloy, C., Orchard-Webb, J., Ranger, S., Ryan, M., Watson, V., Williams, S., 2015. What are shared and social values of ecosystems? Ecol. Econ. 111, 86–99. doi:10.1016/j.ecolecon.2015.01.006.

King, D.M., Wainger, L.A., 2001. Assessing the economic value of biodiversity using indicators of site conditions and landscape context. In: OECD (Ed.), Valuation of biodiversity benefits: Selected studies. OECD, Paris, pp. 121–150.

Kontoleon, A., Pascual, U., Swanson, T.M. (Eds), 2007. Biodiversity economics. Cambridge University Press, Cambridge; New York.

Krutilla, J.V., 1967. Conservation reconsidered. Am. Econ. Rev. 57, 777–786.

Kumar, P. (Ed.), 2010. The economics of ecosystems and biodiversity: Ecological and economic foundations. Routledge, London; New York.

Lamarque, P., Quétier, F., Lavorel, S., 2011. The diversity of the ecosystem services concept and its implications for their assessment and management. C. R. Biol. 334, 441–449. doi:10.1016/j.crvi.2010.11.007.

McAfee, K., 1999. Selling nature to save it? Biodiversity and green developmentalism. Environ. Plan. Soc. Space 17, 133–154. doi:10.1068/d170133.

McCauley, D.J., 2006. Selling out on nature. Nature 443, 27–28. doi:10.1038/443027a.

McConnell, K.E., Bockstael, N.E., 2005. Valuing the environment as a factor of production. In: Mäler, K.-G., Vincent, J.R. (Eds), Handbook of environmental economics: Valuing environmental changes. North Holland, Amsterdam, pp. 621–669.

Mace, G.M., Norris, K., Fitter, A.H., 2012. Biodiversity and ecosystem services: A multilayered relationship. Trends Ecol. Evol. 27, 19–26. doi:10.1016/j.tree.2011.08.006.

Maes, J., Paracchini, M.L., Zulian, G., Dunbar, M.B., Alkemade, R., 2012. Synergies and trade-offs between ecosystem service supply, biodiversity, and habitat conservation status in Europe. Biol. Conserv. 155, 1–12. doi:10.1016/j.biocon.2012.06.016.

Martín-López, B., Gómez-Baggethun, E., García-Llorente, M., Montes, C., 2014. Trade-offs across value-domains in ecosystem services assessment. Ecol. Indic. 37, 220–228. doi:10.1016/j.ecolind.2013.03.003.

Martínez-Alier, J., 2002. The environmentalism of the poor: A study of ecological conflicts and valuation. Edward Elgar, Cheltenham; Northampton, MA.

Matulis, B.S., 2014. The economic valuation of nature: A question of justice? Ecol. Econ. 104, 155–157. doi:10.1016/j.ecolecon.2014.04.010.

MEA, 2005. Ecosystems and human well-being: General synthesis. World Resources Institute, Washington, DC.

Mirrlees, J.A., 1982. The economic uses of utilitarianism. In: Sen, A., Williams, B. (Eds), Utilitarianism and beyond. Cambridge University Press, Cambridge; New York, pp. 63–84.

Mitchell, R.C., Carson, R.T., 1989. Using surveys to value public goods: The contingent valuation method. Resources for the Future, Washington, DC.

Monbiot, G., 2014. Put a price on nature? We must stop this neoliberal road to ruin. *Guardian*, 24 July.

Nahlik, A.M., Kentula, M.E., Fennessy, M.S., Landers, D.H., 2012. Where is the consensus? A proposed foundation for moving ecosystem service concepts into practice. Ecol. Econ. 77, 27–35. doi:10.1016/j.ecolecon.2012.01.001.

Nordhaus, W.D., 2006. Principles of national accounting for nonmarket accounts. In: Jorgenson, D.W., Landefeld, J.S., Nordhaus, W.D. (Eds), A new architecture for the U.S. National Accounts. University of Chicago Press, Chicago, pp. 143–160.

Norgaard, R.B., 2010. Ecosystem services: From eye-opening metaphor to complexity blinder. Ecol. Econ. 69, 1219–1227. doi:10.1016/j.ecolecon.2009.11.009.

Pascual, U., Muradian, R., Brander, L., Gómez-Baggethun, E., Martín-López, B., Verma, M., 2010. The economics of valuing ecosystem services and biodiversity. In: Kumar, P. (Ed.), The economics of ecosystems and biodiversity: Ecological and economic foundations. Routledge, London; New York, pp. 183–256.

Pascual, U., Termansen, M., Hedlund, K., Brussaard, L., Faber, J.H., Foudi, S., Lemanceau, P., Jørgensen, S.L., 2015. On the value of soil biodiversity and ecosystem services. Ecosyst. Serv. 15, 11–18. doi:10.1016/j.ecoser.2015.06.002.

Pearce, D., 1998. Auditing the Earth: The value of the world's ecosystem services and natural capital. Environ. Sci. Policy Sustain. Dev. 40, 23–28. doi:10.1080/00139159 809605092.

Pearce, D.W., 2001. Valuing biological diversity: Issues and overview. In: OECD (Ed.), Valuation of biodiversity benefits: Selected studies. OECD, Paris, pp. 27–44.

Potschin, M.B., Haines-Young, R.H., 2011. Ecosystem services: Exploring a geographical perspective. Prog. Phys. Geogr. 35, 575–594. doi:10.1177/0309133311423172.

Randall, A., 1987. Total Economic Value as a basis for policy. Trans. Am. Fish. Soc. 116, 325–335. doi:10.1577/1548-8659(1987)116<325:TEVAAB>2.0.CO;2.

Randall, A., Stoll, J.R., 1983. Existence value in a total valuation framework. In: Rowe, R.D., Chestnut, L.G. (Eds), Managing air quality and scenic resources at National Parks and Wilderness Areas. Westview Press, Boulder, pp. 265–274.

Robbins, L., 1932. An essay on the nature & significance of economic science. Macmillan, London.

Sagoff, M., 1988. The economy of the earth: Philosophy, law, and the environment. Cambridge University Press, Cambridge; New York.

Samuelson, P.A., 1938. A note on the pure theory of consumer's behaviour. Economica 5, 61–71. doi:10.2307/2548836.

Schläpfer, F., 2016. Democratic valuation (DV): Using majority voting principles to value public services. Ecol. Econ. 122, 36–42. doi:10.1016/j.ecolecon.2015.11.022.

Schmidt, S., Manceur, A.M., Seppelt, R., 2016. Uncertainty of monetary valued ecosystem services: Value transfer functions for global mapping. PLOS ONE 11, e0148524. doi:10.1371/journal.pone.0148524.

Schröter, M., van der Zanden, E.H., van Oudenhoven, A.P.E., Remme, R.P., Serna-Chavez, H.M., de Groot, R.S., Opdam, P., 2014. Ecosystem services as a contested concept: A synthesis of critique and counter-arguments. Conserv. Lett. 7, 514–523. doi:10.1111/conl.12091.

Sen, A., 1977. Rational fools: A critique of the behavioural foundations of economic theory. Philos. Public Aff. 6, 317–344.

Sen, A., 1995. Environmental evaluation and social choice: Contingent valuation and the market analogy. Jpn. Econ. Rev. 46, 23–37. doi:10.1111/j.1468-5876.1995.tb00003.x.

Silvertown, J., 2015. Have ecosystem services been oversold? Trends Ecol. Evol. 30, 641–648. doi:10.1016/j.tree.2015.08.007.

Spangenberg, J.H., Settele, J., 2016. Value pluralism and economic valuation: Defendable if well done. Ecosyst. Serv. 18, 100–109. doi:10.1016/j.ecoser.2016.02.008.

Spangenberg, J.H., Görg, C., Truong, D.T., Tekken, V., Bustamante, J.V., Settele, J., 2014a. Provision of ecosystem services is determined by human agency, not ecosystem functions: Four case studies. Int. J. Biodivers. Sci. Ecosyst. Serv. Manag. 10, 40–53. doi:10.1080/21 513732.2014.884166.

Spangenberg, J.H., von Haaren, C., Settele, J., 2014b. The ecosystem service cascade: Further developing the metaphor – Integrating societal processes to accommodate social processes and planning, and the case of bioenergy. Ecol. Econ. 104, 22–32. doi:10.1016/j.ecolecon.2014.04.025.

Spash, C.L., Vatn, A., 2006. Transferring environmental value estimates: Issues and alternatives. Ecol. Econ., Environmental Benefits Transfer: Methods, Applications and New Directions 60, 379–388. doi:10.1016/j.ecolecon.2006.06.010.

Spash, C.L., Urama, K., Burton, R., Kenyon, W., Shannon, P., Hill, G., 2009. Motives behind willingness to pay for improving biodiversity in a water ecosystem: Economics, ethics and social psychology. Ecol. Econ. 68, 955–964. doi:10.1016/j.ecolecon.2006.09.013.

Stikvoort, B., Lindahl, T., Daw, T.M., 2016. Thou shalt not sell nature: How taboo trade-offs can make us act pro-environmentally, to clear our conscience. Ecol. Econ. 129, 252–259. doi:10.1016/j.ecolecon.2016.05.012.

Sukhdev, P., Wittmer, H., Miller, D., 2014. The Economics of Ecosystems and Biodiversity (TEEB): Challenges and responses. In: Helm, D., Hepburn, C. (Eds), Nature in the balance: The economics of biodiversity. Oxford University Press, New York, pp. 135–150.

TEEB, 2008. The economics of ecosystems & biodiversity: An interim report. European Communities, Germany.

Temper, L., Martínez-Alier, J., 2013. The god of the mountain and Godavarman: Net Present Value, indigenous territorial rights and sacredness in a bauxite mining conflict in India. Ecol. Econ. 96, 79–87. doi:10.1016/j.ecolecon.2013.09.011.

Turner, R.K., Paavola, J., Cooper, P., Farber, S., Jessamy, V., Georgiou, S., 2003. Valuing nature: Lessons learned and future research directions. Ecol. Econ. 46, 493–510. doi:10.1016/S0921-8009(03)00189-7.

Vatn, A., Bromley, D.W., 1994. Choices without prices without apologies. J. Environ. Econ. Manag. 26, 129–148. doi:10.1006/jeem.1994.1008.

Wegner, G., Pascual, U., 2011. Cost–benefit analysis in the context of ecosystem services for human well-being: A multidisciplinary critique. Glob. Environ. Change 21, 492–504. doi:10.1016/j.gloenvcha.2010.12.008.

Weikard, H.-P., 2003. On the quasi-option value of biodiversity and conservation. In: Wesseler, J., Weikard, H.-P., Weaver, R.D. (Eds), Risk and uncertainty in environmental and resource economics. Edward Elgar, Cheltenham, pp. 37–52.

Weisbrod, B.A., 1964. Collective-consumption services of individual-consumption goods. Q. J. Econ. 78, 471–477.

Weitzman, M.L., 1993. What to preserve? An application of diversity theory to crane conservation. Q. J. Econ. 108, 157–183. doi:10.2307/2118499.

3   Definitions, measures and the ecological value of biodiversity

Before we will be able to develop a conceptual framework for the economic valuation of biodiversity, it is necessary to understand what biodiversity really is and why it may be considered of importance from an economic, i.e. essentially anthropocentric point of view. To understand the latter, it is first necessary to know what 'functions' are attributed to biodiversity from an ecological perspective – then, such insights can be used to identify the reasons why biodiversity is *economically* valuable.

In what follows, biodiversity as an ecological concept is discussed, including an overview of definitions, measures and the biodiversity–ecosystem functioning (BEF) literature. The goal of this chapter is to illuminate what biodiversity is and why it is valuable from an ecological point of view.

Despite the not purely scientific origins of the term (see below), biodiversity is essentially an ecological concept. In this chapter, it is shown how it is framed and conceptualised in ecology. First, the debates surrounding biodiversity's definition are briefly sketched. This presentation will then inform the choice of a definition on which the conceptual framework will be based (see Chapter 5). Second, an overview is given about biodiversity measures and indicators. Finally, the BEF literature is reviewed, as it is a crucial element of the conceptual framework proposed in Chapter 5, in that it underlies what is often considered the *ecological value* of biodiversity.

Definitions

Before we will be able to settle on an informed understanding of biodiversity to determine the analysis of its value, it is necessary to have a picture of the debates surrounding this concept's definition, as they illustrate the difficulty of this task.

The term *biodiversity*, which is a contraction of *biological diversity*, was coined in its current form around 1985 by the conservation biologist Walter Rosen for the purposes of the National Forum on BioDiversity in Washington, DC that year (Takacs, 1996). The proceedings of the forum were published by the renowned biologist Edward O. Wilson in his 1988 book *Biodiversity* (Wilson, 1988). However, in its uncontracted form, *biological diversity*, the term has been used at least since 1980 (Harper and Hawksworth, 1994; Koricheva and Siipi, 2004; Swingland, 2013).

It was noted and bemoaned by some commentators that '[s]cientists who love the natural world forged the term *biodiversity* as a weapon to be wielded in these battles [over biological resources]' (Takacs, 1996, p. 3), giving it an emotional and advocative,[1] unscientific connotation. It was also called an 'epistemic-moral hybrid' (Potthast, 2014) and can be understood as a 'boundary concept' (*sensu* Jasanoff, 1987; see also Eser et al., 2014, chap. 1.2), located somewhere between science and politics, as exemplified by the fact that its most influential definition is from a political document (see below).

Whatever the exact motivation behind the coinage of the term, a widely recognised problem with biodiversity is that it does not have a single, clear, agreed-upon definition (Koricheva and Siipi, 2004). Gaston (1996a) calls it a 'pseudocognate' term, which means that its users implicitly assume that others understand it the same way as they themselves do (see also Birnbacher, 2014; Kahn et al., 2001; Meinard et al., 2014). 'The light in which [biodiversity] is viewed may depend on the discipline within whose purviews it is being investigated, on a particular ethical approach or on a given political strategy' (Lanzerath, 2014, p. 1).

So, what is biodiversity then? It is, first and foremost, a form of *diversity*. According to Stirling (2007), diversity in general is a combination of three properties of systems: variety (number of items in a category; the more items, the higher diversity, *ceteris paribus*), balance (distribution of elements across items in a category; the more even the distribution, the higher diversity, *ceteris paribus*) and disparity (degree of difference between items in a category; the less similar the items, the higher diversity, *ceteris paribus*). For biodiversity, these three components correspond to: richness, abundance and phylogenetic distance, respectively. All three properties are relevant and constitutive of diversity (Stirling, 2007).

The most popular and influential definition of *bio*diversity is from the Convention for Biological Diversity (CBD): 'Biodiversity is the variability among living organisms from all sources including, inter alia, terrestrial, marine and other aquatic ecosystems and the ecological complexes of which they are part: this includes diversity within species, between species and of ecosystems' (CBD, 1992). It has been replicated, partly in a slightly modified form, in many publications (e.g. DeLong, 1996; Harper and Hawksworth, 1994; Kumar, 2010; MEA, 2005a; Purvis and Hector, 2000). DeLong (1996) complains that definitions of biodiversity are often *copied* from authorities (as from the CBD in this case) without this choice being sufficiently rationalised. In line with this, Meinard et al. (2014) argue that most definitions used in ecology are based on the CBD definition to such an extent as to make it permissible to summarise them as 'CBD definition and its reformulations' (see also Box 3.1): 'All these definitions are markedly similar, especially in that they are anchored in the notions of diversity, variety and variability, in effect taken as synonyms' (Meinard et al., 2014, p. 88). At the same time, however, they argue that 'although the CBD definition and its reformulations certainly seem unequivocal at first sight, it turns out that they can be understood in markedly different fashions, depending on the method used to clarify and elaborate them' (Meinard et al., 2014, p. 89). This is reflected in the diversity of biodiversity *measures* (see next section).

Box 3.1 Approaches to the definition of biodiversity

Meinard et al. (2014) identify three 'classical approaches toward a general definition of biodiversity'. The *ordinary approach* is based on the (seemingly unequivocal) notion of diversity. They include the *CBD definition and its reformulations* in this class and argue that the basic notion of diversity has been shown to be anything but unequivocal, and so this approach is flawed. In this class appear axiomatic economists such as Weitzman (1992), whose approach will be discussed in more detail in Chapter 4. The *conventionalist approach* advances the use of different surrogates for biodiversity, depending on context. However, the authors argue that in the interdisciplinary landscape of modern biodiversity research this approach leads to large inconsistencies. So, in essence the conventionalist approach effectively precludes the possibility of a general definition of biodiversity. The third approach of *unit and differences* is based on the idea that while biodiversity is irreducible to one single property, 'a phylogenetically informed species count is a good general indicator or surrogate' (Maclaurin and Sterelny, 2008, p. 7; cited in Meinard et al., 2014), the difference from the ordinary approach being the explicit acknowledgement that there cannot be one general definition of biodiversity. Meanwhile, Meinard et al. argue that it is obvious from the frequency with which the term 'biodiversity' is used across disciplines that it is meant to have an overarching, context-independent meaning:

> As soon as one expresses or translates one's disciplinary discourse in the general terms of 'biodiversity', one claims (or at least one is committed to claim) that what one says is relevant beyond one's own disciplinary borders – relevant for all the other disciplines making, as a matter of fact, similar credible claims.
>
> (Meinard et al., 2014, p. 98)

As an alternative, the authors offer a *constructivist approach*, which is based on the premise that 'biodiversity is not a pre-existing entity, but a dynamic concept built by the very fact that several disciplines coherently work together' (2014, p. 90).

Mace et al. (2012) defend the use of broad and inclusive definitions of biodiversity for pragmatic reasons. However, a consequence is that, when it comes to more concrete aspects of the definition, there seem to be a number of points on which biologists have not yet reached agreement. For instance, DeLong (1996) mentions controversies about whether *bio*diversity should only include biotic components of ecosystems or whether abiotic components should also be taken into account.[2] Another point that has been frequently subject to debate is whether *biodiversity* should be used only in the context of 'natural systems' or human-managed systems as well (particularly agriculture).[3] The widely quoted CBD definition seems to include the latter. According to an article in the *Encyclopedia of Biodiversity*, three main attributes of biodiversity can be identified in the literature: composition, including the identity, richness and relative amount of an ecosystem's biotic components; structure, including community/landscape components as well as the organisational levels of species assemblages; and biotic functions, including processes such as nutrient and energy cycles, mutation or food-webs (Swingland, 2013). It is, however, controversial whether all of these are really elements of biodiversity – it might well be argued that the list of attributes is too all-encompassing and unnecessarily stretches the meaning of the term (Faith, 2017; Lyashevska and Farnsworth, 2012; Maier, 2012, chap. 4; Stirling, 2007).

While the CBD definition only names three levels of biodiversity – intraspecies (or genetic) diversity, inter-species diversity (including phylogenetic and taxonomic diversity) and ecosystem diversity (also called *ecological diversity* (Béné and Doyen, 2008; Harper and Hawksworth, 1994)) – further (sub-)levels have been proposed, for example, molecular biodiversity (Campbell, 2003). Also, in addition to different levels, which relate to *structural diversity*, there is the increasingly influential notion of *functional diversity* (Lyashevska and Farnsworth, 2012; Martinez, 1996; Petchey et al., 2009). It is usually understood as 'the diversity in the functional traits of the species in an assemblage' (Mason and Mouillot, 2013, p. 597) and is closely related to the research on biodiversity and ecosystem functioning, which will be discussed below in this chapter.

A flexible definition that encompasses all possible levels and dimensions of biodiversity can be found in Maier (2012): there, biodiversity is defined as the multiplicity or richness of kinds 'in biotic and biota-encompassing categories' (pp. 76–77). This definition implies two conditions: egalitarianism and fungibility. Egalitarianism means that, if we are talking about diversity and, also, its value, all kinds within a category should be viewed as equal – which is another way of stating that biodiversity is not about *identity* of the items under consideration (see also Faith, 2017). The related notion of fungibility, which is close to the economic term *substitutability* (see also Birnbacher, 2014), means that any kind can be substituted by the addition of another, new kind to the diversity mix. Biodiversity consists of a multiplicity of categories, including genes, genomes, species and other taxonomic groups, functions etc., which are not necessarily commensurable (Maier, 2012; but see Lyashevska and Farnsworth, 2012).

To summarise the discussion of the various approaches to defining biodiversity, the following points should be emphasised: There is no single, unequivocally agreed upon definition of biodiversity. It is a highly abstract[4] and complex ecological concept that is used in many different contexts. Calls for precise, one-size-fits-all definitions may well be misguided, as there is a trade-off between vagueness and precision of concepts in modern science – much depends on the specific research context (Strunz, 2012; see also Jax and Heink, 2015; Meinard et al., 2014). Conceptual vagueness can be conducive of pragmatic problem solving and fuel exchange and cooperation across disciplinary borders. Nonetheless,

It is important to be clear about what is meant here by 'diversity'. People frequently cite conservation of diversity as a reason for mounting extraordinary efforts to preserve, say, the whooping crane. What they often really mean is that the whooping crane should be preserved because it is beautiful, or majestic, or inspiring, or because its presence confers some other direct benefit. I would say that these qualities, while important, do not really concern the value of 'diversity' per se.

(Weitzman, 1993, p. 159)

Obviously, there is a need for an encompassing yet precise, flexible definition of biodiversity which would take into account the components of diversity proposed by Stirling (2007), i.e. variety, balance and disparity, while at the same time accounting for the many different perspectives on biodiversity that can be found in the literature. Now that we know the difficulties in providing an operational definition of biodiversity and the various perspectives that should be taken into account, we will be able to formulate a definition of biodiversity to underlie this book's conceptual arguments.

Measures and indicators

[I]t is difficult indeed to contemplate any single general index of diversity that could aggregate properties of variety, balance and disparity in a uniquely robust fashion.

(Stirling, 2007, p. 711)

Since biodiversity is such a complex, multidimensional and abstract concept, its measurement is far from trivial. As Gaston (1996a) emphasised, biodiversity as such cannot be measured – only some of its components/dimensions can (see also Koricheva and Siipi, 2004). It can be said that while the term 'describes variation among units of life, […] the units of biodiversity are themselves many and varied' (Mace, 2014, p. 36). There are two broad categories of biodiversity measures recognised in the literature: those measuring numbers and those concentrating on differences (Gaston, 1996a), with a mixed category of measures attempting to combine these two dimensions (Koricheva and Siipi, 2004). In addition, a number of indicators of biodiversity has been developed and applied in various contexts.[5] How biodiversity can be measured and what indicators can be used to assess its levels has important repercussions for the evaluation of biodiversity proxies used in the economic valuation studies reviewed in Chapter 4. Some of the insights from this section will prove relevant in the discussion of possible ways of coupling the conceptual ideas developed in Chapter 5 with measurable data.

Many different measures of biodiversity have been proposed in various contexts: 'At a global scale, there are roughly 40 potential measures being developed for the Convention on Biological Diversity (CBD) and about 26 indicators being considered in the Streaming Biodiversity Indicators in Europe 2010 process' (Ding and Nunes, 2014, p. 61; see also Polasky et al., 2005). Most diversity measures focus on different components of it. For instance, genetic diversity can be measured by comparing the genotypic differences between species or individuals. Species diversity is mostly measured by means of rather simple indices, such as species richness (number of species) or different indices originating mostly from information theory, in which species numbers are weighted by relative abundances (i.e. they combine variety and balance information according to Stirling, 2007). A typical example is the Shannon index, which is defined as follows:

$$H' = -\sum_i p_i \ln p_i \qquad (3.1)$$

with p_i being the relative abundance of species i, i.e. $p_i = n_i/N$, where n_i is the number of individuals of i and N is the overall population.

Phylogenetic diversity can be measured by combining information on species numbers with genetic dissimilarity between them (phylogenetic distance trees/ dendograms), thus taking into account Stirling's variety and disparity categories (Gotelli and Chao, 2013). Functional diversity measures are closely related to phylogenetic diversity, with the difference that the unit of comparison of species are functional traits (such as, e.g., nutrient capture) instead of genetic information (Petchey and Gaston, 2006). Functional diversity is an attempt to more directly capture the influence of biodiversity on ecosystem functioning (on this, see next section). Table 3.1 provides examples of the measures commonly used to express genetic, species and phylogenetic/functional diversity.

The design and use of biodiversity indices of whichever type/level faces essential data constraints (Mace, 2014; Pereira et al., 2013), which may be the reason why in applications species richness and related measures are by far the most popular.

> Ecosystems are defined as communities of co-occurring species of plants and animals plus the physical environment; as such they are difficult to define and delimit. At the other end of the spectrum, genes are currently still difficult to identify and count. Thus, species counting is the obvious tool for measuring biodiversity.
>
> (Christie et al., 2007, pp. 345–346)

Table 3.1 Common measures of biodiversity

Level of diversity	Measures
Genetic	• Allelic diversity (genotypic differences)
Species	• Shannon index • Gini-Simpson index • Species richness
Phylogenetic/functional	• Rao's quadratic entropy • Phylogenetic entropy • Functional dendograms

Source: compiled from Petchey and Gaston (2006), Gotelli and Chao (2013) and Pereira et al. (2013).

Species richness is sometimes considered a suitable approximation of overall biodiversity (Gaston, 1996b). A similar interpretation is reflected in measuring biodiversity changes in terms of species loss (Lugo, 1988). The problem with this approach, however, is that to date only some 1.7 million species have been documented worldwide – meanwhile, estimates of their real numbers range from around five to more than 100 million (Hunter, 1999; Mainwaring, 2001; Wilson, 1988). While the uncertainty is less pronounced on the level of individual eco-systems,[6] in most cases it is not known how many species live in a given area; even in relatively well studied ecosystems new species are still being found. This problem is additionally aggravated by the fact that there is still no agreement as to what constitutes a species (Isaac et al., 2004). Furthermore, and much more importantly, as shown in an analysis by Lyashevska and Farnsworth (2012), species richness indicators miss much of the diversity information of an eco-system (see also Devictor et al., 2010). Similarly, it was stated in the Millennium Ecosystem Assessment that 'no single component, whether genes, species, or ecosystems, is consistently a good indicator of overall biodiversity, as the components can vary independently' (MEA, 2005b, p. 1).

When data needed to construct diversity indices are not available and the goal is to roughly estimate the state of biodiversity or changes in biodiversity in a given area, various indicators are used, including Red List data, habitat amount, water quality for aquatic biodiversity, so-called indicator species etc. (Butchart et al., 2010). For some purposes, indicators such as population decline, biomass or changes in communities were argued to be more suitable metrics of biodiver-sity change than species numbers (Balmford et al., 2003; Mace, 2014).

While Koricheva and Siipi (2004) maintain that the 'fact that no single measure can capture all the components and attributes of the concept of bio-diversity should not be seen as a weakness but as a manifestation of the concept's flexibility', this supposed flexibility can lead to problems in conveying the message of biodiversity science, be it conservation biology, environmental eco-nomics or any other discipline engaging with this concept. If there are so many differing perspectives on what biodiversity is and how to measure it, transaction costs accrue every time findings that depend on a particular approach have to be communicated and compared with others. For instance, many results of the BEF research are dependent on how biodiversity is measured (see below). Further-more, as will be suggested later (Chapter 4), this multiplicity of views may be confusing even to researchers who deal with biodiversity in their everyday work – not to mention the broader public.

Ecosystem functioning and the ecological value of biodiversity

The biodiversity–ecosystem functioning (BEF) literature reflects a central strand of biodiversity research. The link between biodiversity and various aspects of ecosystem functioning is decisive for biodiversity's influence on human well-being, as will be argued later on in this book. In what follows, an overview of the BEF research is given, including its historical origins, the main findings and some caveats. The relationship between biodiversity and ecosystem functioning is sometimes called the *ecological value* of biodiversity (e.g. Faith, 2017; Farnsworth et al., 2012).

Origins of the debate

As early as 1859, Charles Darwin hypothesised a positive relationship between species diversity and the productivity of an ecosystem (Tilman and Lehman, 2002). In the decades that followed, however, the subject did not attract much attention (Kinzig, 2002). In the second half of the 1950s, a debate set off that still continues to define the importance of the biodiversity concept for ecology and conservation biology – the so-called biodiversity and ecosystem functioning debate (Jax, 2010). At first, the focus was on the hypothesised positive relationship between species richness and the stability of ecosystems. Later, particularly after the introduction of the term *biodiversity* in the late 1980s, the debate broadened significantly – in addition to species richness, many different measures of biodiversity came to be linked, both theoretically and experimentally, to various notions of *ecosystem functioning*.

Biodiversity's influence on ecosystem functioning

The relationship between biodiversity and ecosystem functioning has been studied in many different contexts and by means of different methods and approaches, including conceptual–theoretical considerations, numerical models and field experiments. Experimental evidence comes from both natural and artificial contexts.[7] In different studies, different variables are used both for biodiversity and ecosystem functioning, often leading to different results (Balvanera et al., 2006; Jax, 2010; Pimm, 1984). For instance, Balvanera et al. (2006) found in the empirical literature species richness, functional group richness, evenness and diversity indices as measures of biodiversity, and as many as 29 different types of ecosystem properties used as proxies of functioning. Also, it was pointed out that in some ecosystems keystone species or 'groups with specific functional capabilities' (Haines-Young and Potschin, 2010, p. 127) may be more important than the overall levels of biodiversity (see also Grime, 1997). When ecosystem functioning is identified with the provision of ecosystem services, matters get even more complicated, for there seems to be trade-offs between various service categories, particularly regulating services and provisioning services (Fung et al., 2015; Maes et al., 2012). Nevertheless, there is agreement among most researchers in the field that, while details may be controversial and there remain knowledge gaps, the general picture provided by experimental studies seems to support the initially posed hypothesis that high levels of biodiversity and ecosystem functioning coincide (Balvanera et al., 2006; Cardinale et al., 2012; Elmqvist et al., 2010; Isbell et al., 2015; Maes et al., 2012; Quijas and Balvanera, 2013), even though the magnitude of the respective effects depends on which measure of ecosystem functioning is in focus (Schmid et al., 2002).[8]

Thus, a list of consensus statements summarising the current state of BEF research have been identified (Cardinale et al., 2012):

1 Biodiversity loss leads to a decline in the productive efficiency of eco-systems.
2 Biodiversity increases the temporal stability of ecosystems.
3 The relationship between biodiversity and single ecosystem processes is often non-linear and saturating.
4 Both biodiversity and the existence of key species increase productivity. There are interactions between biodiversity levels and the occurrence of key species.
5 Functional (traits) diversity is crucial for ecosystem functioning.

The central mechanism behind biodiversity's positive influence on ecosystem functioning is *functional redundancy*: the existence of species '[w]ithin the same functional effect type' that, however, exhibit 'different requirements and toler-ances (i.e. belong […] to different functional response types)' (Díaz and Cabido, 2001, p. 653), where *functional response types* are groups of species that exhibit similar responses to the biotic and abiotic environment, and *functional effect types* are groups of species that influence ecosystem processes in similar ways. In fact, the notion of functional redundancy has close links to the so-called *rivet hypothesis* (Ehrlich and Ehrlich, 1981), which states in effect that incremental reductions in biodiversity are possible without immediate breakdown of eco-system functioning – but there is an (uncertain) point beyond which there is too little biodiversity to maintain it (Lawton and Brown, 1994). Usually, the rivet and redundancy hypotheses are viewed as competing hypotheses about the BEF relationship. However, they are actually closely related since redundancy can uphold functioning only given some minimum level, beyond which the function in question breaks down. Thus interpreted, the notion of functional redundancy leads to the so-called *insurance hypothesis* (Folke et al., 1996), which amounts to the 'idea that increasing biodiversity insures ecosystems against declines in their functioning caused by environmental fluctuations' (Yachi and Loreau, 1999, p. 1463). As is sometimes argued in ecological economics literature, this ecological concept can be extended by including human preferences and risk-aversion so as to arrive at the concept of the *insurance value* of biodiversity (see Chapter 4).

Caveats

There are a number of caveats and qualifications that should be mentioned in the context of BEF research. First, as discussed already in the classical paper by Pimm (1984), there exists a number of different measures of both biodiversity and ecosystem functioning (see also Balvanera et al., 2006; Jax, 2010). There-fore, it is not easy to generalise the findings of different studies which use dif-ferent approaches to measurement. Some measures especially of ecosystem functioning (e.g. biomass production) are controversial. On the other hand, it was pointed out that in most studies, only single proxies of ecosystem functioning are used, which might underestimate the effect of biodiversity on overall ecosystem functioning (Gamfeldt et al., 2008).

Another problematic issue is the dominance of small-scale controlled experiments in BEF research, which constrains the external validity and generalisability of their results. Most findings, for example, in the area of forest biodiversity, are based on small-scale, highly artificial experiments – their consequences for complex natural ecosystems are debated (Scherer-Lorenzen et al., 2005). For instance, the most widely cited studies from the Cedar Creek Experiment (e.g. Tilman et al., 2005) are studies of grass diversity, with small numbers of species involved. While there exist studies which investigate the effects of biodiversity in natural ecosystems (cf. Thompson et al., 2009), their number is limited.

A third important issue is more of the epistemological kind: what is measured in BEF studies are *correlations* between (various measures of) biodiversity and ecosystem functioning. It is generally non-trivial to make judgements about causality on the basis of correlations. The theoretical understanding of the respective relationships is limited, despite some recent advances in modelling (cf. Grace et al., 2016). It is especially not clear whether there exist positive feedback loops in the observed systems: initially, biodiversity leads to better ecosystem functioning, but better ecosystem functioning might also have a positive influence on biodiversity levels. For example, it was argued that a well-functioning ecosystem might be less prone to detrimental invasions by exotics (Balvanera et al., 2006) – exotics can thus get into the ecosystem (increase in biodiversity) without harming it (see also Eppink and van den Bergh, 2007, p. 286). Also, a body of literature exists that investigates the effects of ecosystem productivity on biodiversity (e.g. Liang et al., 2016), not the other way around.

A common misunderstanding is behind the critique that the BEF relationship cannot be valid because there exist highly stable and well-functioning ecosystems that at the same time exhibit extremely low levels of biodiversity, such as salt marshes, boreal forests or heathlands (Grime, 1997; Maier, 2012, chap. 6.3). The BEF relationship holds for a given ecosystem type, not across ecosystems. A temperate mountainous forest may require much lower levels of biodiversity to achieve much higher ecosystem functioning than a tropical rainforest. But this does not mean that the association of biodiversity with ecosystem functioning is flawed.

An important point to note at this place is that, in general, biodiversity as such does not have much influence on ecosystem functioning. It is concrete species, groups of them and the interactions between various elements of ecosystems that determine ecosystem functioning. However, as our knowledge of these processes, dynamics and interactions is inherently limited, scientists are forced to recur to the 'crude' notion of biodiversity, which is a useful proxy concept that allows us to approximate the effects of species assemblages on ecosystem functioning. In this sense, the concept of biodiversity is only useful as a second-best solution, where the first-best solution (of knowing the exact roles of the various components of an ecosystem for its proper functioning) is not available.[9]

While BEF research basically involves an ecological perspective on biodiversity, it has important consequences for the economic perspective, which will be explored in Chapters 4 and 5. Particularly, it has relevance for the view of biodiversity as insurance against risks related to the loss of ecosystem intactness, i.e. as underpinning of stable ecosystems.

Summary

The aim of this chapter was to illuminate the valuation object that is at the centre of the focus of the present book. It was shown that the concept of biodiversity is relatively new but highly popular. Because it is quite abstract and complex, the term is often used in very vague and value-laden ways ('epistemic-moral hybrid'). Accordingly, there exist many approaches to defining biodiversity, which encompasses numerous levels and dimensions, including species diversity, genetic diversity, ecosystem diversity, functional diversity. In Chapter 5 we will return to the issue of defining biodiversity. In addition to a presentation of various definitions and the difficulties related to defining biodiversity, it was shown in this chapter how biodiversity can be measured. This discussion will feed into numerous arguments further on in this book, including the critical evaluation of biodiversity proxies used in economic valuation studies and the attempt to provide some insights about how the conceptual framework to be developed in Chapter 5 can be coupled with empirical data.

An important subject of this chapter was biodiversity's *ecological value*. Building upon current ecological literature, it was shown that biodiversity is correlated with ecosystem functioning, particularly with ecosystem stability. Even though there remain unanswered questions and the biodiversity–ecosystem functioning relationship cannot be blindly generalised, it is a crucial aspect for the conceptual arguments developed further on in the book.

Notes

1 In an interview conducted by Edward Grumbine, the acknowledged population geneticist and one of the founding fathers of conservation biology, Michael Soulé, replied to the question why diversity is good that this is based on intuition and aesthetics, while admitting that an important goal of conservation biology is advocacy (Grumbine, 1994).

2 Note that there is a similar discussion regarding ecosystem services, which is the reason why CICES includes an 'accompanying classification of abiotic outputs from natural systems' (CICES V4.3).

3 In recent years, the concept of biocultural diversity has emerged (Maffi and Woodley, 2010), which has an even stronger focus on the interaction between 'natural' and 'artificial' systems.

4 In the present book, this term, when applied to biodiversity, is synonymous with the notion of an 'abstract good', i.e. one which 'cannot exist on its own and cannot be identified without observing and interpreting a wide variety of relevant objects' (Meinard and Grill, 2011, p. 1708).

5 A biodiversity measure or index quantifies one or more aspects of biodiversity directly. A biodiversity indicator, on the other hand, is a proxy, a measure of some other variable that is supposed to be correlated with biodiversity.
6 This is not true for soils – while we do know that soils contain huge numbers of species, only a tiny percentage of them have been characterised (Baveye, 2009).
7 Among the most famous and influential are long-term artificial grassland experiments in the United States (Cedar Creek Experiment) and in Germany (Jena Experiment).
8 For a more sceptical analysis of the empirical evidence, see Schwartz et al. (2000).
9 This point was raised by Mainwaring (2001) in the debate on the Noah's Ark problem initiated by Weitzman (1998), to be discussed in Chapter 4.

References

Balmford, A., Green, R.E., Jenkins, M., 2003. Measuring the changing state of nature. Trends Ecol. Evol. 18, 326–330. doi:10.1016/S0169-5347(03)00067-3.

Balvanera, P., Pfisterer, A.B., Buchmann, N., He, J.-S., Nakashizuka, T., Raffaelli, D., Schmid, B., 2006. Quantifying the evidence for biodiversity effects on ecosystem functioning and services. Ecol. Lett. 9, 1146–1156. doi:10.1111/j.1461-0248.2006.00963.x.

Baveye, P.C., 2009. To sequence or not to sequence the whole-soil metagenome? Nat. Rev. Microbiol. 7, 756–756. doi:10.1038/nrmicro2119-c2.

Béné, C., Doyen, L., 2008. Contribution values of biodiversity to ecosystem performances: A viability perspective. Ecol. Econ. 68, 14–23. doi:10.1016/j.ecolecon.2008.08.015.

Birnbacher, D., 2014. Biodiversity and the 'substitution problem'. In: Lanzerath, D., Friele, M. (Eds), Concepts and values in biodiversity. Routledge, London; New York, pp. 39–54.

Butchart, S.H.M., Walpole, M., Collen, B., Strien, A. van, Scharlemann, J.P.W., Almond, R.E.A., Baillie, J.E.M., Bomhard, B., Brown, C., Bruno, J., Carpenter, K.E., Carr, G.M., Chanson, J., Chenery, A.M., Csirke, J., Davidson, N.C., Dentener, F., Foster, M., Galli, A., Galloway, J.N., Genovesi, P., Gregory, R.D., Hockings, M., Kapos, V., Lamarque, J.-F., Leverington, F., Loh, J., McGeoch, M.A., McRae, L., Minasyan, A., Morcillo, M.H., Oldfield, T.E.E., Pauly, D., Quader, S., Revenga, C., Sauer, J.R., Skolnik, B., Spear, D., Stanwell-Smith, D., Stuart, S.N., Symes, A., Tierney, M., Tyrrell, T.D., Vié, J.-C., Watson, R., 2010. Global biodiversity: Indicators of recent declines. Science 328, 1164–1168. doi:10.1126/science.1187512.

Campbell, A.K., 2003. Save those molecules! Molecular biodiversity and life. J. Appl. Ecol. 40, 193–203. doi:10.1046/j.1365-2664.2003.00803.x.

Cardinale, B.J., Duffy, J.E., Gonzalez, A., Hooper, D.U., Perrings, C., Venail, P., Narwani, A., Mace, G.M., Tilman, D., Wardle, D.A., Kinzig, A.P., Daily, G.C., Loreau, M., Grace, J.B., Larigauderie, A., Srivastava, D.S., Naeem, S., 2012. Biodiversity loss and its impact on humanity. Nature 486, 59–67. doi:10.1038/nature11148.

CBD, 1992. Convention on biological diversity. United Nations, New York.

Christie, M., Hanley, N., Warren, J., Hyde, T., Murphy, K., Wright, R., 2007. Valuing ecological and anthropocentric concepts of biodiversity: A choice experiments application. In: Kontoleon, A., Pascual, U., Swanson, T.M. (Eds), Biodiversity economics. Cambridge University Press, Cambridge; New York, pp. 343–368.

DeLong, D.C., 1996. Defining biodiversity. Wildl. Soc. Bull. 24, 738–749. doi:10.2307/3783168.

Devictor, V., Mouillot, D., Meynard, C., Jiguet, F., Thuiller, W., Mouquet, N., 2010. Spatial mismatch and congruence between taxonomic, phylogenetic and functional diversity: The need for integrative conservation strategies in a changing world. Ecol. Lett. 13, 1030–1040. doi:10.1111/j.1461-0248.2010.01493.x.

Díaz, S., Cabido, M., 2001. Vive la différence: Plant functional diversity matters to ecosystem processes. Trends Ecol. Evol. 16, 646–655. doi:10.1016/S0169-5347(01)02283-2.

Ding, H., Nunes, P.A.L.D., 2014. Modeling the links between biodiversity, ecosystem services and human wellbeing in the context of climate change: Results from an econometric analysis of the European forest ecosystems. Ecol. Econ. 97, 60–73. doi:10.1016/j. ecolecon.2013.11.004.

Ehrlich, P.R., Ehrlich, A.H., 1981. Extinction: The causes and consequences of the disappearance of species. Gollancz, London.

Elmqvist, T., Maltby, E., Barker, T., Mortimer, M., Perrings, C., 2010. Biodiversity, ecosystems and ecosystem services. In: Kumar, P. (Ed.), The economics of ecosystems and biodiversity: Ecological and economic foundations. Routledge, London; New York, pp. 41–111.

Eppink, F.V., van den Bergh, J.C.J.M., 2007. Ecological theories and indicators in economic models of biodiversity loss and conservation: A critical review. Ecol. Econ. 61, 284–293. doi:10.1016/j.ecolecon.2006.01.013.

Eser, U., Neureuther, A.-K., Seyfang, H., Müller, A., 2014. Prudence, justice and the good life: A typology of ethical reasoning in selected European national biodiversity strategies. Bundesamt für Naturschutz, Bonn.

Faith, D.P., 2017. A general model for biodiversity and its value. In: Garson, J., Plutynski, A., Sarkar, S. (Eds), The Routledge handbook of philosophy of biodiversity. Routledge, New York.

Farnsworth, K.D., Lyashevska, O., Fung, T., 2012. Functional complexity: The source of value in biodiversity. Ecol. Complex. 11, 46–52. doi:10.1016/j.ecocom.2012.02.001.

Folke, C., Holling, C.S., Perrings, C., 1996. Biological diversity, ecosystems, and the human scale. Ecol. Appl. 6, 1018–1024. doi:10.2307/2269584.

Fung, T., Farnsworth, K.D., Reid, D.G., Rossberg, A.G., 2015. Impact of biodiversity loss on production in complex marine food webs mitigated by prey-release. Nat. Commun. 6. doi:10.1038/ncomms7657.

Gamfeldt, L., Hillebrand, H., Jonsson, P.R., 2008. Multiple functions increase the importance of biodiversity for overall ecosystem functioning. Ecology 89, 1223–1231. doi:10.1890/06-2091.1.

Gaston, K.J., 1996a. What is biodiversity? In: Gaston, K.J. (Ed.), Biodiversity: A biology of numbers and difference. Blackwell Science, Cambridge, MA, pp. 1–9.

Gaston, K.J., 1996b. Species richness: Measure and measurement. In: Gaston, K.J. (Ed.), Biodiversity: A biology of numbers and difference. Blackwell Science, Cambridge, MA, pp. 77–113.

Gotelli, N.J., Chao, A., 2013. Measuring and estimating species richness, species diversity, and biotic similarity from sampling data. In: Levin, S.A. (Ed.), Encyclopedia of biodiversity. Elsevier, Amsterdam, pp. 195–211.

Grace, J.B., Anderson, T.M., Seabloom, E.W., Borer, E.T., Adler, P.B., Harpole, W.S., Hautier, Y., Hillebrand, H., Lind, E.M., Pärtel, M., Bakker, J.D., Buckley, Y.M., Crawley, M.J., Damschen, E.I., Davies, K.F., Fay, P.A., Firn, J., Gruner, D.S., Hector, A., Knops, J.M.H., MacDougall, A.S., Melbourne, B.A., Morgan, J.W., Orrock, J.L., Prober, S.M., Smith, M.D., 2016. Integrative modelling reveals mechanisms linking productivity and plant species richness. Nature 529, 390–393. doi:10.1038/nature16524.

Grime, J.P., 1997. Biodiversity and ecosystem function: The debate deepens. Science 277, 1260–1261. doi:10.1126/science.277.5330.1260.

Grumbine, R.E., 1994. Conservation biology in context: An interview with Michael Soulé. In: Grumbine, R.E. (Ed.), Environmental policy and biodiversity. Island Press, Washington, DC, pp. 99–105.

Haines-Young, R., Potschin, M., 2010. The links between biodiversity, ecosystem services and human well-being. In: Raffaelli, D.G., Frid, C. (Eds), Ecosystem ecology: A new synthesis. Cambridge University Press, Cambridge; New York, pp. 110–139.

Harper, J.L., Hawksworth, D.L., 1994. Biodiversity: Measurement and estimation. Philos. Trans. R. Soc. Lond. B. Biol. Sci. 345, 5–12. doi:10.1098/rstb.1994.0081.

Hunter, M.L., 1999. Biological diversity. In: Hunter, M.L. (Ed.), Maintaining biodiversity in forest ecosystems. Cambridge University Press, Cambridge; New York, pp. 3–21.

Isaac, N.J.B., Mallet, J., Mace, G.M., 2004. Taxonomic inflation: Its influence on macroecology and conservation. Trends Ecol. Evol. 19, 464–469. doi:10.1016/j.tree.2004.06.004.

Isbell, F., Craven, D., Connolly, J., Loreau, M., Schmid, B., Beierkuhnlein, C., Bezemer, T.M., Bonin, C., Bruelheide, H., de Luca, E., Ebeling, A., Griffin, J.N., Guo, Q., Hautier, Y., Hector, A., Jentsch, A., Kreyling, J., Lanta, V., Manning, P., Meyer, S.T., Mori, A.S., Naeem, S., Niklaus, P.A., Polley, H.W., Reich, P.B., Roscher, C., Seabloom, E.W., Smith, M.D., Thakur, M.P., Tilman, D., Tracy, B.F., van der Putten, W.H., van Ruijven, J., Weigelt, A., Weisser, W.W., Wilsey, B., Eisenhauer, N., 2015. Biodiversity increases the resistance of ecosystem productivity to climate extremes. Nature 526, 574–577. doi:10.1038/nature15374.

Jasanoff, S.S., 1987. Contested boundaries in policy-relevant science. Soc. Stud. Sci. 17, 195–230. doi:10.1177/030631287017002001.

Jax, K., 2010. Ecosystem functioning. Cambridge University Press, Cambridge; New York.

Jax, K., Heink, U., 2015. Searching for the place of biodiversity in the ecosystem services discourse. Biol. Conserv. 191, 198–205. doi:10.1016/j.biocon.2015.06.032.

Kahn, J.R., O'Neill, R., Stewart, S., 2001. Stated preference approaches to the measurement of the value of biodiversity. In: OECD (Ed.), Valuation of biodiversity benefits: Selected studies. OECD, Paris, pp. 91–119.

Kinzig, A.P., 2002. Opening remarks. In: Kinzig, A.P., Pacala, S.W., Tilman, D. (Eds), The functional consequences of biodiversity: Empirical progress and theoretical extensions. Princeton University Press, Princeton, pp. 1–6.

Koricheva, J., Siipi, H., 2004. The phenomenon of biodiversity. In: Oksanen, M., Pietarinen, J. (Eds), Philosophy and biodiversity. Cambridge University Press, Cambridge, pp. 27–53.

Kumar, P. (Ed.), 2010. The economics of ecosystems and biodiversity: Ecological and economic foundations. Routledge, London; New York.

Lanzerath, D., 2014. Biodiversity as an ethical concept: An introduction. In: Lanzerath, D., Friele, M. (Eds), Concepts and values in biodiversity. Routledge, London; New York, pp. 1–17.

Lawton, J.H., Brown, V.K., 1994. Redundancy in ecosystems. In: Schulze, E.-D., Mooney, H.A. (Eds), Biodiversity and ecosystem function. Springer, Berlin; New York.

Liang, J., Watson, J.V., Zhou, M., Lei, X., 2016. Effects of productivity on biodiversity in forest ecosystems across the United States and China. Conserv. Biol. 30, 308–317. doi:10.1111/cobi.12636.

Lugo, A.E., 1988. Estimating reductions in the diversity of tropical forest species. In: Wilson, E.O. (Ed.), Biodiversity. National Academy Press, Washington, DC, pp. 58–70.

Lyashevska, O., Farnsworth, K.D., 2012. How many dimensions of biodiversity do we need? Ecol. Indic. 18, 485–492. doi:10.1016/j.ecolind.2011.12.016.

Mace, G.M., 2014. Biodiversity: Its meanings, roles, and status. In: Helm, D., Hepburn, C. (Eds), Nature in the balance: The economics of biodiversity. Oxford University Press, New York, pp. 35–56.

Mace, G.M., Norris, K., Fitter, A.H., 2012. Biodiversity and ecosystem services: A multi-layered relationship. Trends Ecol. Evol. 27, 19–26. doi:10.1016/j.tree.2011.08.006.

Maclaurin, J., Sterelny, K., 2008. What is biodiversity? University of Chicago Press, Chicago.

Maes, J., Paracchini, M.L., Zulian, G., Dunbar, M.B., Alkemade, R., 2012. Synergies and trade-offs between ecosystem service supply, biodiversity, and habitat conservation status in Europe. Biol. Conserv. 155, 1–12. doi:10.1016/j.biocon.2012.06.016.

Maffi, L., Woodley, E., 2010. Biocultural diversity conservation: A global sourcebook. Earthscan, London; Washington, DC.

Maier, D.S., 2012. What's so good about biodiversity? A call for better reasoning about nature's value. Springer, Dordrecht; New York.

Mainwaring, L., 2001. Biodiversity, biocomplexity, and the economics of genetic dissimilarity. Land Econ. 77, 79. doi:10.2307/3146982.

Martinez, N.D., 1996. Defining and measuring functional aspects of biodiversity. In: Gaston, K.J. (Ed.), Biodiversity: A biology of numbers and difference. Blackwell Science, Cambridge, MA, pp. 114–148.

Mason, N.W.H., Mouillot, D., 2013. Functional diversity measures. In: Levin, S.A. (Ed.), Encyclopedia of biodiversity. Elsevier, Amsterdam, pp. 597–608.

MEA, 2005a. Ecosystems and human well-being: Biodiversity synthesis. World Resources Institute, Washington, DC.

MEA, 2005b. Ecosystems and human well-being: General synthesis. World Resources Institute, Washington, DC.

Meinard, Y., Grill, P., 2011. The economic valuation of biodiversity as an abstract good. Ecol. Econ. 70, 1707–1714. doi:10.1016/j.ecolecon.2011.05.003.

Meinard, Y., Coq, S., Schmid, B., 2014. A constructivist approach toward a general definition of biodiversity. Ethics Policy Environ. 17, 88–104. doi:10.1080/21550085.2014.885490.

Pereira, H.M., Ferrier, S., Walters, M., Geller, G.N., Jongman, R.H.G., Scholes, R.J., Bruford, M.W., Brummitt, N., Butchart, S.H.M., Cardoso, A.C., Coops, N.C., Dulloo, E., Faith, D.P., Freyhof, J., Gregory, R.D., Heip, C., Höft, R., Hurtt, G., Jetz, W., Karp, D.S., McGeoch, M.A., Obura, D., Onoda, Y., Pettorelli, N., Reyers, B., Sayre, R., Scharlemann, J.P.W., Stuart, S.N., Turak, E., Walpole, M., Wegmann, M., 2013. Essential biodiversity variables. Science 339, 277–278. doi:10.1126/science.1229931.

Petchey, O.L., Gaston, K.J., 2006. Functional diversity: Back to basics and looking forward. Ecol. Lett. 9, 741–758. doi:10.1111/j.1461-0248.2006.00924.x.

Petchey, O.L., O'Gorman, E.J., Flynn, A., 2009. A functional guide to functional diversity measures. In: Naeem, S., Bunker, D.E., Hector, A., Loreau, M., Perrings, C. (Eds), Biodiversity, ecosystem functioning, & human wellbeing: An ecological and economic perspective. Oxford University Press, Oxford, pp. 49–59.

Pimm, S.L., 1984. The complexity and stability of ecosystems. Nature 307, 321–326. doi:10.1038/307321a0.

Polasky, S., Costello, C., Solow, A., 2005. The economics of biodiversity. In: Mäler, K.-G., Vincent, J.R. (Eds), Handbook of environmental economics: Economywide and international environmental issues. North Holland, Amsterdam, pp. 1517–1560.

Potthast, T., 2014. The values of biodiversity: Philosophical considerations connecting theory and practice. In: Lanzerath, D., Friele, M. (Eds), Concepts and values in biodiversity. Routledge, London; New York, pp. 132–146.

Purvis, A., Hector, A., 2000. Getting the measure of biodiversity. Nature 405, 212–219. doi:10.1038/35012221.

Quijas, S., Balvanera, P., 2013. Biodiversity and ecosystem services. In: Levin, S.A. (Ed.), Encyclopedia of biodiversity. Elsevier, Amsterdam, pp. 341–356.

Scherer-Lorenzen, M., Körner, C., Schulze, E.-D., 2005. The functional significance of forest diversity: A synthesis. In: Scherer-Lorenzen, M., Körner, C., Schulze, E.-D. (Eds), Forest diversity and function: Temperate and boreal systems. Springer, Berlin; New York, pp. 377–389.

Schmid, B., Joshi, J., Schläpfer, F., 2002. Empirical evidence for biodiversity–ecosystem functioning relationships. In: Kinzig, A.P., Pacala, S.W., Tilman, D. (Eds), The functional consequences of biodiversity: Empirical progress and theoretical extensions. Princeton University Press, Princeton, pp. 120–150.

Schwartz, M.W., Brigham, C.A., Hoeksema, J.D., Lyons, K.G., Mills, M.H., Mantgem, P.J. van, 2000. Linking biodiversity to ecosystem function: Implications for conservation ecology. Oecologia 122, 297–305. doi:10.1007/s004420050035.

Stirling, A., 2007. A general framework for analysing diversity in science, technology and society. J. R. Soc. Interface 4, 707–719. doi:10.1098/rsif.2007.0213.

Strunz, S., 2012. Is conceptual vagueness an asset? Arguments from philosophy of science applied to the concept of resilience. Ecol. Econ. 76, 112–118. doi:10.1016/j.ecolecon.2012.02.012.

Swingland, I.R., 2013. Definition of biodiversity. In: Levin, S.A. (Ed.), Encyclopedia of biodiversity. Elsevier, Amsterdam, pp. 399–410.

Takacs, D., 1996. The idea of biodiversity: Philosophies of paradise. Johns Hopkins University Press, Baltimore.

Thompson, I., Mackey, B., McNulty, S., Mosseler, A., 2009. Forest resilience, biodiversity, and climate change: A synthesis of the biodiversity/resilience/stability relationship in forest ecosystems (No. 43), CBD Technical Series. Secretariat of the Convention on Biological Diversity, Montreal.

Tilman, D., Lehman, C., 2002. Biodiversity, composition, and ecosystem processes: Theory and concepts. In: Kinzig, A.P., Pacala, S.W., Tilman, D. (Eds), The functional consequences of biodiversity: Empirical progress and theoretical extensions. Princeton University Press, Princeton, pp. 9–41.

Tilman, D., Polasky, S., Lehman, C., 2005. Diversity, productivity and temporal stability in the economies of humans and nature. J. Environ. Econ. Manag. 49, 405–426. doi:10.1016/j.jeem.2004.03.008.

Weitzman, M.L., 1992. On diversity. Q. J. Econ. 107, 363–405.

Weitzman, M.L., 1993. What to preserve? An application of diversity theory to crane conservation. Q. J. Econ. 108, 157–183. doi:10.2307/2118499.

Weitzman, M.L., 1998. The Noah's ark problem. Econometrica 66, 1279. doi:10.2307/2999617.

Wilson, E.O. (Ed.), 1988. Biodiversity. National Academy Press, Washington, DC.

Yachi, S., Loreau, M., 1999. Biodiversity and ecosystem productivity in a fluctuating environment: The insurance hypothesis. Proc. Natl. Acad. Sci. 96, 1463–1468. doi:10.1073/pnas.96.4.1463.

Excursus

Biodiversity value in environmental ethics

In the previous chapter, we looked at biodiversity from a primarily descriptive, ecological perspective, focusing on its definition, measurement and its relevance for ecosystem functioning. Positive insights are crucial for the proper identification of the *valuation object* biodiversity. A properly specified valuation object can then be valued, which is a normative exercise.[1] The goal of the present book is to conceptually identify sources of the economic value of biodiversity and to suggest viable ways and means of its estimation. In other words, the ultimate goal is to illuminate the normative dimension of biodiversity (with the qualification that economics links value with the preferences of individuals). Given this, environmental ethics, which also has a lot to say about biodiversity and its value, can provide some useful insights. Particularly, it illuminates the ethical relevance and status of economic valuation (an issue related to those already discussed in Chapter 2); and it offers useful arguments regarding biodiversity's value, especially its intrinsic and existence value, which will be taken up in Chapter 4, where economically relevant sources of the value of biodiversity will be discussed.

Economic theory, especially neoclassical economics, has a quite clear ethical background, namely a combination of anthropocentrism and utilitarianism/welfarism (see Chapter 2). In particular, the utilitarian perspective is often criticised as very narrow by ethicists (Sen and Williams, 1982). Therefore, as shown in the debate about the relationship between ecological economics and neoclassical theory (Spash, 2012, 2013; Strunz et al., 2016) and in the literature critical of the conventional economic valuation approach (Jax et al., 2013; Kenter et al., 2015; Lo and Spash, 2013), there is a lot that environmental and ecological economics can learn from ethics in general and environmental ethics in particular.[2] Even if the lessons learned lead 'only' to the clarification of one's own standpoint, they can still be intellectually fruitful by providing reasoned arguments for this standpoint. As there exists much ethical literature on the value(s) of biodiversity, it might be useful to consider the main points made by environmental ethicists and their implications for the economic valuation approach advanced here. The field of environmental ethics is vast and diverse, so the presentation here is only cursory by necessity, yet the selected arguments should suffice to strengthen and/ or qualify some of the arguments made later in this book, particularly in Chapters 4 and 5.

One of the basic analytical concepts of environmental ethics is the classification of axiological (value-theoretic) arguments according to how they respond to the so-called *demarcation problem*, i.e. the identification of the *moral community*, the group of entities towards which people have moral duties or, in the language of value theories, members of which have intrinsic or inherent values.[3] There exist two large classes of demarcation arguments, anthropocentric and non-anthropocentric (physiocentric).[4] The latter can be further subdivided into pathocentrism, biocentrism, ecocentrism and holism, but these distinctions are of less relevance here. Each of the 'centrisms' defines the moral community. The anthropocentric perspective confines its reach to human beings and admits only instrumental values to other entities, while physiocentric perspectives further include non-human entities (e.g. sentient organisms in the case of pathocentrism). Economics is often criticised for its exclusively anthropocentric perspective. Yet it should be acknowledged that many environmental ethicists consider physiocentrism as problematic (DesJardins, 2006, pp. 114–115; Eser et al., 2014, pp. 34–35; Potthast, 2014, pp. 140–142), especially because it seems to require a definition of nature's or natural things' interest or well-being (Maier, 2012, pp. 395–396). Also, some ethicists view intrinsic values as compatible with economic valuation, at least under some specific interpretations. For instance, Davidson (2013) argues that economic valuation is reconcilable with a consequentialist interpretation of intrinsic value, as 'our willingness to pay may also directly reflect benefits to other people or nature instead of benefits to ourselves' (p. 173). Similarly, it was noted by Dasgupta (2001, p. 260) that

> [p]urists would say that including a resource's intrinsic value in U [utility] is a misuse of terminology, since U is being interpreted as human well-being. It is a misuse of terminology, but no harm is done to our understanding of matters as long as we know that it is a misuse.

Whether this interpretation is appropriate is debated, for example by McShane (2017b), who shows that none of the many possible interpretations of intrinsic value is compatible with the economic perspective.

Eser et al. (2014) distinguish three types of arguments used in environmental debates, which can be loosely connected to three major strands in ethical theory: prudential arguments (consequentialism/utilitarianism), justice arguments (deontology) and good life arguments (virtue ethics) (see also Díaz et al., 2015; Spangenberg and Settele, 2016). It is often claimed that economics, being based on a utilitarian framework, does not take into account other, non-utilitarian types of arguments. However, it has been shown that in economic valuation the motivations behind the (hypothetical) choices people make, from which willingness-to-pay (WTP) measures can be subsequently derived, are by no means restricted to utilitarian considerations and include many other kinds of ethical reasoning as well (Spash, 2006; Spash et al., 2009; see also Aldred, 1994; Davidson, 2013; Martín-López et al., 2007). Thus, it may be argued that using WTP and cost–benefit analyses as arguments for or against the protection of biodiversity is utilitarian. Yet the basis of the WTP is not, at least not necessarily. In this sense, economic valuation can be viewed as a liberal approach, in that it is based on the preferences of humans, without being concerned with the origin of these preferences.[5]

In a similar vein, it has often been emphasised by environmental ethicists that the

> subtlest sense in which the environment is a public good is that it is an aspect of the common good. [...] That is, valued parts of the natural world are widely regarded as goods to society, over and above the benefits they provide to individuals.
>
> (Jacobs, 1997, p. 212)

Accordingly, there has been much emphasis on social or cultural values of bio-diversity and ecosystem services (Chan et al., 2012; Kenter, 2016; Kenter et al., 2015; Scholte et al., 2015), which are often viewed as being in opposition to the supposedly self-interested preferences elicited in economic valuation studies. Whether this view really applies is, however, a controversial issue (Jacobs, 1997; Jax et al., 2013), and some scholars have argued that both individual and social values are relevant (Bartkowski and Lienhoop, 2016; Lo and Spash, 2013). The crux of all this is that, irrespective of the ethical source of a particular value/valuation of biodiversity, it can be captured by economic valuation as long as it is reflected in (broadly defined) *individual* preferences.

Another, more general problem identified in environmental ethics literature is the issue of representation of and taking into account the interests of future generations (O'Neill, 2001). Biodiversity's importance is often primarily seen in our moral obligation not to 'rob' future generations of the possibility to enjoy a quality of life at least similar to ours (Wägele, 2014). This is, of course, a rather difficult starting point, as we cannot know the preferences and possibilities of future generations (Krysiak and Krysiak, 2006; Scholtes, 2010). This means that uncertainty about the future is a central consideration in the context of biodiversity's (economic) value. We will come back to this issue in more detail in Chapters 4 and 5.

A number of ethical arguments can be made for the conservation of biodiversity (few if any have been made against it). Biodiversity can be viewed, among others, as a resource, provider of services, 'pharmacopoeia' (source of pharmaceutically useful substances), container of knowledge or carrier of option value (cf. Eser et al., 2014; Maier, 2012; Potthast, 2014). Many of these ideas will be taken up in Chapter 4, since they can be and have been framed in economic terms; in the remainder of this section, however, we focus on the issue of biodiversity's 'value on its own'.

An interesting and economically relevant question, controversially debated in environmental ethics, is whether biodiversity has intrinsic/inherent value (or, for that matter, existence value; one may summarise these notions as 'value on its own'). Highly divergent views on that matter have emerged. The oldest arguments suggesting that diversity in general is good (in the sense of intrinsic-ally valuable) go back to Gottfried Wilhelm Leibniz and Thomas Aquinas, who saw an inherent link between diversity/variety and divine order. However, their reasoning is dependent on a quite specific religious inclination and, stripped of it, is rather arbitrary. In fact, it is very difficult to offer an alternative argument showing that diversity as such is good (Maier, 2012, chap. 2.3.2). With regard to biodiversity, arguments for its general *goodness* or *value* are often linked to the so-called deep ecology movement:

> Value is an intrinsic part of diversity; it does not depend on the properties of the species in question, the uses to which particular species may or may not be put, or their alleged role in the balance of global ecosystems. For biologi-cal diversity, value is. Nothing more and nothing less. No cottage industry of expert evaluators is needed to assess this kind of value.
>
> (Ehrenfeld, 1988, p. 214)

The problem here appears to be that the focus is on the species that 'compose' biodiversity, which can be argued to be intrinsically valuable – yet to conclude that since single species have value on their own, biodiversity, i.e. the diversity of living things (including, but not limited to species), must have it too, is a fallacy of composition. This view is nonetheless common in the discussion about the link between biodiversity and ecosystem services, where biodiversity is meant to be preserved because of the intrinsic value of species (Jax and Heink, 2015), or its preservation is framed as an ecosystem service: 'regarding biodiver-sity itself as an ecosystem service reflects an intrinsic value for biodiversity, whereby organisms have value that is by definition unquantifiable and therefore nontransactable' (Mace et al., 2012, p. 20).

Some base their arguments in favour of biodiversity having intrinsic value on a differentiation between natural (intrinsically valuable, good) and human-made diversity (e.g. Lee, 2004). Such arguments suffer from two problems: first, the distinction between natural/native and human-made/artificial/exotic/alien is contestable, both as a descriptive and a normative concept (see Box E.1); second, the implied source of intrinsic value in this case appears to be naturalness, not diversity. Similarly, many proponents of biodiversity's intrinsic value do not make a clear distinction between biodiversity and nature, and use these terms effectively as synonymous (e.g. Deliège and Neuteleers, 2015). But if biodiver-sity really is the same as nature, what do we need two different terms for?

Another approach to the problem is based on the identification of diversity with *difference*,[6] where it is argued that interactions with nature are constitutive of human existence and that 'differences are also psychologically important for humans' (Eser et al., 2014, chap. 8.1.2):

> Difference matters for accepting responsibility for someone or something. In all these cases, it is not the sheer number of diverse things, but the experi-ence of difference that gives value to a particular aspect of nature, a

particular landscape or a particular object. In fact, people do also value monotonous landscapes like deserts or the quiet sea – exactly because they offer a unique experience of difference.

(p. 173)

This essentially eudaimonistic argument is, however, based on two problematic assumptions. First, there is the claim that 'differences are psychologically important for humans', which might be granted on the basis of analogy to psychological findings from other fields (e.g. Plaut, 2014), though it is at least not obvious that this statement can be generalised. Second, this notion is extended to biodiversity, which is less convincing – as forcefully argued by Maier (2012, chap. 6.6), it is unclear why the supposed (and debatable) constitutiveness of interactions with nature for human beings would necessitate any *diversity* of natural things. Furthermore, the argument by Eser et al. (2014) is not an argument in favour of valuing diversity as such, but of valuing it for its contribution to 'psychologically proper' human development. It may be concluded, however tentatively, that it is difficult to find convincing arguments in the literature on environmental ethics that would speak in favour of attributing 'value on its own' to biodiversity.

A recent review of different interpretations of the concept of intrinsic value and their applicability to biodiversity can be found in McShane (2017a). She distinguishes the following interpretations:

- moral standing, which links intrinsic value to the demarcation problem and is based on our moral duties towards entities;
- objective value, which is close to what was called non-anthropogeneity above, i.e. the question of whether something has value irrespective of the existence of any valuers;
- non-instrumental value, i.e. a value not resulting from the respective entity being a means (an instrument) towards an end;
- non-extrinsic value, which means that the entity in question is valuable 'independently of any connections to any [other] valuable thing' (p. 421);
- final value, which is similar to the latter, but focuses on our attitude towards things, not directly on their value;
- unconditional value, i.e. value irrespective of context;
- overriding value, i.e. value that overrides any other value (in economic terms, one would call it lexicographic);
- non-anthropocentric value, which means that something is valuable irrespective of human interests.

Clearly, all these interpretations are more or less related. Nonetheless, the conclusion of the author is quite frank:

While there might be arguments that could succeed in establishing the final and/or non-anthropocentric value of biodiversity, my own view is that intrinsic value claims about particular parts of the world tend to do a better job of capturing concerns that many people express in terms of biodiversity, which are often concerns about particular things in the world that are threatened.

(p. 435)

This is fortunate because if biodiversity would have intrinsic value, this would severely confine the reach of any economic, preference-based reasoning (McShane, 2017b).

Box E.1 Native vs non-native biodiversity

One of the many unresolved debates regarding both definition and measurement of biodiversity concerns the question whether there should be a distinction between *native* (i.e. presumably 'good') and *non-native/exotic/alien/invasive* ('bad') biodiversity (Heink and Jax, 2014). For instance, Hunter (1999) criticises the supposedly misleading use of common measures of biological diversity, as they do not reflect links and interdependencies among species and may also invite the introduction of non-native species as a move to enhance local biodiversity. In line with this critique, Dasgupta (2001, p. 128) stresses that biodiversity is about species that 'have co-evolved under selection pressure[, not] a simple head-count of "objects"'.

Under this interpretation, which is the basis of the field of *invasion biology*, biodiversity is implicitly identified with a notion of 'original pristinity'. This identification has been criticised as naive since truly pristine ecosystems hardly exist (Ellis et al., 2013; Maier, 2012, chap. 4), as recognised by those studying *biocultural diversity* (Maffi and Woodley, 2010). Most if not all ecosystems on Earth are what they are because of different degrees of human influence at least since the Neolithic Age. Moreover, the very notions of *alien* and *native* species can be challenged for conceptual reasons – numerous authors have argued that they cannot be defined without a considerable degree of arbitrariness (cf. Davis et al., 2011; Thompson, 2014; Sagoff, 2005).

Even under the assumption that 'nativeness' can be defined in a non-arbitrary way, alien species' effects on biodiversity are very case-specific (Gurevitch and Padilla, 2004; Warren, 2007) and not generally negative (Reise et al., 2006; Rodriguez, 2006; Sax and Gaines, 2008).

Furthermore, a fundamental problem of the distinction 'native vs non-native' is that it is highly normative. It injects a normative twist into the very notion of biodiversity. For instance, there exist arguments for favouring 'natural' biodiversity over 'man-made' biodiversity (Lee, 2004) – the arbitrariness of any dividing line between the two notwithstanding, there is no clearly identifiable reason for actually preferring 'natural' over 'man-made' intrinsically. It can be argued that since human beings have been part of evolutionary processes for millennia, and evolutionary processes (including extinctions, creation of new species, relocations etc.) are an integral part of the dynamic system we call *nature*, the division between 'natural' or 'native' and 'man-made' or 'non-native' spuriously suggests that natural systems are static – which they clearly are not. In fact, it was observed that 'artificial' habitats can be important refuges for species that lost their original habitats (Martínez-Abraín and Jiménez, 2016).

In the end, one of the main arguments of the present book is that to use bio-diversity as a valuation object, it is essential to take as much of the 'moral' out of the 'epistemic-moral hybrid' (Potthast, 2014) as possible. Thus, the notion of nativeness seems to conflate more than it enlightens.

However, it should be kept in mind that laypeople seem to be influenced by the public debates regarding alien species and tend to prefer those species they con-sider to be natives (e.g. Lundhede et al., 2015; see also Schüttler et al., 2011). This is especially important given economics' utilitarian approach. It is an open question how to deal with such dissonances between conceptual coherence and seemingly 'irrational' preferences (see also the discussion of the case study in Chapter 5).

Summary

The goal of this Excursus into the realm of environmental ethics and its views on biodiversity value was to broaden the perspective for the economic analysis thereof. The main findings of this exercise are: (i) even though economic valu-ation is controversial because of its utilitarian basis, it can to some extent take into account preferences based on different ethical stances; (ii) despite the popularity of the claim that biodiversity has intrinsic value (or, more gener-ally, value on its own), especially in conservation biology and deep ecology, there appear to be no convincing arguments to support this claim. If we want to identify the value of biodiversity, we have to look elsewhere. (iii) One place where we might find answers is the future – our responsibility towards future generations and the uncertainty surrounding the specifics of this responsibility. In the next two chapters, we will adopt an economic perspective to tackle these issues.

Notes

1 Economic valuation is sometimes described by economists as a positive exercise, since it consists in eliciting and aggregating the values held by individuals. However, in the process of eliciting and aggregating values/preferences, a number of implicit normative judgements are made, e.g. which values to include, how to aggregate differing values etc. (cf. Aldred, 2010, chap. 6).
2 On the potential of fruitful bidirectional exchange between economics and ethics in general, see Sen (1987). Aldred (2010) argues in his illuminating book that economics is generally much more normative than usually believed – engaging with ethics can thus help economists make clear their own normative assumptions.
3 It is somewhat typical of philosophy that different authors use different terms to describe seemingly similar concepts. *Inherent*, *intrinsic* and *existence* value is one primary example. For an overview about the different uses of these terms, see Eser et al. (2014, p. 152); also McShane (2017a, 2017b), Spangenberg and Settele (2016) and Chan et al. (2016). A category which seems to be outside the classic demarcation problem distinction is eudaimonistic value (see Eser et al., 2014; Jax et al., 2013;

Muraca, 2011), which derives from Aristotelian virtue ethics and assigns value to things because they are essential for a *good life* (eudaimonia, εὐδαιμονία). Note also that intrinsic value of nature is among the 'core beliefs' of ecological economics (Røpke, 2005), in whose tradition much of the present book is written. This strengthens the rationale for engaging with the question whether biodiversity *can* have value on its own.

4 A different question altogether is whether the values nature is supposed to have are believed to be anthropogenic/anthroporelational, i.e. whether they exist independently of human existence (cf. Lanzerath, 2014; Maier, 2012, pp. 19–20). These two questions are sometimes problematically intermingled. The issue of anthropogenicity, however, is quite metaphysical and will not be further discussed here. But see McShane (2017a).

5 This can be and has been, of course, validly criticised, because economics implicitly treats sadistic or otherwise perversely motivated preferences equally with others (cf. Sen, 1977). On the limitations of utilitarianism, in and beyond economics, see Sen and Williams (1982). See also Chapter 2.

6 This view is closely related to the economics literature on diversity value (e.g. Klemisch-Ahlert, 1993; Nehring and Puppe, 2002; Weitzman, 1992). See also Chapter 4.

References

Aldred, J., 1994. Existence value, welfare and altruism. Environ. Values 3, 381–402.

Aldred, J., 2010. The skeptical economist: Revealing the ethics inside economics. Earthscan, London; Washington, DC.

Bartkowski, B., Lienhoop, N., 2016. Beyond rationality, towards reasonableness: Deliberative monetary valuation and Amartya Sen's approach to rationality. Presented at the AES 2016, Warwick.

Chan, K.M.A., Balvanera, P., Benessaiah, K., Chapman, M., Díaz, S., Gómez-Baggethun, E., Gould, R., Hannahs, N., Jax, K., Klain, S., Luck, G.W., Martín-López, B., Muraca, B., Norton, B., Ott, K., Pascual, U., Satterfield, T., Tadaki, M., Taggart, J., Turner, N., 2016. Opinion: Why protect nature? Rethinking values and the environment. Proc. Natl. Acad. Sci. 113, 1462–1465.

Chan, K.M.A., Satterfield, T., Goldstein, J., 2012. Rethinking ecosystem services to better address and navigate cultural values. Ecol. Econ. 74, 8–18.

Dasgupta, P., 2001. Human well-being and the natural environment. Oxford University Press, Oxford; New York.

Davidson, M.D., 2013. On the relation between ecosystem services, intrinsic value, existence value and economic valuation. Ecol. Econ. 95, 171–177.

Davis, M.A., Chew, M.K., Hobbs, R.J., Lugo, A.E., Ewel, J.J., Vermeij, G.J., Brown, J.H., Rosenzweig, M.L., Gardener, M.R., Carroll, S.P., Thompson, K., Pickett, S.T.A., Stromberg, J.C., Tredici, P.D., Suding, K.N., Ehrenfeld, J.G., Grime, J.P., Mascaro, J., Briggs, J.C., 2011. Don't judge species on their origins. Nature 474, 153–154.

Deliège, G., Neuteleers, S., 2015. Should biodiversity be useful? Scope and limits of ecosystem services as an argument for biodiversity conservation. Environ. Values 24, 165–182.

DesJardins, J.R., 2006. Environmental ethics: An introduction to environmental philosophy, 4th edn. Wadsworth, Belmont; London.

Díaz, S., Demissew, S., Carabias, J., Joly, C., Lonsdale, M., Ash, N., Larigauderie, A., Adhikari, J.R., Arico, S., Báldi, A., Bartuska, A., Baste, I.A., Bilgin, A., Brondizio, E., Chan, K.M., Figueroa, V.E., Duraiappah, A., Fischer, M., Hill, R., Koetz, T., Leadley,

P., Lyver, P., Mace, G.M., Martin-Lopez, B., Okumura, M., Pacheco, D., Pascual, U., Pérez, E.S., Reyers, B., Roth, E., Saito, O., Scholes, R.J., Sharma, N., Tallis, H., Thaman, R., Watson, R., Yahara, T., Hamid, Z.A., Akosim, C., Al-Hafedh, Y., Allah-verdiyev, R., Amankwah, E., Asah, S.T., Asfaw, Z., Bartus, G., Brooks, L.A., Caillaux, J., Dalle, G., Darnaedi, D., Driver, A., Erpul, G., Escobar-Eyzaguirre, P., Failler, P., Fouda, A.M.M., Fu, B., Gundimeda, H., Hashimoto, S., Homer, F., Lavorel, S., Lichtenstein, G., Mala, W.A., Mandivenyi, W., Matczak, P., Mbizvo, C., Mehrdadi, M., Metzger, J.P., Mikissa, J.B., Moller, H., Mooney, H.A., Mumby, P., Nagendra, H., Nesshover, C., Oteng-Yeboah, A.A., Pataki, G., Roué, M., Rubis, J., Schultz, M., Smith, P., Sumaila, R., Takeuchi, K., Thomas, S., Verma, M., Yeo-Chang, Y., Zlatanova, D., 2015. The IPBES Conceptual framework: Connecting nature and people. Curr. Opin. Environ. Sustain. 14, 1–16.

Ehrenfeld, D., 1988. Why put a value on biodiversity? In: Wilson, E.O. (Ed.), Biodiversity. National Academy Press, Washington, DC, pp. 212–216.

Ellis, E.C., Kaplan, J.O., Fuller, D.Q., Vavrus, S., Goldewijk, K.K., Verburg, P.H., 2013. Used planet: A global history. Proc. Natl. Acad. Sci. 110, 7978–7985.

Eser, U., Neureuther, A.-K., Seyfang, H., Müller, A., 2014. Prudence, justice and the good life: A typology of ethical reasoning in selected European national biodiversity strategies. Bundesamt für Naturschutz, Bonn.

Gurevitch, J., Padilla, D.K., 2004. Are invasive species a major cause of extinctions? Trends Ecol. Evol. 19, 470–474.

Heink, U., Jax, K., 2014. Framing biodiversity: The case of 'invasive alien species'. In: Lanzerath, D., Friele, M. (Eds), Concepts and values in biodiversity. Routledge, London; New York, pp. 73–98.

Hunter, M.L., 1999. Biological diversity. In: Hunter, M.L. (Ed.), Maintaining biodiversity in forest ecosystems. Cambridge University Press, Cambridge; New York, pp. 3–21.

Jacobs, M., 1997. Environmental valuation, deliberative democracy and public decision-making institutions. In: Foster, J. (Ed.), Valuing nature? Ethics, economics and the environment. Routledge, London; New York, pp. 211–231.

Jax, K., Heink, U., 2015. Searching for the place of biodiversity in the ecosystem services discourse. Biol. Conserv. 191, 198–205.

Jax, K., Barton, D.N., Chan, K.M.A., de Groot, R., Doyle, U., Eser, U., Görg, C., Gómez-Baggethun, E., Griewald, Y., Haber, W., Haines-Young, R., Heink, U., Jahn, T., Joosten, H., Kerschbaumer, L., Korn, H., Luck, G.W., Matzdorf, B., Muraca, B., Neßhöver, C., Norton, B., Ott, K., Potschin, M., Rauschmayer, F., von Haaren, C., Wichmann, S., 2013. Ecosystem services and ethics. Ecol. Econ. 93, 260–268.

Kenter, J.O., 2016. Editorial: Shared, plural and cultural values. Ecosyst. Serv.

Kenter, J.O., O'Brien, L., Hockley, N., Ravenscroft, N., Fazey, I., Irvine, K.N., Reed, M.S., Christie, M., Brady, E., Bryce, R., Church, A., Cooper, N., Davies, A., Evely, A., Everard, M., Fish, R., Fisher, J.A., Jobstvogt, N., Molloy, C., Orchard-Webb, J., Ranger, S., Ryan, M., Watson, V., Williams, S., 2015. What are shared and social values of ecosystems? Ecol. Econ. 111, 86–99.

Klemisch-Ahlert, M., 1993. Freedom of choice: A comparison of different rankings of opportunity sets. Soc. Choice Welf. 10, 189–207.

Krysiak, F.C., Krysiak, D., 2006. Sustainability with uncertain future preferences. Environ. Resour. Econ. 33, 511–531.

Lanzerath, D., 2014. Biodiversity as an ethical concept: An introduction. In: Lanzerath, D., Friele, M. (Eds), Concepts and values in biodiversity. Routledge, London; New York, pp. 1–17.

Lee, K., 2004. There is biodiversity and biodiversity: Implications for environmental philosophy. In: Oksanen, M., Pietarinen, J. (Eds), Philosophy and biodiversity. Cambridge University Press, Cambridge, pp. 152–171.

Lo, A.Y., Spash, C.L., 2013. Deliberative Monetary Valuation: In search of a democratic and value plural approach to environmental policy. J. Econ. Surv. 27, 768–789.

Lundhede, T., Jacobsen, J.B., Hanley, N., Strange, N., Thorsen, B.J., 2015. Incorporating outcome uncertainty and prior outcome beliefs in stated preferences. Land Econ. 91, 296–316.

Mace, G.M., Norris, K., Fitter, A.H., 2012. Biodiversity and ecosystem services: A multi-layered relationship. Trends Ecol. Evol. 27, 19–26.

McShane, K., 2017a. Is biodiversity intrinsically valuable? (And what might that mean?). In: Garson, J., Plutynski, A., Sarkar, S. (Eds), Routledge handbook of philosophy of biodiversity. Routledge, New York, pp. 410–443.

McShane, K., 2017b. Intrinsic values and economic valuation. In: Spash, C.L. (Ed.), Routledge handbook of ecological economics: Nature and society. Routledge, New York.

Maffi, L., Woodley, E., 2010. Biocultural diversity conservation: A global sourcebook. Earthscan, London; Washington, DC.

Maier, D.S., 2012. What's so good about biodiversity? A call for better reasoning about nature's value. Springer, Dordrecht; New York.

Martín-López, B., Montes, C., Benayas, J., 2007. The non-economic motives behind the willingness to pay for biodiversity conservation. Biol. Conserv. 139, 67–82.

Martínez-Abraín, A., Jiménez, J., 2016. Anthropogenic areas as incidental substitutes for original habitat. Conserv. Biol. 30, 593–598.

Muraca, B., 2011. The map of moral significance: A new axiological matrix for environmental ethics. Environ. Values 20, 375–396.

Nehring, K., Puppe, C., 2002. A theory of diversity. Econometrica 70, 1155–1198.

O'Neill, J., 2001. Representing people, representing nature, representing the world. Environ. Plan. C Gov. Policy 19, 483–500.

Plaut, V.C., 2014. Diversity science and institutional design. Policy Insights Behav. Brain Sci. 1, 72–80.

Potthast, T., 2014. The values of biodiversity: Philosophical considerations connecting theory and practice. In: Lanzerath, D., Friele, M. (Eds), Concepts and values in biodiversity. Routledge, London; New York, pp. 132–146.

Reise, K., Olenin, S., Thieltges, D.W., 2006. Are aliens threatening European aquatic coastal ecosystems? Helgol. Mar. Res. 60, 77–83.

Rodriguez, L.F., 2006. Can invasive species facilitate native species? Evidence of how, when, and why these impacts occur. Biol. Invasions 8, 927–939.

Røpke, I., 2005. Trends in the development of ecological economics from the late 1980s to the early 2000s. Ecol. Econ. 55, 262–290.

Sagoff, M., 2005. Do non-native species threaten the natural environment? J. Agric. Environ. Ethics 18, 215–236.

Sax, D.F., Gaines, S.D., 2008. Species invasions and extinction: The future of native biodiversity on islands. Proc. Natl. Acad. Sci. 105, 11490–11497.

Scholte, S.S.K., van Teeffelen, A.J.A., Verburg, P.H., 2015. Integrating socio-cultural perspectives into ecosystem service valuation: A review of concepts and methods. Ecol. Econ. 114, 67–78.

Scholtes, F., 2010. Whose sustainability? Environmental domination and Sen's capability approach. Oxf. Dev. Stud. 38, 289–307.

Schüttler, E., Rozzi, R., Jax, K., 2011. Towards a societal discourse on invasive species management: A case study of public perceptions of mink and beavers in Cape Horn. J. Nat. Conserv. 19, 175–184.

Sen, A., 1977. Rational fools: A critique of the behavioural foundations of economic theory. Philos. Public Aff. 6, 317–344.

Sen, A., 1987. On ethics and economics. Blackwell, Oxford; New York.

Sen, A., Williams, B. (Eds), 1982. Utilitarianism and beyond. Cambridge University Press, Cambridge; New York.

Spangenberg, J.H., Settele, J., 2016. Value pluralism and economic valuation: Defendable if well done. Ecosyst. Serv. 18, 100–109.

Spash, C.L., 2006. Non-economic motivation for contingent values: Rights and attitudinal beliefs in the willingness to pay for environmental improvements. Land Econ. 82, 602–622.

Spash, C.L., 2012. New foundations for ecological economics. Ecol. Econ. 77, 36–47.

Spash, C.L., 2013. The shallow or the deep ecological economics movement? Ecol. Econ. 93, 351–362.

Spash, C.L., Urama, K., Burton, R., Kenyon, W., Shannon, P., Hill, G., 2009. Motives behind willingness to pay for improving biodiversity in a water ecosystem: Economics, ethics and social psychology. Ecol. Econ. 68, 955–964.

Strunz, S., Klauer, B., Ring, I., Schiller, J., 2016. Between Scylla and Charybdis? On the place of economic methods in sustainability science. Sustain. Sci. 1–12.

Thompson, K., 2014. Where do camels belong? The story and science of invasive species. Profile Books, London.

Wägele, J.-W., 2014. The necessity for biodiversity research: We are responsible for the quality of life of coming generations. In: Lanzerath, D., Friele, M. (Eds), Concepts and values in biodiversity. Routledge, London; New York, pp. 24–38.

Warren, C.R., 2007. Perspectives on the 'alien' versus 'native' species debate: A critique of concepts, language and practice. Prog. Hum. Geogr. 31, 427–446.

Weitzman, M.L., 1992. On diversity. Q. J. Econ. 107, 363–405.

4   State of the art in the economic valuation of biodiversity

In the previous chapters, we focused on particular aspects of this book's over-arching theme, namely, the economic valuation of biodiversity. In Chapter 2 the focus was on economic valuation: its theoretical foundations and its conceptual reach. Chapter 3 took a closer look at the concept of biodiversity: its definition, approaches to measurement and its 'ecological value'. In the environmental ethics excursus we then looked at issues of biodiversity value from a more abstract, philosophical perspective. Before we will be able to combine these insights, which will culminate in a conceptual framework for the economic valuation of biodiversity (Chapter 5), in this chapter we review the state of the art of the economics literature on biodiversity value. This review has two parts – its first part focuses on the empirics of economic valuation and presents a comprehensive critical review of existing biodiversity valuation studies; the second part presents selected conceptual arguments about the sources and nature of the economic value of biodiversity. This rather unusual and somewhat counterintuitive order is dictated both by the fact that the author started working on the subject by looking at the empirical literature and by the relative detachment of the latter and the conceptual perspectives. This detachment means that, given the conceptual focus of the present book, the theoretical and conceptual literature can be viewed as refining the 'raw' insights provided by empirical valuation studies.

Empirics

This section provides a review of all economic valuation studies published through October 2014 that included biodiversity as a valuation object. It is a slightly extended and modified version of Bartkowski et al. (2015), which reports the search strategy used in conducting the review as well as a list of all reviewed studies. The review is structured as follows: first, a classification of proxies used in order to estimate WTPs (willingness-to-pay) for biodiversity is offered. The second subsection summarises the results with respect to proxy use, methods applied and interactions between methods and proxies. The third subsection offers a discussion of the results, especially an evaluation of the proxies defined previously, and identifies best-practice studies. The overarching goal of this section is (i) to show what approaches are used in biodiversity valuation studies and, especially, how they rely on ecological concepts of biodiversity discussed in Chapter 3; (ii) to identify, against this background, the limitations and potential of current approaches, which, together with the overview of the conceptual state of the art in this field, will then feed into the adjacent major chapter of the present book, where a conceptual framework for the economic valuation of biodiversity will be developed.

Biodiversity proxies

The measurement and operationalisation of biodiversity are all but trivial tasks. Since there is no single 'right' indicator of biodiversity and since data constraints abound, economists who aim at valuing biodiversity use various different proxies for it. In what follows, a classification of the attributes valuation practitioners used as proxies is offered. Note that the use of the word *proxies* instead of *indicators* is deliberate, as the proxies used by valuation practitioners cannot always be identified with the indicators ecologists use in biodiversity research. The classification was specifically designed for the purposes of the review. It is inspired by classifications proposed by Nunes et al. (2003) and Pearce (2001), but it deviates from them, first, in that it is based on a more strict understanding of biodiversity, and second, in that it was adapted during the process of reviewing the valuation studies so as to enable the full attribution of all studies to the respective categories. As a result, six attribute categories were identified (Table 4.1).

An important criterion according to which the categories defined above can be grouped is whether they are framed in terms of biodiversity components or in terms of its functions. Components are the various physical levels or aspects of biodiversity, such as species, genes, landscapes etc. Functions of biodiversity include insurance, carrier of future options or underpinning of ecosystems – in other words, 'functions' are the particular ways through which biodiversity

Table 4.1 Classification of biodiversity proxies used in valuation studies

Proxy	Description
Numbers	Species richness or biodiversity indices (e.g. the Shannon index)
Species	Rare/threatened/endangered species, invasive species or changes in the abundance of (particular) species
Genetics	Expenditures on research or bioprospecting or preferences of consumers and farmers for different varieties of agricultural crops
Functions	Via biodiversity's role in underpinning and facilitating the functions and processes of ecosystems
Habitats	Preservation of habitats (similar to the use of the biodiversity indicator *habitat amount* by ecologists) or the ecosystem service *biodiversity protection*
Abstract	Stated preference studies with scenarios of 'low', 'medium' or 'high' levels of biodiversity, without more thorough specification within the questionnaire

influences human well-being (note that this is different from the commonly used concept of *ecosystem functions*). As can be easily seen, Numbers and Species focus on components of biodiversity; Genetics and Functions are rather framed in terms of roles. Meanwhile, the two remaining categories Habitats and Abstract cannot be easily attributed – they seem too general to fit the distinction between roles and components in a meaningful and sensible way.

Two qualifications should be made regarding the studies included in the categories Genetics and Species. Within the Genetics category, studies based on the (implicit) valuations expressed in bioprospecting contracts[1] were only included if they explicitly valued genetic diversity. No attention is paid to the contracts themselves. In contrast, Nunes et al. (2003) included a list of such contracts in their overview of different valuation approaches. For an extensive study of bioprospecting, see ten Kate and Laird (2000). In the Species category, only those studies were included whose authors specifically mentioned that they used rare/threatened/endangered species as a proxy for biodiversity. However, there are many valuation studies in which these species were chosen as valuation objects for other reasons, particularly because they are often well-known, iconic species, for which values can be elicited relatively easily. These were obviously omitted from the review.

Existing biodiversity valuation studies

This subsection presents the results of a review of all existing economic valuation studies of biodiversity published through October 2014. Here, only raw results are presented; the discussion of the most important results will take place in the next subsection.

Some 123 distinct studies were found that provide economic value estimates for biodiversity. Of these, 58 aimed at valuing biodiversity primarily (as judged based on titles and abstracts of the resulting publications), while 65 included biodiversity while following other objectives (e.g. valuation of a specific ecosystem).

As can be seen in Figure 4.1, 60 studies were conducted in Europe and 23 in Asia, the other continents being represented much less frequently. Even though it is widely recognised that most biodiversity hotspots are located in the tropics, particularly in South America, equatorial Africa and South-east Asia (Myers et al., 2000), only a few economic valuation studies of biodiversity were conducted in these extremely biodiverse areas. This finding is in accordance with a more general pattern identified by Christie et al. (2012), who found that most valuation studies are conducted in developed countries, whereas ecologically more valuable areas in the developing world remain clearly understudied (see also Seppelt et al., 2011). This might reflect both the lack of data and skills among practitioners in developing countries and problems related to usage of monetary value categories in these regions (Norgaard, 2010).[2]

Figure 4.2 shows the distribution of the studies with regard to ecosystem types covered (their classification follows the TEEB classification of biomes (de Groot et al., 2010)). Some 44 studies investigated the value of biodiversity in

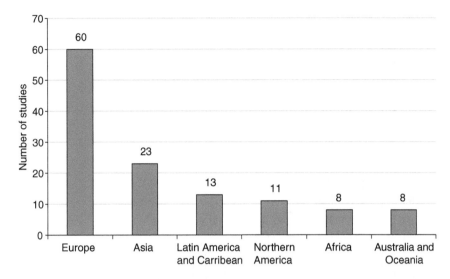

Figure 4.1 Number of biodiversity valuation studies by continent.

forest ecosystems (13 of which were tropical forests); in 19 cases the study area was marine. More than one ecosystem type was covered by 17 studies; 13 cultivated areas were studied. The other ecosystem types categories are less frequent, wetlands (nine studies) being the only remaining with more than five occurrences.

Figure 4.3 depicts the temporal distribution of the studies included in the review. The two oldest studies were conducted in 1992 (Garrod and Willis, 1994; Veisten et al., 2004). Note, however, that the figure shows number of studies *published* in a given year. The year when they were conducted was not always recoverable. Nonetheless, the overall trend appears similar in both cases: After a rather slow start during the 1990s, when only a few attempts to identify the economic value of biodiversity were undertaken, after 2000 the number of studies conducted each year more than doubled. This rise in the wake of the new millennium coincides with the publication of David Pearce's complaint about the lack of studies valuing diversity rather than biological resources (Pearce, 2001).

The single most important insight from the review is the use of various biodiversity proxies. As shown in Figure 4.4, the most common proxies are Habitat and Species, which were used 51 and 44 times, respectively. The other proxy categories are much less frequent: Numbers was used in 15 studies, Genetics in 11, Functions in nine and Abstract in seven. Ten studies used multiple proxies, which is why the numbers in Figure 4.4 add to more than 123, the number of studies reviewed.

There were two large types of studies in the review (Figure 4.5): those which explicitly focused on biodiversity as their main valuation object (58 studies), and

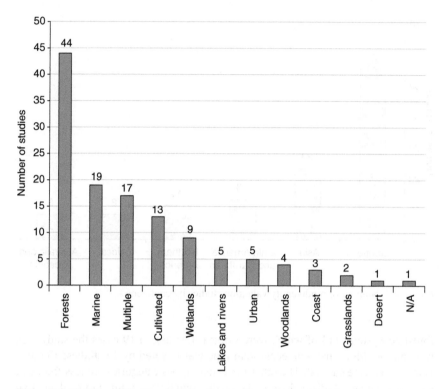

Figure 4.2 Number of biodiversity valuation studies by ecosystem types.

those which included it only as one object among others, with main focus on other issues (65 studies).

Willingness-to-pay for biodiversity can be determined in two ways: either in an *isolated* way, where only biodiversity is valued, or in an *embedded* way, where biodiversity is the main valuation object, but is nevertheless valued as one attribute among many of a given ecosystem. Obviously, the 65 studies that valued biodiversity but focused on other objectives all implicitly belong to the 'embedded' category. Of the remaining 58 biodiversity-focused studies, 24 studies chose isolated valuation as their approach. Of the 34 non-isolated studies, 17 used only proxies belonging to the Habitat category (see above), which does not allow for isolated valuation because, as will be argued below, it cannot distinguish between biodiversity and other attributes of an ecosystem. The remainder are 17 biodiversity-focused, non-isolated, non-habitat studies.

The biodiversity valuation studies reviewed here used an array of valuation methods. However, in a vast majority of them stated preference methods were used. Only in a few cases either market-based or revealed preference methods were applied (see Figure 4.6).

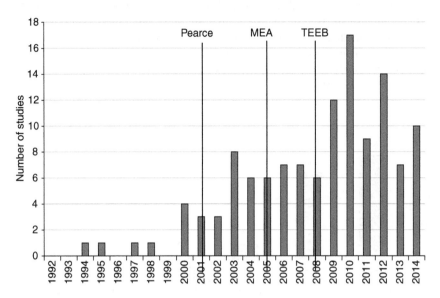

Figure 4.3 Number of published biodiversity valuation studies per year.

Note
The vertical lines indicate important events in the history of economic valuation of biodiversity: David Pearce's complaint about valuation of biological resources rather than diversity; publication of the Millennium Ecosystem Assessment (MEA); and publication of TEEB's Interim Report.

Deliberative monetary valuation (DMV) will be an important theme in Chapter 5 of this book, as it will be argued there that it is an approach particularly well-suited to the valuation of biodiversity. Therefore, it is interesting to look at its frequency in the reviewed field. DMV was applied four times in the studies reviewed here: Szabó (2011) showed in the context of biodiversity valuation that deliberative approaches significantly reduce the incidence of protest bids; both Wätzold et al. (2008) and Christie et al. (2006) applied deliberative methods in the hope of learning effects and to overcome issues of unfamiliarity and complexity of the valued goods; so did Anthony and Bellinger (2007) in a developing country context.

The results presented above can be combined so as to provide some additional insights. In Table 4.2, the use of proxies and methods are mapped against each other.

Travel cost (TC) and 'other stated preferences' (Other SP) can be ignored here because there are only very few studies using these methods. When the other three method classes are compared (CE, CV, MB), two patterns are visible: first, studies that used market-based methods (mainly production function methods) made use of the attributes belonging to the Functions category relatively often (27 per cent of cases, against only 7 per cent of all studies using

Functions proxies). Second, there is a difference between choice experiments and contingent valuation in that the former are more often used in combination with Species, the latter with Habitats. However, at least the second pattern seems to be a coincidence, as no sensible explanation comes to mind why Species would be relatively better suited for choice experiments than Habitats, as compared with contingent valuation.

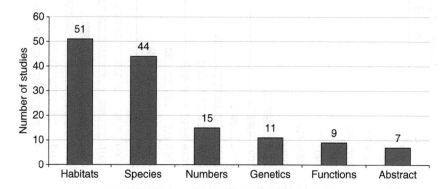

Figure 4.4 Number of biodiversity valuation studies by proxy.

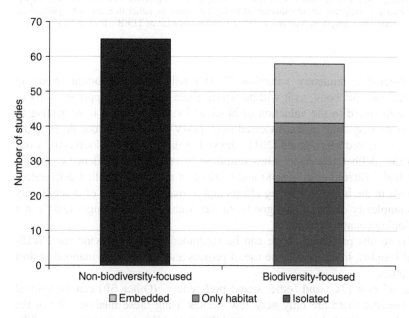

Figure 4.5 Embedded vs isolated valuation of biodiversity.

Note
The additional categories of embedded, only habitat and isolated are relevant only for the right-hand bar (for explanation, see text).

Another interesting combination of the previously presented general results might be how the 'isolated' vs 'embedded' approaches coincide with the use of methods in studies with a clear biodiversity focus (see above). For this exercise (Table 4.3), only the three largest method classes are taken into account (CV, CE, MB):

'Isolated' biodiversity valuation is comparatively frequently done by means of CV (55 per cent of isolated studies used this method). The relative frequency of CV is even more pronounced in embedded studies which approximated

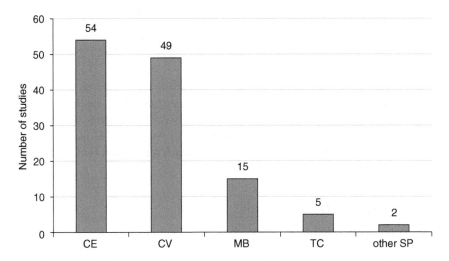

Figure 4.6 Distribution of biodiversity valuation studies by valuation method.

Note
CE=discrete choice experiments, CV=contingent valuation, MB=market-based methods, TC=travel cost method (including contingent behaviour), other SP=stated preference methods other than CE/CV; note that two studies applied two methods each.

Table 4.2 Dependence of proxies on methods

Attributes/methods	CE	CV	Other SP	TC	MB	Sum
Habitats	11 *(0.18)*	28 *(0.54)*	0	5 *(1.0)*	7 *(0.47)*	51 *(0.37)*
Species	31 *(0.49)*	12 *(0.23)*	0	0	1 *(0.07)*	44 *(0.32)*
Numbers	10 *(0.16)*	3 *(0.06)*	1 *(0.5)*	0	1 *(0.07)*	15 *(0.11)*
Abstract	3 *(0.05)*	3 *(0.06)*	1 *(0.5)*	0	0	7 *(0.05)*
Functions	4 *(0.06)*	1 *(0.02)*	0	0	4 *(0.27)*	9 *(0.07)*
Genetics	4 *(0.06)*	5 *(0.10)*	0	0	2 *(0.13)*	11 *(0.08)*
Sum	63	52	2	5	15	137

Notes
Each cell contains the absolute number of studies using the respective combination of method and attribute. Italic numbers in brackets inform about the proportion of studies that used the specific attribute–method combination compared to the number of studies using the respective method. The bottom row and the last column indicate sums. The abbreviations are the same as in Figure 4.6.

Table 4.3 Relationship between methods and approaches ('isolated' vs 'embedded') used

Approaches/methods	CV	CE	MB
Total	54 *(0.43)*	49 *(0.39)*	15 *(0.12)*
Biodiversity in focus total	26 *(0.45)*	21 *(0.36)*	8 *(0.14)*
• isolated	12 *(0.46/0.55)*	7 *(0.33/0.32)*	3 *(0.38/0.14)*
• embedded, Habitat only	11 *(0.42/0.73)*	3 *(0.14/0.2)*	1 *(0.13/0.07)*
• embedded, not only Habitat	3 *(0.12/0.17)*	11 *(0.52/0.61)*	4 *(0.5/0.22)*

Notes
Each cell contains the absolute number of studies using the respective combination of methods and approaches. Relative frequencies are given in brackets: if there is only a single number, it gives the proportion with regard to the category constituting the row; if there are two numbers separated by a slash, the former gives the proportion with regard to the category constituting the column, the other the row.

biodiversity solely by means of a Habitat proxy. Embedded studies without Habitat or with more than one biodiversity proxy were conducted more often by means of CE and market-based methods than CV. For both (CE and MB), the proportion of embedded non-Habitat studies is much higher than for CV (52 per cent and 50 per cent versus 12 per cent).

Evaluation of the field

This section is devoted to a discussion and evaluation of the above-presented results regarding the use of biodiversity proxies in valuation studies. The main focus is on the proxies found in the literature and their potential to capture biodiversity. The goal of this exercise is to identify limitations and best-practice approaches found in biodiversity valuation studies. Both their weaknesses and strengths can then be used to inform the development of the conceptual framework in Chapter 5; particularly, they can suggest whether there are limitations that cannot be overcome (due to lack of data or inherent limitations of valuation methods). First, criteria for evaluation of biodiversity proxies will be presented. Second, limitations of the approaches found in the literature will be pointed out. The third part of this section identifies a small number of studies which use a comparatively promising approach, given our perspective and the evaluation criteria, in that they frame biodiversity in terms of multiple proxies.[3]

Any evaluation needs transparent criteria along which it is conducted. For the evaluation of the biodiversity valuation literature, the following criteria have been developed during the process of reviewing the 123 biodiversity valuation studies:

1   *A biodiversity proxy should credibly approximate biodiversity.* Biodiversity is a complex and multi-faceted entity, thus it is difficult to identify proxies that cover its full extent. For example, a small sub-category of species cannot properly capture biodiversity and its value on its own. Indeed, it

might well be impossible to construct a proxy that captures all aspects of biodiversity. Nonetheless, a proper proxy (or set of proxies, see below) should cover as many aspects and dimensions of biodiversity as possible, given data, resources and other constraints. It should also be kept in mind in this context that 'no single component, whether genes, species, or ecosystems, is consistently a good indicator of overall biodiversity, as the components can vary independently' (MEA, 2005, p. 1; see also Lyashevska and Farnsworth, 2012).

2   *A biodiversity proxy should not cover more than biodiversity.* As we are concerned here with the economic value of the diversity of living entities, the identity of the latter and other valuable aspects/components of natural systems are less relevant, for example, wilderness, ecosystem services or abiotic components of ecosystems. It is crucial that biodiversity not be taken to be a synonym for *nature* or *ecosystem*, as these are distinct concepts; a concept only has analytic value if its distinctness from other related concepts is kept in mind. Good biodiversity proxies should be as precise as possible, being neither too narrow nor too encompassing.

3   *The connection between the chosen biodiversity proxy and biodiversity's contribution to human well-being should be clear.* This is particularly relevant in stated preference studies, where willingness to pay (WTP) or willingness to accept compensation (WTA) for changes in biodiversity is directly elicited from members of the general public. It is not enough for respondents to be aware of what biodiversity generally means for human well-being (e.g. as underpinning the stability of ecosystem services provision) – it should also be made clear to them what the specific *change* in biodiversity which is the basis of the WTP/WTA elicitation means in terms of their well-being. This calls for explicitly incorporating the change's effects on human well-being into WTP/WTA questions. Where possible, the analysed changes should also be quantified. However, in some cases it might not be possible to quantify a change in biodiversity without making it incomprehensible to respondents. A mere statement that, for example, the number of species has changed from X to Y is unlikely to be relevant for a respondent's assessment of her well-being. In studies not based on stated preference elicitation the link between biodiversity proxy and human well-being should be comprehensible as well.

4   *It does not make much sense to estimate the economic value of biodiversity in isolation.* Unlike the three previous criteria, this is independent of the specific biodiversity proxies used – rather, it has to do with the overall design of valuation studies. Of course, many valuation studies included in the present review do not focus on biodiversity, but estimate its value along with other valuation objects. Only a limited number of studies explicitly focus on the value of biodiversity. However, even if biodiversity value is in focus, the question remains: what does a specific WTP for biodiversity in a given ecosystem tell us? It cannot be easily generalised to other ecosystems, nor does it provide information about the *relative* importance of

biodiversity-related benefits within the studied ecosystem. Furthermore, valuing biodiversity in an 'embedded' way can help to separate it from other valuable attributes of ecosystems, thus contributing to fulfilling criterion 2. Accordingly, biodiversity should be valued as embedded in valuation of the ecosystem as a whole, so as to assess its relative contribution to the ecosystem's value.

For the moment, the more practical criterion of data availability is ignored. Of course, the data requirements of some biodiversity proxies are more easily satisfied – indeed, this might be the ultimate reason why the proxy categories Habitats and Species are by far the most frequent in biodiversity valuation studies.

In general, it should be emphasised that sometimes biodiversity indicators, as they are defined in ecology, are used as proxies in valuation studies – but often the proxies cannot be identified with indicators. This is especially the case in stated preference based studies, which is understandable insofar as a biodiversity proxy fulfils a different role in such a study than a biodiversity indicator normally does – rather than just indicating the state of or changes in biodiversity in an ecosystem, a proxy used in a questionnaire-based study is meant to symbolise biodiversity in a way that makes clear its link and contribution to human well-being. In what follows, we contrast the proxies introduced in Table 4.1 with the criteria developed above.

Habitats: This proxy covers many more aspects than just the diversity of an ecosystem's components and hence it is impossible to separate out the biodiversity aspect. Furthermore, habitats include many abiotic components, whereas biodiversity is by its name restricted to the biotic dimension of ecosystems. Some studies have included *biodiversity protection* as an ecosystem service, possibly following the idea behind the new service category of *habitat services* introduced in the TEEB classification of ecosystem services (de Groot et al., 2010). While it was shown that biomes are a relatively good predictor of species richness (Gerstner et al., 2014), the identification of biodiversity changes with changes in the extent of habitat protection appears unwarranted, at least as a generalisation (cf. Brown and Williams, 2016), even though there happens to be an established relationship in specific cases. See, for example, the justification offered by Kragt et al. (2009) in the context of coral reefs. Having said that, it should be added that to determine the value of an ecosystem, it might be more sensible to value it as a whole, rather than to value single ecosystem services separately, possibly by use of different valuation methods, and to subsequently aggregate their values additively. This reflects the contention that an ecosystem is 'more than the sum of its parts' (cf. Banzhaf and Boyd, 2012, pp. 437–438; Bockstael et al., 2000). Furthermore, the additive aggregation of the values of single ecosystem services can lead to double-counting (Fu et al., 2011). As a proxy for biodiversity in valuation studies, however, habitat protection is not sufficient and too imprecise.

Species: The use of rare/threatened/endangered or invasive species as biodiversity proxy covers only one single component of biodiversity. While it may be argued that in some cases keystone species are a good indicator of biodiversity (Haines-Young and Potschin, 2010), it is in most cases far from trivial to identify them. The species chosen in the studies reviewed here were mostly species too marginal in an ecosystem to have meaningful influence on its biodiversity levels – indeed, their being endangered and/or rare was mostly the reason why they were chosen, not their ecosystemic importance. Thus, the sole focus on single species appears unsatisfactory and likely obscures the complex relationships within an ecosystem (Mainwaring, 2001), as it suggests that the fate of single species has a general impact on overall biodiversity. Furthermore, it was pointed out that the definition of rarity of species may itself be problematic and of limited usefulness (McIntyre, 1992). When (invasive) alien species are used as a proxy, additional problems ensue, which are related to the difficulties of the notion of *nativeness* (cf. Box E.1).

Numbers: The use of species numbers species or biodiversity indices is restricted almost exclusively to stated preference studies, with the exception of one study, which used Simpson's diversity index in a model fed by life satisfaction and market price data (Ambrey and Fleming, 2014). Stated preference methods necessitate making clear to respondents the links between the biodiversity proxy and human well-being. For this, the informational basis of ecological biodiversity measures is very limited. For example, for a layperson it may be unclear what the actual meaning of a specific number of species is. Jacobsen et al. (2008) showed that knowledge of concrete species in the 'biodiversity mix' increases people's WTP for biodiversity, which may be due to the otherwise insufficient understanding on the side of surveyed persons (see also Martín-López et al., 2008). Also, and importantly, it has been shown that most common biodiversity indices misrepresent the actual levels of biodiversity in ecosystems (Lyashevska and Farnsworth, 2012).

Abstract: The criticism directed at the category of Numbers also holds in a very similar way for the Abstract category, i.e. a general reference in stated preference studies to the concept of biodiversity (e.g. in that respondents are asked to evaluate changes between 'low' and 'medium' levels of biodiversity). Even if participants in such surveys were informed previously about the general effects and ecological importance of biodiversity, it can hardly be expected that they can translate a vaguely described change in biodiversity into specific effects that influence their well-being. Also, population surveys reveal that laypeople often do not know what biodiversity is, which makes the general reference to it unsatisfactory when economic values are to be elicited (UEBT, 2013).

Functions: This and the following category (Genetics) both emphasise functions rather than components of biodiversity. Thus, the link to human well-being is relatively clear. However, one might be tempted to argue that this approach is redundant because the chain of reasoning behind the Functions category is mostly the following: biodiversity positively influences the stability and resilience of ecosystems (Balvanera et al., 2006), thus also stabilising the generation and provision of ecosystem services (Mace et al., 2012). The latter have a direct influence on human well-being and are therefore the appropriate objects of valuation (Boyd and Banzhaf, 2007). Under this perspective, valuation of bio-diversity would result in double-counting (Hamilton, 2013), i.e. considering both the value of direct effects on human well-being (ecosystem services) and the value of mere intermediate 'inputs' to these direct effects. However, it is pos-sible to argue that (i) the double-counting issue only arises in accounting-like applications, not when the goal of valuation is to provide information about and to communicate the value of biodiversity, and (ii) the stabilising effect of bio-diversity has a value going beyond that of the services 'reliably' provided by a stable ecosystem (see also the discussion of similar issues in Chapter 5 below).

Genetics: A closely related approach is the one behind the valuation studies falling in the Genetics category, which can be linked to the concept of option value (Box 2.2). Two main sub-approaches can be distinguished here – one group of studies concentrated on agricultural varieties and their attractiveness for either farmers or consumers (e.g. Birol et al., 2009b; Dinis et al., 2011), while others based their estimates of biodiversity's value on information about bio-prospecting contracts and research expenditures (e.g. Erwin et al., 2010; Jobst-vogt et al., 2014). Both implicitly emphasised an important role of biodiversity as a 'library' (Goeschl and Swanson, 2007; Weitzman, 1995), which contains information that may have value in the future (see also Farnsworth et al., 2012). As a standalone biodiversity proxy, however, Genetics is also insufficient, even though it points in the right direction according to the criteria developed in the previous section.

According to the interpretation presented in this section, the most common approaches to the economic valuation of biodiversity do not fulfil the criteria presented in the previous section. Especially, they are often too unspecific, either being too broad or too narrow to capture the essence of biodiversity. In fact, even the two approaches that appear most promising, namely Functions and Genetics, are by themselves limited in their comprehensiveness and cannot capture the whole complexity of the notion of biodiversity. In some studies, however, the attempt was made to operationalise biodiversity by use of more than one proxy/attribute. Below, these studies will be discussed in some more detail, as they offer an approach that comes close to fulfilling the two precision criteria (evaluation criteria 1 and 2) proposed above. Before that, we briefly discuss the studies reviewed here in terms of evaluation criterion 4.

Of the 123 valuation studies reviewed here, 58 focused on biodiversity. Only for these the distinction between embedded and isolated valuation is relevant (i.e. between valuation of biodiversity as a standalone valuation object or as part of a more broad ecosystem valuation, in which non-biodiversity elements are included). Most of them either valued biodiversity in an isolated way or used a single Habitat proxy, which by construction excludes isolated valuation but suffers from other problems (see above). Thus, a very small number of studies have actually focused on biodiversity valuation and did this in an embedded way without, however, relying solely on a Habitat proxy.[4] Not surprisingly, in most of the 'embedded' studies discrete choice experiments (CE) were the method of choice – this method allows for a distinction between the relative contributions of different factors (attributes) to the overall WTP for a good (here: ecosystem). Since biodiversity is itself multidimensional, but at the same time only one property of an ecosystem, the use of CE appears particularly opportune (we will pick up this consideration in Chapter 5).

The general message is that a non-negligible number of studies (particularly when we focus on those which explicitly chose biodiversity as their main object of interest) committed the fallacy of valuing (changes in) biodiversity only, which is problematic for numerous reasons (see criterion 4 above). This is particularly disappointing because some of these studies exhibit best-practice approaches in other respects (see below in the text). Perhaps most importantly, a change in biodiversity is usually the result of a change in the state of the ecosystem under investigation; other attributes of the ecosystem are likely to change as well. Leaving them out in the valuation study leads to a serious risk of omitted variable bias: those whose preferences are analysed implicitly include in their considerations of the presented change in the ecosystem's state more attributes than just biodiversity. The results are thus biased. Only the inclusion of further, non-biodiversity attributes can prevent this.

Biodiversity is a multidimensional concept; hence describing biodiversity with multiple proxies or attributes seems to be an obvious approach. Thus, studies using such an approach can be viewed as representing best practice, at least in one (important) respect. The review reveals that there are 10 such studies (Birol et al., 2009a; Christie et al., 2006; Czajkowski et al., 2009; Eggert and Olsson, 2009; Garber-Yonts et al., 2004; Jobstvogt et al., 2014; Lehtonen et al., 2003; Liebe and Preisendörfer, 2007; MacMillan et al., 2001; Rajmis et al., 2009). Table 4.4 presents a list of these studies and the attributes their authors used to describe biodiversity in the respective studies (quoted literally).

In all multi-attribute studies some version of the proxy category Species was applied – mostly involving rare or endangered species, in one case alien species (Rajmis et al., 2009).[5] Furthermore, seven of these 10 studies used a proxy belonging to the Habitat category in their multi-attribute description of biodiversity. Also, a Functions proxy occurred four times in these multi-attribute studies, being used only nine times in the overall sample of 123 studies. This confirms the intuition that, while Functions alone might be viewed as too imprecise and thus uninformative, it still reflects an important aspect of biodiversity's value. Last but not least, attributes belonging to the categories Numbers and Genetics were used once each in the sub-sample presented here.

Two interesting attributes proposed are 'landscape diversity' in Liebe and Preisendörfer (2007) and 'ecosystem components' in Czajkowski et al. (2009) (by which the latter mean dead wood, ponds, streams etc.). Prima facie, both seem to emphasise abiotic components of ecosystems, which per definition are not part of biodiversity. However, this critique would appear to be overly pedantic: landscapes are defined mainly in terms of their biotic elements. The problem here rather is that landscape diversity concerns a different spatial level than the other attributes chosen by Liebe and Preisendörfer. In the case of Czajkowski et al., it might be argued that ecosystem components such as dead wood or aquifers can be considered potentially

Table 4.4 Multi-attribute descriptions of biodiversity in valuation studies

Study	Attributes
Birol et al. (2009)	• 'number of different species [and] their population levels' • 'number of different habitats and their size'
Christie et al. (2006)	• 'familiar species of wildlife' • 'rare (unfamiliar) species of wildlife' • 'habitat' • 'ecosystem processes'
Czajkowski et al. (2009)	• 'natural ecological processes' • 'rare species of fauna and flora' • 'ecosystem components'
Eggert and Olsson (2009)	• 'richness in species and richness within each species' • 'important for the sea's capacity to handle environmental disturbances, but also for productivity'
Garber-Yonts et al. (2004)	• 'biodiversity reserves' • 'endangered species' • 'forest age management'
Jobstvogt et al. (2014)	• 'number of protected species' • '[potential] new medicinal products'
Lehtonen et al. (2003)	• 'number of endangered species' • 'conservation areas' • '[number of] biotopes at favourable levels of conservation'
Liebe and Preisendörfer (2007)	• 'biotopes of rare species' • 'species richness' • 'age structure of the forests' • 'landscape diversity'
MacMillan et al. (2001)	• 'restoration of native forest' • 'reintroduction of the beaver/wolf'
Rajmis et al. (2009)	• 'dangers from alien species' • 'resilience'

diverse *micro-habitats*,[6] which would mean, on the one hand, that the critique of the Habitats attribute category applies at least partly. On the other hand, this attribute is an important attempt to take into account the astonishing biodiversity of insects and microbes living largely unnoticed in such micro-biotopes.

While the emphasis on the functions biodiversity has in enhancing human well-being was explicit in some of the attributes found here, most studies focused on components, Rajmis et al. (2009) being the only study with a clearly functional focus, stressing the *functionality* of biodiversity (Bakhtiari et al., 2014). As will be suggested in the next chapter, this constitutes a major research gap and an opportunity to enhance the practice of economic valuation of biodiversity.

Given the breadth and specificity of the chosen biodiversity proxies, three multi-attribute studies should be singled out as best practice: Christie et al. (2006), Czajkowski et al. (2009) (which explicitly builds upon the approach of Christie et al.) and Liebe and Preisendörfer (2007). Each of these three studies covered multiple dimensions of biodiversity and defined them in a relatively precise way. The main missing element – or, rather, the main difference between their approach and the approach advanced in the present work – is that (i) they all focused on components of biodiversity, without a clear, pronounced and explicit link to its influence on human well-being and (ii) they all analysed the value of biodiversity in an isolated way.

Given biodiversity's predominantly indirect value, the most encompassing way to value it is by means of stated preference methods (see Chapter 5 for a more detailed argument). In a multi-attribute approach, indirect values are likely to be relevant for at least some of the proxies used. Hence it is not surprising that all 10 studies applied either discrete choice experiments or contingent valuation. Also, as choice experiments are a method specifically designed to take into account the multitude of good characteristics (attributes) and their respective influence on utility, this method was applied in eight of the multi-attribute studies. Interestingly, while it will be argued further on in this book that deliberative monetary valuation (DMV) is particularly well-suited to handle the uniqueness of biodiversity as a valuation object, only Christie et al. (2006) used this approach in a subsample of their study (without significant differences to the larger 'conventional' subsample). We will come back to this and other methodological issues in Chapter 5.

In general, the multi-attribute approach to the economic valuation of biodiversity appears very promising, especially because it overcomes some of the shortcomings of attempts to reduce the vast complexity of the concept of biodiversity to one single attribute or component. At the same time, it allows us to keep the underlying description of biodiversity specific without becoming too encompassing. However, it might be worth putting more emphasis on the functions of biodiversity instead of describing it in terms of its components (with the functions only implicitly behind those). This approach, too, has limitations, of course. One clear limitation is data – our understanding of biodiversity and its effects on both eco- and human systems is still very limited, and for many ecosystems data related to biodiversity are hard to come by (UNEP-WCMC, 2015). Furthermore, when biodiversity is valued via stated preference methods, the main challenge is to determine the right amount of information provided to respondents that allows them to thoroughly understand the valuation object without leading to a cognitive overstrain (MacMillan et al., 2006). As already mentioned, this might be viewed as an opportunity to employ deliberation-based methods, as those are believed to ease the uptake of information and the formation of informed preferences for complex environmental public goods (e.g. Lienhoop and Völker, 2016).

Having gained a broad overview of the praxis of economic valuation of biodiversity, we now turn to the theoretical and conceptual literature available.

Theory and concepts

In the previous section, a critical review of all existing economic valuation studies of biodiversity was presented. In what follows, the focus will be on theoretical and conceptual arguments: how have economists conceptualised biodiversity value? What is its relationship with considerations of uncertainty, which the ecological and ethical perspectives have suggested as important? This section can thus be viewed as refining the insights gained up to now.

First, an important strand of the economics literature concerned with biodiversity will be presented, which has to do with the measurement of diversity and has its origins in axiomatic social choice theory. Much of the discussion in this strand has gone under the heading of the 'Noah's Ark Problem', a term coined by Martin Weitzman. After this discussion, we will then take on a broader perspective and review various other economics literature on biodiversity value. Since much of the work reviewed here has to do with issues of risk and uncertainty, in the last subsection we will take a step back and focus on the links between biodiversity, uncertainty in the context of ecosystems, and how uncertainty is usually dealt with in economic valuation. All these diverging issues and strands will then be combined and unified in a conceptual framework for the economic valuation of biodiversity presented in Chapter 5.

Noah's Ark or the economist's measures of diversity

Although there exist a vast number of different measures of biodiversity in the ecological literature, some economists have argued that these are not useful for economic analysis, whose main goal is optimisation of the use of scarce goods, including biodiversity. The rationale behind the ensuing strand of research is that (i) some ecosystem components provide us with benefits and (ii) trade-offs are involved, regarding, for example, financial resources and land-use options, which effectively prevent us from being able to preserve all ecosystem components. This gave rise to the idea that some components of ecosystems may be redundant in the sense that they fulfil functions or occupy niches that could also be fulfilled by other, possibly taxonomically related species – the so-called Noah's Ark Problem, proposed by Weitzman (1998), in line with the ecological *redundancy hypothesis*, discussed in Chapter 3.

The main argument made by Weitzman (1992, 1993, 1995, 1998) and other economists dealing with this problem (e.g. Nehring and Puppe, 2002; Solow et al., 1993; Weikard, 2002) is that *dissimilarity* is the most relevant concept in operationalising diversity. This literature was triggered by Weitzman (1992), who showed that optimal preservation involves a strong focus on distantly related species. Solow et al. (1993) added the insight that the preservation value of a species 'depends not only on its genetic distinctiveness, but also on the effect that its extinction would have on the extinction probabilities of other species' (p. 67). Weitzman (1998) then extended the list of 'fundamental ingredients' for ranking conservation priorities by adding the utility of each species and the cost of its preservation to the calculus.

Further publications refined Weitzman's results by linking them to the concepts of existence and intrinsic value (Nehring and Puppe, 2002), shifting the focus from species to ecosystems and the services they provide (Kassar and Lasserre, 2004; Weikard, 2002) or including a still broader range of 'fundamental ingredients' (Martin, 2016). Baumgärtner (2007a) nicely contrasts this economic approach to biodiversity measurement and the ecological approach (presented in Chapter 3, above). He argues that they differ because of the different conceptual foundations of each discipline, and traces these back to the respective philosophical roots of the two, identifying ecology with the more conservative philosophical approaches of Gottfried Wilhelm Leibniz and Immanuel Kant and economics with the liberal tradition of David Hume, John Locke or René Descartes. According to him, in economics, 'relative abundances are usually considered irrelevant for the measurement of diversity. The reason is that in economics the diversity issue is usually framed as a choice problem' (Baumgärtner, 2007a, p. 304), while ecologists refuse this perspective because they do not see species as individual 'goods', but rather as integral parts of a complex, dynamically interacting system.

In line with this, Nehring and Puppe (2002)[7] point out that there is a difference between 'valuing diversity' (which they equate to the economic approach advanced by, e.g., themselves and Weitzman) and 'measuring diversity', which for them amounts to additive counting of one way or another. However, as implied above, the analysis of Noah's Ark Problem is essentially a cost-effectiveness analysis[8] and requires prior information on the preferences for different species, genes and other biodiversity components to be operational. Thus, valuation has to take place before this kind of analysis can become relevant. Furthermore, Nehring and Puppe's (2002) use of the terms 'existence value' and 'intrinsic value' is mistaken. As the authors themselves admit, option value is a more related concept (see also below). As discussed in the Excursus, biodiversity cannot sensibly have intrinsic or existence value.

Furthermore, a more fundamental limitation of the Noah's Ark approach is that it downplays the uncertainties and complexities of ecosystems and their functioning. Accordingly, the approach has been criticised in the subsequent literature (Dasgupta et al., 2013; Mainwaring, 2001). Among other points of critique it was pointed out that, first, there may exist important but unknown threshold effects (the *rivet hypothesis* mentioned in Chapter 3); and second, the axiomatic economists' approach supposedly ignores evolution, which leads to a specialisation and multi-functionality of species (biocomplexity). We simply do not know which elements of biodiversity are redundant and which are not. Optimal selection of those elements that are 'worth preserving' is thus hardly possible, despite being a nice intellectual exercise.

Nonetheless, the Noah's Ark literature has motivated much research on the economic value of biodiversity and directed the attention of economists towards the diversity of living things; also, it contributed significantly to our understanding of biodiversity as a pool of options. In what follows, these issues and the literature targeting the economic value of biodiversity in a less abstract sense will be presented.

Concepts of biodiversity's economic value

When it comes to economic valuation *sensu stricto* (see Chapter 2), biodiversity has not been seen as a valuation object all too often. Rather, the understanding has been that biodiversity underpins the provision of ecosystem services but has no economic value itself, as it does not contribute directly to human well-being (cf. Boyd and Banzhaf, 2007; Hamilton, 2013). For example, in a conceptual figure in the first TEEB report (see Figure 4.7), no direct link from biodiversity to human well-being is recognised. A similar figure can be found in Nunes et al. (2003, fig. 5.1). Biodiversity is only seen there as underpinning the provision of ecosystem services, which influence human well-being directly. This is, of course, in line with ecological research showing that biodiversity correlates not only with ecosystem stability and resilience (see Chapter 3), but also with productivity or biomass production (e.g. Costanza et al., 2007). However, the role of biodiversity is in this case obviously secondary and it is the ecosystem goods and services that are of primary economic value; thus the common perception of biodiversity as underpinning the provision of ecosystem goods and services without primary economic value.[9]

On the other hand, in the same TEEB report on *Ecological and Economic Foundations* from which Figure 4.7 is derived, the insurance value of an ecosystem was indirectly linked to biodiversity (Pascual et al., 2010). However, the application of valuation techniques to biodiversity is not an easy task (Reyers et al., 2010) and it was noted more than once that 'there is certainly not yet an established framework for valuing biological variety' (Nijkamp et al., 2008, p. 218). Nonetheless, a number of approaches have been suggested in the literature. We turn to these now.

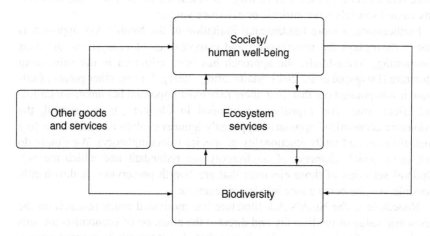

Figure 4.7 The role of biodiversity according to TEEB.

Note
Simplified version of an unpublished figure by Ann Kinzig, Charles Perrings and Robert Scholes, reprinted as fig. 2.8 in Elmqvist et al. (2010).

Two large overviews about the economic valuation of biodiversity and eco-system services should be mentioned first. Nunes et al. (2003; see also Nunes and van den Bergh, 2001) offer an ecological economic perspective on biodiver-sity, a large part of which focuses on valuation. However, while very informa-tive in many respects, their overview is based on a very broad understanding of 'biodiversity', which allows them to discuss its economic value in terms of the provision of ecosystem services, habitats etc. Those aspects of their book that are really biodiversity-specific are considered in what follows. The other important overview is the already repeatedly mentioned first TEEB report on *Ecological and Economic Foundations* (Kumar, 2010). Here, however, the focus is even broader and while many of the threads discussed below can be found there, they are scattered and lack a consistent unifying perspective. Such a per-spective will be provided in the next chapter.

A very common thread in the economics literature on biodiversity value sees biodiversity as a portfolio – a perspective inherently related to that offered in the Noah's Ark literature discussed above. As will be argued in the next chapter, the portfolio or, following Figge (2004), 'bio-folio' perspective actu-ally spans two different aspects and relates to two different types of uncertainty (supply uncertainty and demand uncertainty). While they should be treated sep-arately for analytical reasons, it is often not clear which is the relevant one in a particular context.

Figge (2004) proposes the metaphor of biodiversity as a 'bio-folio', using the analogy from financial economics and portfolio theory (Markowitz, 1952). Port-folio theory posits that in order to minimise the risk of holding financial assets, one should spread this risk by investing one's money in a portfolio of different, uncorrelated assets. Thus, at the so-called efficient frontier, one might be able to significantly reduce risk of losses for a given expected gain as compared with investments in single or correlated assets. Obviously, the analogy between bio-diversity and a financial portfolio is rather metaphorical, for numerous reasons. Above all, a financial portfolio consists of individual assets all of which have *positive expected values*. Otherwise, they wouldn't be bought and held. The idea of the portfolio is solely to dampen fluctuations in the realised value of these assets. In contrast, biodiversity includes 'assets' whose (expected) value is not positive – for example, pathogens or pests. However, due to ecosystem complex-ity, it is not possible to 'eliminate' the 'assets' with negative expected value from the portfolio, as these can play an important role in the overall functioning of the ecosystem in question (see the related criticism of the Noah's Ark approach in the previous section). In addition, while in financial economics the assumption is usually made that probability distributions and expected values can be calculated exactly, this does not hold for biodiversity (Rajmis et al., 2010).[10] Still, the portfolio metaphor highlights the way in which the diversity of biological assets in an ecosystem can contribute to the latter's stability and, eventually, to human well-being.

Much of the 'portfolio' research has happened in recent years under the heading of *insurance value*, in implicit or explicit relation to the insurance hypothesis discussed in Chapter 3. Most basically, the broad concept of insurance can be framed as follows:

> Any idea of 'insurance' fundamentally refers to a combination of three elements: (i) the objective characteristics of risk in terms of different possible states of nature, (ii) the decision maker's subjective risk preferences over these states, and (iii) a mechanism that allows mitigation of (i) in view of (ii).
>
> (Baumgärtner and Strunz, 2014, p. 22)

Actually, the concept of insurance value can be conceived in two ways in the context of natural ecosystems. First, certain ecosystems provide *insurance services* to society; for instance, a riparian forest influences the probability with which downstream human dwellings will be hit by floods, as well as the severity of these floods. This type of insurance value is usually accounted for within the ESS framework (mainly within the category of regulating ecosystem services) and is not obviously linked to biodiversity. The other, biodiversity-relevant type of insurance value results from biodiversity's influence on the stability and resilience of ecosystems and thus on their ability to continuously and 'safely' provide ecosystem services. The latter type is in focus here. It reflects the contribution of biodiversity to the proper functioning of ecosystems, namely, the temporal and spatial stability of these complex systems, whereby 'stability' does not mean a non-changing state, but rather the continued capacity to fulfil ecological functions and provide services. Of course, behind this reasoning lurks the assumption that stability has value in and of itself, i.e. that people prefer a supply of some goods and services when they deem it stable to the same supply deemed unstable (risk-aversion). The assumption here is that, just as people are willing to pay insurance premiums to insure against, say, fire, they are also willing to pay for the stability of an ecosystem, beyond the specific services and functions it provides/fulfils.

Baumgärtner (2007b, p. 90) defines insurance value as 'a value component in addition to the usual value arguments (such as direct or indirect use or non-use values, or existence values) which hold in a world of certainty' (see also Fromm, 2000). Following Ehrlich and Becker's (1972) work on insurance in general, Baumgärtner and Strunz (2014) differentiate between two basic forms of insurance: an insurance contract and *self-protection*, the latter amounting to attempts of the interested actor herself to reduce uncertainty on her own. The insurance role of biodiversity is much closer to this latter notion, as societies can 'insure' against future declines in the provision of ecosystem services by deliberately maintaining and increasing biodiversity in ecosystems. In a similar vein, Pascual et al. (2015) differentiate in the context of soil biodiversity between the 'insurance value components' of *self-protection* and *self-insurance*, where the former is 'the value of lowering the risk (probability) of being negatively affected by a disturbance' and the latter is 'associated with lowering the size of the loss due to such event occurring' (p. 14).

The role of biodiversity as a *natural insurance* against exogenous shocks is perhaps most obvious in agriculture. The use of different varieties of crops (or different races of livestock), including crop rotation, decreases the proneness of a harvest to pests. There exists, however, a trade-off between high yields and vulnerability to pests since exceptionally high yields are guaranteed by special-isation, i.e. in this case, monocultures:

> [T]he more prevalent is the host, the bigger is the size of the evolutionary dining-room area within which the host-specific parasites have leeway to play with new genetic combinations, or to experiment with the increased comparative advantage that comes from specializing to finer-grained sub-niches within the host organism.
>
> (Weitzman, 2000, p. 237)

Preservation of biodiversity of wild forms can have direct implications for agriculture. There are many cases of non-commercial wild varieties of agricul-tural crops such as rice or coffee whose genetic material could be used to counter diseases or pests (Di Falco, 2012; Di Falco and Chavas, 2009). A prominent example was the grassy stunt virus epidemic that was a big problem for rice cultivation in Asia in the 1970s – the International Rice Research Institute (IRRI) succeeded in breeding a resistant variety from a wild rice variety with no commercial value (Heal, 2000, p. 15). In times of increasingly widespread use of biotechnology, wild biodiversity has gained even more importance in this context: genetic engineering makes possible the use of genetic information from completely unrelated organisms, which increases the significance of (the diversity of) non-agricultural wild species for agriculture. While in traditional agriculture only genetic material found in varieties of the same species or, sometimes, some related species could be used to create new, better crop varieties, today such limits do not apply any more, as DNA snip-pets can be potentially transferred between very different organisms. Further-more, modern genome editing techniques allow for introduction of genes from related (wild) varieties much faster and with more precision than via tradi-tional breeding (Palmgren et al., 2015). Thus, the range of options available to respond to future preference changes has become much larger than before the advent of modern biotechnology (Carroll and Charo, 2015).[11] To put it poign-antly, 'a relatively cheap way of buying catastrophe insurance is to cultivate or hold small positive amounts of as many different kinds of potential domest-icates as it may be possible to preserve' (Weitzman, 2000, p. 261).[12] In a recent application along these lines, Henselek et al. (2016) investigate the insurance effect of the diversity of wild pollinators in Californian almond orchards and show that it increases the expected income of almond farmers (see also Baumgärtner, 2007b; Klein et al., 2012). In a similar vein, Finger and Buchmann (2015) use empirical data from the large-scale Jena Experi-ment in a model that studies the influence of biodiversity in grassland on the behaviour of hypothetical farmers.

The view of biodiversity's role as insurance is closely related to the notion of resilience (Admiraal et al., 2013; Baumgärtner and Strunz, 2014). The diversity of biotic components of an ecosystem is widely believed to be linked to its resilience, i.e. the ability of the system to return to its initial *basin of attraction*, i.e. 'a region in state space in which the system tends to remain' (Walker et al., 2004) after a disturbance (Holling, 1973).[13] The idea here is that biodiversity protects us from negative effects caused by the combination of uncertainty and irreversibility of changes (regime shifts) in the state of ecosystems (Binder and Polasky, 2013; Chavas, 2009).

According to Goeschl and Swanson (2007, p. 273), '[o]f the many ways in which biodiversity might be conceptualised, one of the most important is as the diversity of the set of genetic resources'. They go on to revisit Weitzman's (1995) concept of biodiversity as a library, i.e. a carrier of (especially genetic) information (see also Farnsworth et al., 2012) and extend it to the notion of a 'legacy library', thus stressing the intergenerational component of biodiversity value. The legacy library metaphor can be interpreted as a combination of the concept of option value (see Box 2.2) with intergenerational equity concerns. Under this perspective, biodiverse ecosystems are potential sources of basically three categories of future benefits: genetic knowledge (relevant especially for agriculture), models or blueprints for new technologies (a classic example being aircraft, which is an attempt to mimic birds) and substances for future use in the chemical and pharmaceutical industries (Myers, 1997). Especially the recognition of the latter aspect has had direct economic repercussions, as exemplified by the phenomenon of bioprospecting (Costello and Ward, 2006; Goeschl and Swanson, 2002; ten Kate and Laird, 2000). The most famous case of bioprospecting was the 1991 agreement between the National Biodiversity Institute of Costa Rica (INBio) and the pharmaceutical company Merck, which allowed the latter to commercially use samples from 11 Costa Rican conservation areas; however, the profitability of bioprospecting has been debated in the literature (Clapp and Crook, 2002; Costello and Ward, 2006; Crook, 2001). Furthermore, especially when bioprospecting is based on using indigenous knowledge, it often results in accusations of biopiracy (Shiva, 1997). Nonetheless, the very fact that firms are from time to time engaging in bioprospecting suggests that biodiversity has option value to them.

Insurance and options, which can both be summarised under the portfolio metaphor, are the two main reasons why biodiversity is associated with economic value in the literature. Another, less prominent argument has been made, for example, in the work of TEEB, where biodiversity was explicitly linked with the TEEB-specific category of habitat services (Elmqvist et al., 2010). In particular, the maintenance of genetic diversity is an ecosystem service in the TEEB classification. It seems, however, that the importance of maintaining genetic diversity is mainly due to the portfolio perspective discussed above. In Chapter 5 we will see that another sub-category of habitat services, namely the maintenance of life cycle of migrating species, can also be linked with biodiversity and constitutes a value type different from both option and insurance value.

Another possible way through which biodiversity can contribute to the value of an ecosystem is via aesthetics. It is well established that aesthetic reasons have a large influence on how people perceive and value an ecosystem (e.g. Lienhoop and Völker, 2016). It may be argued that exceptionally biodiverse ecosystems are also perceived as exceptionally beautiful. Thus, ecosystems might be valuable partly because they are biodiverse, as reflected, for example, in the appreciation of diverse forests indicated by related tourist and recreational activities: in a recent study it was found that indicators of habitat diversity and species diversity are good predictors of visitor numbers in Finnish national parks (Siikamäki et al., 2015). Although the link to the *biophilia hypothesis*[14] that the authors suggest appears to be an over-interpretation of their data, their results do indicate a relationship between biodiversity and the recreational appreciation of ecosystems. Another recent study found that species diversity has a significant influence on the recreational value of forests (Giergiczny et al., 2015). However, the opposite might also be the case, i.e. biodiverse ecosystems might be conceived by some people as 'unsightly' (see Horne et al., 2005; Kimmins, 1999). Whether the effect of biodiversity on subjective appreciation of an ecosystem's 'beauty' is positive or negative is a matter of empirical investigation. But biodiversity seems to have influence on the aesthetic value of an ecosystem.

Both species diversity and landscape/ecosystem diversity were shown to influence the aesthetic perception of nature by people (Dallimer et al., 2012; Lindemann-Matthies et al., 2010). Empirical studies also indicate that laypeople's ability to distinguish species is very limited (Bebbington, 2005; Pilgrim et al., 2008; Voigt and Wurster, 2015). This is potentially problematic because it can lead to differences between actual and perceived diversity; the problem arises irrespective of whether stated preference or revealed preference methods are applied. Another caveat is that it is important to distinguish the appreciation of the diversity of ecosystem components (species, landscapes etc.) from the appreciation of some specific elements in the mix (Jacobsen et al., 2008): for instance, the different appreciation of two forest patches may be due to the difference in biodiversity levels between them, but it may also be due to one particular species that one patch includes while the other does not. In a more general sense, it might be very difficult to disentangle the various components of the aesthetic value of an ecosystem, so as to filter out biodiversity's contribution to it. It is important for conceptual reasons to keep in mind that biodiversity influences aesthetics, but it seems inadvisable to distinguish between the different factors which determine aesthetic appreciation in actual valuation studies. As it was already argued in this chapter that it is not sensible to estimate the economic value of biodiversity in isolation, it is manifest that when a change in an ecosystem is valued, aesthetics is an important component along with biodiversity and other relevant ecosystem goods and services. Yet it is not sensible and, in fact, not necessary to distinguish between the relative contributions of biodiversity and other factors (such as the presence of particular species or landscape structure) to aesthetics.

It was already discussed in the Excursus and mentioned again in the discussion of the Noah's Ark approach that despite occasional claims in the literature to the contrary, biodiversity, properly defined, cannot sensibly have existence or intrinsic value. An argument can be made that biodiversity exhibits the other two sub-categories of non-use values: that bequest value, i.e. the consideration of the interests of future generations, is a significant component of biodiversity's economic value will be argued in the next chapter. Altruistic value, which can be interpreted as reflecting sympathy and/or commitment towards other individuals (*sensu* Sen, 1977),[15] is generally compatible with any environmental good and service – it is entirely dependent on the altruistic preferences of the individual, not on any additional distinct characteristics of biodiversity.

In the context of the ecosystem services concept, the notion of ecosystem dis-services, i.e. 'functions of ecosystems that are perceived as negative for human well-being' (Lyytimäki and Sipilä, 2009, p. 311), recently emerged (for a review, see von Döhren and Haase, 2015). Similarly, it was argued that biodiversity is not always beneficial to people. For example, there is an established and rather obvious positive relationship between general biodiversity levels and pathogen diversity (Lafferty, 2014; Thomas et al., 2009). Another, more anecdotal example is provided by a study of Canadian lakes in which it was shown that higher levels of aquatic species diversity are correlated with longer food chains – as a result, mercury concentrations in top predators (which happen to be the fish people like eating) were relatively high (Mazmunder, 2009). Also, for many people, highly biodiverse ecosystems, particularly forests, may seem 'untidy' or even 'scary' (Bixler and Floyd, 1997; Horne et al., 2005; Kimmins, 1999).

Two questions emerge: first, can these negative effects be attributed to biodiversity at all? And second, if yes, are they not already captured within the other value categories presented above? That biodiversity contains not only items that positively influence human well-being, but also pathogens, pests and the like, was already mentioned above when biodiversity was compared to a financial portfolio. However, in this case it might be argued that the problem is not biodiversity itself but the identity of its elements or instances. Furthermore, many more factors influence the presence of pathogens and severity thereof, so attaching it to biodiversity would be problematic. It appears to be more sensible to account for such negative effects or ecosystem disservices using additional, non-diversity attributes when the value of ecosystem is to be determined. These arguments hold even more for the anecdotal example of mercury concentrations – here, reference to biodiversity is not sensible, as the actual carrier of value can be easily identified (mercury concentration in edible fish). With regard to bio-diversity's negative influence on aesthetics, this effect can be attributed to it, but it is easily captured as aesthetic value with a negative sign. Thus, a separate category of biodiversity disvalue does not appear to have much merit.

Uncertainty and biodiversity

The discussion in the previous section suggests that a significant part of bio diversity's economic value is the result of uncertainty: both interpretations of the portfolio metaphor, i.e. insurance value and option value, are only relevant in a non-deterministic world in which the future (and aspects of the present) is uncertain and human beings are risk-averse. That the latter is generally true was shown repeatedly in empirical investigations (e.g. Dohmen et al., 2011; Holt and Laury, 2002). In what follows, we will take a closer look at the nexus between biodiversity, uncertainty and economic valuation.

In the most general sense, uncertainty can be defined as a situation in which '[a] person [...] lacks confidence about his knowledge relating to a specific question' (Sigel et al., 2010, p. 504). In economics it is common, building upon Knight (1921), to differentiate between *risk* and *uncertainty* or *ambiguity*; later contributions added the notion of *ignorance* (Faber et al., 1992). Risk prevails in the 'world of classical statistics', where there is a known set of possible future events and every event can be attributed a probability based on past frequencies of their occurrence. Ambiguity is more severe – it prevails where possible future events are known but not all can be assigned probability. This is, in a sense, the 'world of Bayesian statistics', as in the latter probability distributions need not be based on previously observed frequencies of events, but can be derived, at least in theory, from subjective 'gut feeling' (Tschirk, 2014). Ignorance is the most problematic issue: not only are probability distributions unknown, so also are possible future events. This is, so to speak, the world of 'anything can happen'.

Economic analysis mostly focuses on risk because ambiguity and ignorance cannot be easily formalised. This is, of course, an abstraction, because for many economically relevant phenomena objective probabilities are not known. Yet for many applications the assumption of risk is 'good enough' to provide analytical insights. However, if there are reasons to assume that we have to do with ambiguity or ignorance, the reach of economic valuation is limited (Vardas and Xepapadeas, 2010; Wegner and Pascual, 2011).[16] Table 4.5 summarises the implications of each of these three types of uncertainty for economic valuation and assesses their prevalence in biodiversity-relevant contexts. With regard to the applicability of economic valuation, ambiguity is rather controversial. On the one hand, it can be argued that when possible outcomes are known, people should be able to assign some subjective probability to them (except for extremely rare events); however, this assumption has been contested in the literature (Aldred, 2010, chap. 6). It seems that it is a matter for empirical investigation whether it can be safely assumed in a given context that people are able to assign subjective probability; how this issue can be dealt with in the economic valuation of biodiversity will be briefly discussed in Chapter 5. For ignorance, it can be safely stated that it precludes the application of economic valuation (an important issue, of course, is whether we are aware of our ignorance (see Faber et al., 1992)). Regarding the prevalence of each in the context of biodiversity and its economic value, it seems that risk is an acceptable assumption regarding biodiversity's function as natural insurance in some well-studied ecosystems (e.g. Henselek et al., 2016); in others, it is more realistic to speak of ambiguity. For instance, the functional redundancy hypothesis is sometimes interpreted in such a way that 'redundant' elements of ecosystems can potentially be identified and 'sacrificed' to achieve higher efficiency in the use of these ecosystems (see

Table 4.5 Uncertainty types and economic valuation of biodiversity

Uncertainty type	Applicability of economic valuation	Prevalence in biodiversity-related contexts
Risk	Applicable	Biodiversity–ecosystem functioning relationship in well-studied ecosystem types
Ambiguity	Applicable under the assumption of purely subjective probabilities	Biodiversity–ecosystem functioning relationship in less well-studied ecosystem types; future development of preferences for ecosystem elements (partly)
Ignorance	Not applicable	Future development of preferences for ecosystem elements (partly)

the discussion of Noah's Ark problem above). Whether this is indeed so is a highly contested issue at the intersection between ecology and economics (Hector and Bagchi, 2007; Mainwaring, 2001). The complexity of interdependencies within ecosystems is so high that we cannot know *ex ante* which entities, if any, are truly redundant – our knowledge of the actual interactions of ecosystems is limited and biodiversity thus serves as an approximation. In fact, 'we often fail to learn of the benefits provided by a given species or ecosystem until it is gone' (Pascual et al., 2010, p. 223; see also Ehrenfeld, 1988; Vatn and Bromley, 1994). In this case, the main source of uncertainty is the future behaviour of ecosystems. However, the view of biodiversity as a pool of options has more to do with the uncertainty surrounding future preferences of human beings – here, the assumption of risk seems inappropriate; rather, ambiguity and, in some cases at least, ignorance are more realistic assumptions (cf. Faber et al., 1992). In general, we cannot know *ex ante* which entities will be needed in the future to satisfy the preferences of coming generations (Scholtes, 2007, 2010). Human needs and preferences are highly dynamic and respond to a complex network of drivers such as technological innovations and scientific discoveries, cultural trends etc. We have some experiences of finding useful elements in ecosystems, such as bioactive substances used in medicines: for instance, some taxol-based cytotoxic drugs used in cancer therapy are based on substances found only recently in Pacific yew (*Taxus brevifolia*) (Oberlies and Kroll, 2004). However, it is still very difficult and essentially subjective to decide on a probability of making similar discoveries in the future, especially in less well-studied ecosystems.

The portfolio metaphor suggests that biodiversity as a pool of options and biodiversity as natural insurance are closely related concepts. Nonetheless, there is a difference between the two: they focus on two different 'market sides' to which uncertainty applies. When biodiversity is viewed as a pool of options to accommodate future preferences, this has obviously to do with demand-side uncertainty – it is the future demand for various elements of ecosystems that is uncertain. Conversely, the natural insurance via functional redundancy 'responds' to uncertainty in the supply of ecosystem goods and services.

Ecosystems are inherently dynamic systems; they are constantly exposed to both anthropogenic (Pereira et al., 2012) and non-anthropogenic disturbances. These act as selective mechanisms and lead to changes in ecosystems on various levels of organisation. Therefore, importantly, it is unrealistic to expect that biodiversity as natural insurance can prevent any changes, i.e. make ecosystems stable in the sense of a non-changing state; however, it can make them stable and resilient enough to stabilise their capacity to provide ecosystem goods and services.

Of course, despite being linked to two different types of uncertainty which, as was argued above, are differently severe, the two value-inducing functions of biodiversity are closely intertwined. From a conceptual point of view, they are two distinct effects. However, without a minimum amount of stability and resilience, a pool of options is not of much use because it can break down at any moment.

In the context of value estimation, particularly the natural insurance effect of biodiversity poses a problem: while it responds to (supply) uncertainty, the effect itself is uncertain. Specifically, economic valuation involves a perspective of change; so when the economic value of biodiversity is to be estimated, one needs to start with an ecosystem change. It is uncertain, however, how a given ecosystem change will translate into a change in biodiversity levels; furthermore, as was discussed in Chapter 3, the exact relationship between biodiversity and ecosystem functioning varies among ecosystems in magnitude and in some cases even in direction. The first- and second-order uncertainties involved in the actual estimation of biodiversity's economic value will be discussed in more detail in the methodological part of Chapter 5. It will be shown there how this and other challenges posed by the valuation object biodiversity can be handled in valuation studies and how they can inform the choice of appropriate valuation methods.

Summary

This chapter started with a critical review of all biodiversity valuation studies published up to October 2014. The central results concern the use of biodiversity proxies and the choice of methods in these studies. It was shown that the most common proxies are habitat protection and particular species (95 of 137 cases). These are also the most problematic, in that they do not really capture biodiversity, by either being too narrow (species) or too encompassing (habitats). Only 10 of the 123 studies accounted for the multidimensionality of biodiversity by using multiple proxies to describe it. Furthermore, of the 58 studies that explicitly focused on biodiversity primarily, 24 valued it in an isolated way, as a standalone environmental good – which is problematic because biodiversity changes are inherently linked to changes in the ecosystem whose biodiversity is in focus. With regard to methods, a clear tendency towards stated preference methods could be identified: they were used in 105 studies. This confirms the contention expressed, for example, by Meinard and Grill (2011) that the complexity and abstractness of biodiversity makes it necessary to approach it by means of stated preference methods.

What can we learn from this literature review? The general insight is that the conceptual situation in the field of economic valuation of biodiversity is precarious in many respects. First and foremost, an established framework for estimating the economic value of biodiversity does not yet exist. Different studies use highly divergent approaches, regarding both methods and, especially, the choice of biodiversity proxies. So, the field is inconsistent, the results of the studies not comparable to each other. Furthermore, as was extensively discussed in this chapter, most biodiversity proxies used in the literature are deficient. They are so in multiple ways: first, the most commonly used proxies, in particular, actually miss the target of capturing biodiversity; second, only a handful of studies use multiple biodiversity proxies so as to capture its multidimensionality; third, even among those best-practice studies, most chose the approach of valuing components of biodiversity, rather than translating it into well-being-influencing effects such as its importance for ecosystem functioning.

On the other hand, as was shown in the second part of this chapter, the environmental economics literature offers a number of useful concepts and theories of biodiversity's economic value. First, there is the older literature on the Noah's Ark problem, which is not really about biodiversity value, but rather about measurement and prioritisation mechanisms for conservation; however, it makes some very important points, including a clear definition of biodiversity that underlies the analysis, and a focus on aspects of functional redundancy. Many concepts of biodiversity's economic value discussed in this chapter explicitly or implicitly build upon this strand of literature. It turns out that viewing biodiversity as a portfolio is a powerful metaphor from which many important contributions emerged; depending on the underlying source of uncertainty, one can distinguish here between the insurance value and the option value of biodiversity. Based on that, the last section of the present chapter discussed in more detail the nexus between biodiversity, uncertainty and economic valuation, pointing to the limits of standard economic analysis that assumes risk rather than ambiguity or even ignorance. Further conceptual and empirical arguments showing why biodiversity is valuable from an economic point of view include its influence on aesthetics; its (secondary) role as underpinning the provision of ecosystem services and providing hatcheries for migratory species; conversely, as was shown in the Excursus, despite arguments to the contrary biodiversity cannot sensibly have existence value; and the notion of disvalue (borrowing conceptually from the concept of ecosystem disservices) does not appear sensible either.

This chapter provided us with a critical overview about existing empirical and conceptual approaches to the economic valuation of biodiversity. By identifying their usefulness as well as their limits, it allows us to turn in the next chapter to the main aim of the present book – developing, on this basis, a conceptual framework for the economic valuation of biodiversity; a framework that combines in a consistent, unifying manner and expands the existing literature on biodiversity's economic value.

Notes

1 'Bioprospecting refers to the assessment of life forms for development of unique molecules, biological entities, or structures that have potential utility in the economic sphere' (Cox and King, 2013, p. 588).

2 In one of the studies included in the review (Anthony and Bellinger, 2007), which was conducted in Zambia, the 'payment vehicle' was pebbles because the indigenous participants had had little experience of money. Similarly innovative approaches may help close the gap identified by Christie and colleagues.

3 For a somewhat different interpretation and evaluation of the same data, see Farnsworth et al. (2015). In their reply to the published version of the literature review (Bartkowski et al., 2015) they offer a 'biologist's perspective' on the problem.

4 Of course, this result might be skewed due to the way valuation studies are reported in publications. It is well conceivable that a study focused on biodiversity valued it in an embedded way, but did not report its results so as to make the original focus clear, because it had much more to report regarding the whole studied ecosystem, not only its diversity.

5 However, contrary to the common use of the occurrence of invasive alien species as a proxy for biodiversity, Rajmis et al. seem to emphasise the role of biodiversity in protecting ecosystems against negative effects of alien species, which would actually fit the Functions category.

6 A related idea, also based on the notion of (micro-)habitats and their diversity, will be discussed in Chapter 5.

7 Their research is explicitly inspired by the social choice theoretic literature on the axiomatisation of freedom of choice (e.g. Klemisch-Ahlert, 1993; Pattanaik and Xu, 1990).

8 Accordingly, Weikard (2003) introduces the concept of quasi-option value into this 'diversity theory'. In line with the criticism that quasi-option value is rather a decision rule than a value category (see Box 2.2), he frames his contribution as 'the development of a framework for the choice of conservation policies under uncertainty' (p. 49).

9 For a detailed analysis of the *productive value* of biodiversity that results from its contribution to ecosystem productivity, see Chavas (2009).

10 Note, however, that in formalised models of the insurance value of biodiversity, Knightian risk (known probability distributions for known potential outcomes) is usually assumed for reasons of mathematical tractability (Baumgärtner, 2007b; Pascual et al., 2015). Also, the reasonableness of portfolio theory's usual assumptions regarding probability distributions have been challenged in the wake of the recent financial crisis (e.g. Taleb, 2010).

11 In this context, so-called CRISPR/Cas genome editing has a huge potential, as it is a very cheap, easy to use and highly precise technique that allows the insertion, removal or silencing of single or multiple genes at once (Bartkowski et al., unpublished).

12 A controversially discussed issue is whether this kind of precautionary preservation of varieties should happen *in situ* or *ex situ* (Maier, 2012, chap. 7.2.3).

13 There exist a number of specific definitions of resilience (cf. Brand and Jax, 2007; Strunz, 2012). Yet the general meaning of the concept is the ability of a system (ecosystem, population etc.) to absorb disturbances, and this is sufficiently precise for our purposes.

14 The biophilia hypothesis has its foundation in Fromm's (1973) concept of biophilia, i.e. 'love of life', which he originally used in a psychological context. Wilson (1984) and Kellert and Wilson (1993) developed the concept further into an evolutionary psychology hypothesis that human beings have a natural, inherent affinity towards other living organisms and the biosphere in general.

15 Sympathy means that the well-being of individual Y is included in the utility function of individual X. Commitment means that individual X acts against her preferences and in accordance to the preferences of Y due to a sense of duty (e.g. to adhere to social norms). For more on that, see Sen (1977) and Bartkowski and Lienhoop (2016).

16 In a different yet related context, Stirling (2010) called upon scientists to face the
    uncertainties pertaining to their areas of research and to communicate them accord-
    ingly. A realistic approach to issues of ambiguity and ignorance, as called for here,
    reflects the contention that uncertainty has to be taken seriously, also in the area of
    economic valuation of biodiversity.

References

Admiraal, J.F., Wossink, A., de Groot, W.T., de Snoo, G.R., 2013. More than total eco-
    nomic value: How to combine economic valuation of biodiversity with ecological
    resilience. Ecol. Econ. 89, 115–122. doi:10.1016/j.ecolecon.2013.02.009.
Aldred, J., 2010. The skeptical economist: Revealing the ethics inside economics. Earth-
    scan, London; Washington, DC.
Ambrey, C.L., Fleming, C.M., 2014. Valuing ecosystem diversity in South East Queens-
    land: A life satisfaction approach. Soc. Indic. Res. 115, 45–65. doi:10.1007/s11205-
    012-0208-4.
Anthony, B.P., Bellinger, E.G., 2007. Importance value of landscapes, flora and fauna to
    Tsonga communities in the rural areas of Limpopo province, South Africa. South Afr.
    J. Sci. 103, 148–154.
Bakhtiari, F., Jacobsen, J.B., Strange, N., Helles, F., 2014. Revealing lay people's percep-
    tions of forest biodiversity value components and their application in valuation method.
    Glob. Ecol. Conserv. 1, 27–42. doi:10.1016/j.gecco.2014.07.003.
Balvanera, P., Pfisterer, A.B., Buchmann, N., He, J.-S., Nakashizuka, T., Raffaelli, D.,
    Schmid, B., 2006. Quantifying the evidence for biodiversity effects on ecosystem func-
    tioning and services. Ecol. Lett. 9, 1146–1156. doi:10.1111/j.1461-0248.2006.00963.x.
Banzhaf, H.S., Boyd, J., 2012. The architecture and measurement of an ecosystem
    services index. Sustainability 4, 430–461. doi:10.3390/su4040430.
Bartkowski, B., Lienhoop, N., 2016. Beyond rationality, towards reasonableness: Delib-
    erative monetary valuation and Amartya Sen's approach to rationality. Presented at the
    AES 2016, Warwick.
Bartkowski, B., Lienhoop, N., Hansjürgens, B., 2015. Capturing the complexity of bio-
    diversity: A critical review of economic valuation studies of biological diversity. Ecol.
    Econ. 113, 1–14. doi:10.1016/j.ecolecon.2015.02.023.
Bartkowski, B., Pirscher, F., Theesfeld, I., Timaeus, J., unpublished. CRISPR/Cas genome
    editing: Opportunity and challenge for agricultural production, research and regulation.
Baumgärtner, S., 2007a. Why the measurement of species diversity requires prior value
    judgements. In: Kontoleon, A., Pascual, U., Swanson, T.M. (Eds), Biodiversity eco-
    nomics. Cambridge University Press, Cambridge; New York, pp. 293–310.
Baumgärtner, S., 2007b. The insurance value of biodiversity in the provision of ecosystem
    services. Nat. Resour. Model. 20, 87–127. doi:10.1111/j.1939-7445.2007.tb00202.x.
Baumgärtner, S., Strunz, S., 2014. The economic insurance value of ecosystem resilience.
    Ecol. Econ. 101, 21–32. doi:http://dx.doi.org/10.1016/j.ecolecon.2014.02.012.
Bebbington, A., 2005. The ability of A-level students to name plants. J. Biol. Educ. 39,
    63–67. doi:10.1080/00219266.2005.9655963.
Binder, S., Polasky, S., 2013. Biodiversity, human well-being, and markets. In: Levin,
    S.A. (Ed.), Encyclopedia of biodiversity. Elsevier, Amsterdam, pp. 435–439.
Birol, E., Hanley, N., Koundouri, P., Kountouris, Y., 2009a. Optimal management of wet-
    lands: Quantifying trade-offs between flood risks, recreation, and biodiversity conser-
    vation. Water Resour. Res. 45. doi:10.1029/2008WR006955.

Birol, E., Villalba, E.R., Smale, M., 2009b. Farmer preferences for milpa diversity and genetically modified maize in Mexico: A latent class approach. Environ. Dev. Econ. 14, 521–540. doi:10.1017/S1355770X08004944.

Bixler, R.D., Floyd, M.F., 1997. Nature is scary, disgusting, and uncomfortable. Environ. Behav. 29, 443–467. doi:10.1177/001391659702900401.

Bockstael, N.E., Freeman, A.M., Kopp, R.J., Portney, P.R., Smith, V.K., 2000. On measuring economic values for nature. Environ. Sci. Technol. 34, 1384–1389. doi:10.1021/es990673l.

Boyd, J., Banzhaf, S., 2007. What are ecosystem services? The need for standardized environmental accounting units. Ecol. Econ. 63, 616–626. doi:10.1016/j.ecolecon.2007.01.002.

Brand, F.S., Jax, K., 2007. Focusing the meaning(s) of resilience: Resilience as a descriptive concept and a boundary object. Ecol. Soc. 12, 23.

Brown, E.D., Williams, B.K., 2016. Ecological integrity assessment as a metric of biodiversity: Are we measuring what we say we are? Biodivers. Conserv. 25, 1011–1035. doi:10.1007/s10531-016-1111-0.

Carroll, D., Charo, R.A., 2015. The societal opportunities and challenges of genome editing. Genome Biol. 16, 242. doi:10.1186/s13059-015-0812-0.

Chavas, J.-P., 2009. On the productive value of biodiversity. Environ. Resour. Econ. 42, 109–131. doi:10.1007/s10640-008-9206-z.

Christie, M., Fazey, I., Cooper, R., Hyde, T., Kenter, J.O., 2012. An evaluation of monetary and non-monetary techniques for assessing the importance of biodiversity and ecosystem services to people in countries with developing economies. Ecol. Econ. 83, 67–78. doi:10.1016/j.ecolecon.2012.08.012.

Christie, M., Hanley, N., Warren, J., Murphy, K., Wright, R., Hyde, T., 2006. Valuing the diversity of biodiversity. Ecol. Econ. 58, 304–317. doi:10.1016/j.ecolecon.2005.07.034.

Clapp, R.A., Crook, C., 2002. Drowning in the magic well: Shaman pharmaceuticals and the elusive value of traditional knowledge. J. Environ. Dev. 11, 79–102. doi:10.1177/10704 9650201100104.

Costanza, R., Fisher, B., Mulder, K., Liu, S., Christopher, T., 2007. Biodiversity and ecosystem services: A multi-scale empirical study of the relationship between species richness and net primary production. Ecol. Econ. 61, 478–491. doi:10.1016/j.ecolecon.2006.03.021.

Costello, C., Ward, M., 2006. Search, bioprospecting and biodiversity conservation. J. Environ. Econ. Manag. 52, 615–626. doi:10.1016/j.jeem.2006.04.001.

Cox, P.A., King, S., 2013. Bioprospecting. In: Levin, S.A. (Ed.), Encyclopedia of biodiversity. Elsevier, Amsterdam, pp. 588–599.

Crook, C., 2001. Biodiversity prospecting agreements: Evaluating their economic and conservation benefits in Costa Rica and Peru. University of Toronto, Toronto.

Czajkowski, M., Buszko-Briggs, M., Hanley, N., 2009. Valuing changes in forest biodiversity. Ecol. Econ. 68, 2910–2917. doi:10.1016/j.ecolecon.2009.06.016.

Dallimer, M., Irvine, K.N., Skinner, A.M.J., Davies, Z.G., Rouquette, J.R., Maltby, L.L., Warren, P.H., Armsworth, P.R., Gaston, K.J., 2012. Biodiversity and the feel-good factor: Understanding associations between self-reported human well-being and species richness. BioScience 62, 47–55. doi:10.1525/bio.2012.62.1.9.

Dasgupta, P., Kinzig, A.P., Perrings, C., 2013. The value of biodiversity. In: Levin, S.A. (Ed.), Encyclopedia of biodiversity. Elsevier, Amsterdam, pp. 167–179.

de Groot, R.S., Fisher, B., Christie, M., 2010. Integrating the ecological and economic dimensions in biodiversity and ecosystem service valuation. In: Kumar, P. (Ed.), The economics of ecosystems and biodiversity: Ecological and economic foundations. Routledge, London; New York, pp. 9–40.

Di Falco, S., 2012. On the value of agricultural biodiversity. In: Rausser, G.C. (Ed.), Annual review of resource economics, Vol. 4. Annual Reviews, Palo Alto, pp. 207–223.

Di Falco, S., Chavas, J.-P., 2009. On crop biodiversity, risk exposure, and food security in the highlands of Ethiopia. Am. J. Agric. Econ. 91, 599–611. doi:10.1111/j.1467-8276. 2009.01265.x.

Dinis, I., Simoes, O., Moreira, J., 2011. Using sensory experiments to determine consumers' willingness to pay for traditional apple varieties. Span. J. Agric. Res. 9. doi:10.5424/sjar/ 20110902-133-10.

Dohmen, T., Falk, A., Huffman, D., Sunde, U., Schupp, J., Wagner, G.G., 2011. Individual risk attitudes: Measurement, determinants, and behavioral consequences. J. Eur. Econ. Assoc. 9, 522–550. doi:10.1111/j.1542-4774.2011.01015.x.

Eggert, H., Olsson, B., 2009. Valuing multi-attribute marine water quality. Mar. Policy 33, 201–206. doi:10.1016/j.marpol.2008.05.011.

Ehrenfeld, D., 1988. Why put a value on biodiversity? In: Wilson, E.O. (Ed.), Biodiversity. National Academy Press, Washington, DC, pp. 212–216.

Ehrlich, I., Becker, G.S., 1972. Market insurance, self-insurance, and self-protection. J. Polit. Econ. 80, 623–648.

Elmqvist, T., Maltby, E., Barker, T., Mortimer, M., Perrings, C., 2010. Biodiversity, ecosystems and ecosystem services. In: Kumar, P. (Ed.), The economics of ecosystems and biodiversity: Ecological and economic foundations. Routledge, London; New York, pp. 41–111.

Erwin, P.M., López-Legentil, S., Schuhmann, P.W., 2010. The pharmaceutical value of marine biodiversity for anti-cancer drug discovery. Ecol. Econ. 70, 445–451. doi:10.1016/ j.ecolecon.2010.09.030.

Faber, M., Manstetten, R., Proops, J.L.R., 1992. Humankind and the environment: An anatomy of surprise and ignorance. Environ. Values 1, 217–241. doi:10.3197/ 096327192776680089.

Farnsworth, K.D., Adenuga, A.H., de Groot, R.S., 2015. The complexity of biodiversity: A biological perspective on economic valuation. Ecol. Econ. 120, 350–354. doi:10.1016/j.ecolecon.2015.10.003.

Farnsworth, K.D., Lyashevska, O., Fung, T., 2012. Functional complexity: The source of value in biodiversity. Ecol. Complex. 11, 46–52. doi:10.1016/j.ecocom.2012.02.001.

Figge, F., 2004. Bio-folio: Applying portfolio theory to biodiversity. Biodivers. Conserv. 13, 827–849. doi:10.1023/B:BIOC.0000011729.93889.34.

Finger, R., Buchmann, N., 2015. An ecological economic assessment of risk-reducing effects of species diversity in managed grasslands. Ecol. Econ. 110, 89–97. doi:10.1016/j.ecolecon.2014.12.019.

Fromm, E., 1973. The anatomy of human destructiveness. Holt Rinehart & Winston, New York.

Fromm, O., 2000. Ecological structure and functions of biodiversity as elements of its total economic value. Environ. Resour. Econ. 16, 303–328. doi:10.1023/ A:1008359022814.

Fu, B.-J., Su, C.-H., Wei, Y.-P., Willett, I.R., Lü, Y.-H., Liu, G.-H., 2011. Double counting in ecosystem services valuation: Causes and countermeasures. Ecol. Res. 26, 1–14. doi:10.1007/s11284-010-0766-3.

Garber-Yonts, B., Kerkvliet, J., Johnson, R., 2004. Public values for biodiversity conservation policies in the Oregon coast range. For. Sci. 50, 589–602.

Garrod, G.D., Willis, K.G., 1994. Valuing biodiversity and nature conservation at a local level. Biodivers. Conserv. 3, 555–565. doi:10.1007/BF00115161.

Gerstner, K., Dormann, C.F., Václavík, T., Kreft, H., Seppelt, R., 2014. Accounting for geographical variation in species–area relationships improves the prediction of plant species richness at the global scale. J. Biogeogr. 41, 261–273. doi:10.1111/jbi.12213.

Giergiczny, M., Czajkowski, M., Żylicz, T., Angelstam, P., 2015. Choice experiment assessment of public preferences for forest structural attributes. Ecol. Econ. 119, 8–23. doi:10.1016/j.ecolecon.2015.07.032.

Goeschl, T., Swanson, T.M., 2002. The social value of biodiversity for R&D. Environ. Resour. Econ. 22, 477–504. doi:10.1023/A:1019869119754.

Goeschl, T., Swanson, T.M., 2007. Designing the legacy library of genetic resources: Approaches, methods and results. In: Kontoleon, A., Pascual, U., Swanson, T.M. (Eds), Biodiversity economics. Cambridge University Press, Cambridge; New York, pp. 273–292.

Haines-Young, R., Potschin, M., 2010. The links between biodiversity, ecosystem services and human well-being. In: Raffaelli, D.G., Frid, C. (Eds), Ecosystem ecology: A new synthesis. Cambridge University Press, Cambridge; New York, pp. 110–139.

Hamilton, K., 2013. Biodiversity and national accounting (No. WPS 6441). World Bank, Washington, DC.

Heal, G.M., 2000. Nature and the marketplace: Capturing the value of ecosystem services. Island Press, Washington, DC.

Hector, A., Bagchi, R., 2007. Biodiversity and ecosystem multifunctionality. Nature 448, 188–190. doi:10.1038/nature05947.

Henselek, Y., Klein, A.-M., Baumgärtner, S., 2016. The economic insurance value of wild pollinators in almond orchards in California. Presented at the 18th Annual BIOECON Conference, Cambridge.

Holling, C.S., 1973. Resilience and stability of ecological systems. Annu. Rev. Ecol. Syst. 4, 1–23.

Holt, C.A., Laury, S.K., 2002. Risk aversion and incentive effects. Am. Econ. Rev. 92, 1644–1655. doi:10.1257/000282802762024700.

Horne, P., Boxall, P.C., Adamowicz, W.L., 2005. Multiple-use management of forest recreation sites: A spatially explicit choice experiment. For. Ecol. Manag. 207, 189–199. doi:10.1016/j.foreco.2004.10.026.

Jacobsen, J.B., Boiesen, J.H., Thorsen, B.J., Strange, N., 2008. What's in a name? The use of quantitative measures versus 'iconised' species when valuing biodiversity. Environ. Resour. Econ. 39, 247–263. doi:10.1007/s10640-007-9107-6.

Jobstvogt, N., Hanley, N., Hynes, S., Kenter, J., Witte, U., 2014. Twenty thousand sterling under the sea: Estimating the value of protecting deep-sea biodiversity. Ecol. Econ. 97, 10–19. doi:10.1016/j.ecolecon.2013.10.019.

Kassar, I., Lasserre, P., 2004. Species preservation and biodiversity value: A real options approach. J. Environ. Econ. Manag. 48, 857–879. doi:10.1016/j.jeem.2003.11.005.

Kellert, S.R., Wilson, E.O. (Eds), 1993. The biophilia hypothesis. Island Press, Washington, DC.

Kimmins, J.P., 1999. Biodiversity, beauty and the 'beast': Are beautiful forests sustainable, are sustainable forests beautiful, and is 'small' always ecologically desirable? For. Chron. 75, 955–960. doi:10.5558/tfc75955-6.

Klein, A.-M., Brittain, C., Hendrix, S.D., Thorp, R., Williams, N., Kremen, C., 2012. Wild pollination services to California almond rely on semi-natural habitat. J. Appl. Ecol. 49, 723–732. doi:10.1111/j.1365-2664.2012.02144.x.

Klemisch-Ahlert, M., 1993. Freedom of choice: A comparison of different rankings of opportunity sets. Soc. Choice Welf. 10, 189–207. doi:10.1007/BF00182505.

Knight, F.H., 1921. Risk, uncertainty and profit. Hart, Schaffner and Marx, New York.

Kragt, M.E., Roebeling, P.C., Ruijs, A., 2009. Effects of Great Barrier Reef degradation on recreational reef-trip demand: A contingent behaviour approach. Aust. J. Agric. Resour. Econ. 53, 213–229. doi:10.1111/j.1467-8489.2007.00444.x.

Kumar, P. (Ed.), 2010. The economics of ecosystems and biodiversity: Ecological and economic foundations. Routledge, London; New York.

Lafferty, K.D., 2014. Biodiversity loss and infectious diseases. In: Verdade, L.M., Lyra-Jorge, M.C., Piña, C.I. (Eds), Applied ecology and human dimensions in biological conservation. Springer, Berlin Heidelberg, pp. 73–89.

Lehtonen, E., Kuuluvainen, J., Pouta, E., Rekola, M., Li, C.-Z., 2003. Non-market benefits of forest conservation in southern Finland. Environ. Sci. Policy 6, 195–204. doi:10.1016/S1462-9011(03)00035-2.

Liebe, U., Preisendörfer, P., 2007. Zahlungsbereitschaft für kollektive Umweltgüter. Theoretische Grundlagen und empirische Analysen am Fallbeispiel der Wertschätzung biologischer Vielfalt im Wald. Z. Für Soziol. 36, 326–345.

Lienhoop, N., Völker, M., 2016. Preference refinement in deliberative choice experiments. Land Econ. 92, 555–557. doi:10.3368/le.92.3.555.

Lindemann-Matthies, P., Junge, X., Matthies, D., 2010. The influence of plant diversity on people's perception and aesthetic appreciation of grassland vegetation. Biol. Conserv. 143, 195–202. doi:10.1016/j.biocon.2009.10.003.

Lyashevska, O., Farnsworth, K.D., 2012. How many dimensions of biodiversity do we need? Ecol. Indic. 18, 485–492. doi:10.1016/j.ecolind.2011.12.016.

Lyytimäki, J., Sipilä, M., 2009. Hopping on one leg: The challenge of ecosystem disservices for urban green management. Urban For. Urban Green. 8, 309–315. doi:10.1016/j.ufug.2009.09.003.

Mace, G.M., Norris, K., Fitter, A.H., 2012. Biodiversity and ecosystem services: A multilayered relationship. Trends Ecol. Evol. 27, 19–26. doi:10.1016/j.tree.2011.08.006.

McIntyre, S., 1992. Risks associated with the setting of conservation priorities from rare plant species lists. Biol. Conserv. 60, 31–37. doi:10.1016/0006-3207(92)90796-P.

MacMillan, D.C., Duff, E.I., Elston, D.A., 2001. Modelling the non-market environmental costs and benefits of biodiversity projects using contingent valuation data. Environ. Resour. Econ. 18, 391–410. doi:10.1023/A:1011169413639.

MacMillan, D.C., Hanley, N., Lienhoop, N., 2006. Contingent valuation: Environmental polling or preference engine? Ecol. Econ. 60, 299–307. doi:10.1016/j.ecolecon.2005.11.031.

Maier, D.S., 2012. What's so good about biodiversity? A call for better reasoning about nature's value. Springer, Dordrecht; New York.

Mainwaring, L., 2001. Biodiversity, biocomplexity, and the economics of genetic dissimilarity. Land Econ. 77, 79. doi:10.2307/3146982.

Markowitz, H., 1952. Portfolio selection. J. Finance 7, 77–91. doi:10.1111/j.1540-6261.1952.tb01525.x.

Martin, D.W., 2016. Noah revisits biodiversity prioritization. Mod. Econ. 07, 1272–1289. doi:10.4236/me.2016.711122.

Martín-López, B., Montes, C., Benayas, J., 2008. Economic valuation of biodiversity conservation: The meaning of numbers. Conserv. Biol. 22, 624–635. doi:http://dx.doi.org/10.1111/j.1523-1739.2008.00921.x.

Mazmunder, A., 2009. Consequences of aquatic biodiversity for water quality and health. In: Sala, O.E., Meyerson, L.A., Parmesan, C. (Eds), Biodiversity change and human health: From ecosystem services to spread of disease. Island Press, Washington, DC; Covelo, CA; London, pp. 143–157.

MEA, 2005. Ecosystems and human well-being: General synthesis. World Resources Institute, Washington, DC.

Meinard, Y., Grill, P., 2011. The economic valuation of biodiversity as an abstract good. Ecol. Econ. 70, 1707–1714. doi:10.1016/j.ecolecon.2011.05.003.

Myers, N., 1997. Biodiversity's genetic library. In: Daily, G.C. (Ed.), Nature's services: Societal dependence on natural ecosystems. Island Press, Washington, DC, pp. 255–273.

Myers, N., Mittermeier, R.A., Mittermeier, C.G., da Fonseca, G.A.B., Kent, J., 2000. Biodiversity hotspots for conservation priorities. Nature 403, 853–858. doi:10.1038/35002501.

Nehring, K., Puppe, C., 2002. A theory of diversity. Econometrica 70, 1155–1198. doi:10.1111/1468-0262.00321.

Nijkamp, P., Vindigni, G., Nunes, P.A.L.D., 2008. Economic valuation of biodiversity: A comparative study. Ecol. Econ. 67, 217–231. doi:10.1016/j.ecolecon.2008.03.003.

Norgaard, R.B., 2010. Ecosystem services: From eye-opening metaphor to complexity blinder. Ecol. Econ. 69, 1219–1227. doi:10.1016/j.ecolecon.2009.11.009.

Nunes, P.A.L.D., van den Bergh, J.C.J.M., 2001. Economic valuation of biodiversity: Sense or nonsense? Ecol. Econ. 39, 203–222. doi:10.1016/S0921-8009(01)00233-6.

Nunes, P.A.L.D., van den Bergh, J.C.J.M., Nijkamp, P., 2003. The ecological economics of biodiversity: Methods and applications. Edward Elgar, Cheltenham; Northampton, MA.

Oberlies, N.H., Kroll, D.J., 2004. Camptothecin and taxol: Historic achievements in natural products research. J. Nat. Prod. 67, 129–135. doi:10.1021/np030498t.

Palmgren, M.G., Edenbrandt, A.K., Vedel, S.E., Andersen, M.M., Landes, X., Østerberg, J.T., Falhof, J., Olsen, L.I., Christensen, S.B., Sandøe, P., Gamborg, C., Kappel, K., Thorsen, B.J., Pagh, P., 2015. Are we ready for back-to-nature crop breeding? Trends Plant Sci. 20, 155–164. doi:10.1016/j.tplants.2014.11.003.

Pascual, U., Muradian, R., Brander, L., Gómez-Baggethun, E., Martín-López, B., Verma, M., 2010. The economics of valuing ecosystem services and biodiversity. In: Kumar, P. (Ed.), The economics of ecosystems and biodiversity: Ecological and economic foundations. Routledge, London; New York, pp. 183–256.

Pascual, U., Termansen, M., Hedlund, K., Brussaard, L., Faber, J.H., Foudi, S., Lemanceau, P., Jørgensen, S.L., 2015. On the value of soil biodiversity and ecosystem services. Ecosyst. Serv. 15, 11–18. doi:10.1016/j.ecoser.2015.06.002.

Pattanaik, P.K., Xu, Y., 1990. On ranking opportunity sets in terms of freedom of choice. Rech. Économiques Louvain Louvain Econ. Rev. 56, 383–390.

Pearce, D.W., 2001. Valuing biological diversity: Issues and overview. In: OECD (Ed.), Valuation of biodiversity benefits: Selected studies. OECD, Paris, pp. 27–44.

Pereira, H.M., Navarro, L.M., Martins, I.S., 2012. Global biodiversity change: The bad, the good, and the unknown. Annu. Rev. Environ. Resour. 37, 25–50. doi:10.1146/annurev-environ-042911-093511.

Pilgrim, S.E., Cullen, L.C., Smith, D.J., Pretty, J., 2008. Ecological knowledge is lost in wealthier communities and countries. Environ. Sci. Technol. 42, 1004–1009. doi:10.1021/es070837v.

Rajmis, S., Barkmann, J., Marggraf, R., 2009. User community preferences for climate change mitigation and adaptation measures around Hainich National Park, Germany. Clim. Res. 40, 61–73. doi:10.3354/cr00803.

Rajmis, S., Barkmann, J., Marggraf, R., 2010. Pythias Rache: zum ökonomischen Wert ökologischer Risikovorsorge. GAIA 19, 114–121.

Reyers, B., Bidoglio, G., O'Farrell, P., Schutyser, F., 2010. Measuring biophysical quantities and the use of indicators. In: Kumar, P. (Ed.), The economics of ecosystems and biodiversity: Ecological and economic foundations. Routledge, London; New York, pp. 113–147.

Scholtes, F., 2007. Umweltherrschaft und Freiheit: Naturbewertung im Anschluss an Amartya K. Sen, Edition panta rei. transcript-Verl, Bielefeld.

Scholtes, F., 2010. Whose sustainability? Environmental domination and Sen's capability approach. Oxf. Dev. Stud. 38, 289–307. doi:10.1080/13600818.2010.505683.

Sen, A., 1977. Rational fools: A critique of the behavioural foundations of economic theory. Philos. Public Aff. 6, 317–344.

Seppelt, R., Dormann, C.F., Eppink, F.V., Lautenbach, S., Schmidt, S., 2011. A quantitative review of ecosystem service studies: Approaches, shortcomings and the road ahead. J. Appl. Ecol. 48, 630–636. doi:10.1111/j.1365-2664.2010.01952.x.

Shiva, V., 1997. Biopiracy: The plunder of nature and knowledge. South End Press, Boston, MA.

Sigel, K., Klauer, B., Pahl-Wostl, C., 2010. Conceptualising uncertainty in environmental decision-making: The example of the EU water framework directive. Ecol. Econ. 69, 502–510. doi:10.1016/j.ecolecon.2009.11.012.

Siikamäki, P., Kangas, K., Paasivaara, A., Schroderus, S., 2015. Biodiversity attracts visitors to national parks. Biodivers. Conserv. 24, 2521–2534. doi:10.1007/s10531-015-0941-5.

Solow, A., Polasky, S., Broadus, J., 1993. On the measurement of biological diversity. J. Environ. Econ. Manag. 24, 60–68. doi:10.1006/jeem.1993.1004.

Stirling, A., 2010. Keep it complex. Nature 468, 1029–1031. doi:10.1038/4681029a.

Strunz, S., 2012. Is conceptual vagueness an asset? Arguments from philosophy of science applied to the concept of resilience. Ecol. Econ. 76, 112–118. doi:10.1016/j. ecolecon.2012.02.012.

Szabó, Z., 2011. Reducing protest responses by deliberative monetary valuation: Improving the validity of biodiversity valuation. Ecol. Econ. 72, 37–44. doi:10.1016/j. ecolecon.2011.09.025.

Taleb, N.N., 2010. The Black Swan: The impact of the highly improbable, 2nd edn. Random House, New York.

ten Kate, K., Laird, S.A., 2000. The commercial use of biodiversity: Access to genetic resources and benefit-sharing. Earthscan, London.

Thomas, M.B., Lafferty, K.D., Friedman, C.S., 2009. Biodiversity and disease. In: Sala, O.E., Meyerson, L.A., Parmesan, C. (Eds), Biodiversity change and human health: From ecosystem services to spread of disease. Island Press, Washington, DC; Covelo, CA; London, pp. 229–244.

Tschirk, W., 2014. Statistik: Klassisch oder Bayes: zwei Wege im Vergleich, Springer-Lehrbuch. Springer Spektrum, Berlin.

UEBT, 2013. Biodiversity Barometer 2013.

UNEP-WCMC, 2015. Experimental Biodiversity Accounting as a component of the System of Environmental-Economic Accounting Experimental Ecosystem Accounting (SEEA-EEA) (Supporting document to Advancing the SEEA Experimental Ecosystem Accounting project). United Nations.

Vardas, G., Xepapadeas, A., 2010. Model uncertainty, ambiguity and the precautionary principle: Implications for biodiversity management. Environ. Resour. Econ. 45, 379–404. doi:10.1007/s10640-009-9319-z.

Vatn, A., Bromley, D.W., 1994. Choices without prices without apologies. J. Environ. Econ. Manag. 26, 129–148. doi:10.1006/jeem.1994.1008.

Veisten, K., Fredrik Hoen, H., Navrud, S., Strand, J., 2004. Scope insensitivity in contingent valuation of complex environmental amenities. J. Environ. Manage. 73, 317–331. doi:10.1016/j.jenvman.2004.07.008.

Voigt, A., Wurster, D., 2015. Does diversity matter? The experience of urban nature's diversity: Case study and cultural concept. Ecosyst. Serv. 12, 200–208. doi:10.1016/j.ecoser.2014.12.005.

von Döhren, P., Haase, D., 2015. Ecosystem disservices research: A review of the state of the art with a focus on cities. Ecol. Indic. 52, 490–497. doi:10.1016/j.ecolind.2014.12.027.

Walker, B., Holling, C.S., Carpenter, S.R., Kinzig, A., 2004. Resilience, adaptability and transformability in social–ecological systems. Ecol. Soc. 9, 5.

Wätzold, F., Lienhoop, N., Drechsler, M., Settele, J., 2008. Estimating optimal conservation in the context of agri-environmental schemes. Ecol. Econ. 68, 295–305. doi:10.1016/j.ecolecon.2008.03.007.

Wegner, G., Pascual, U., 2011. Cost–benefit analysis in the context of ecosystem services for human well-being: A multidisciplinary critique. Glob. Environ. Change 21, 492–504. doi:10.1016/j.gloenvcha.2010.12.008.

Weikard, H.-P., 2002. Diversity functions and the value of biodiversity. Land Econ. 78, 20. doi:10.2307/3146920.

Weikard, H.-P., 2003. On the quasi-option value of biodiversity and conservation. In: Wesseler, J., Weikard, H.-P., Weaver, R.D. (Eds), Risk and uncertainty in environmental and resource economics. Edward Elgar, Cheltenham, pp. 37–52.

Weitzman, M.L., 1992. On diversity. Q. J. Econ. 107, 363–405. doi:10.2307/2118476.

Weitzman, M.L., 1993. What to preserve? An application of diversity theory to crane conservation. Q. J. Econ. 108, 157–183. doi:10.2307/2118499.

Weitzman, M.L., 1995. Diversity functions. In: Perrings, C., Folke, C., Mäler, K.-G., Holling, C.S., Jansson, B.-O. (Eds), Biodiversity loss: Economic and ecological issues. Cambridge University Press, Cambridge, pp. 21–43.

Weitzman, M.L., 1998. The Noah's ark problem. Econometrica 66, 1279. doi:10.2307/2999617.

Weitzman, M.L., 2000. Economic profitability versus ecological entropy. Q. J. Econ. 115, 237–263. doi:10.1162/003355300554728.

Wilson, E.O., 1984. Biophilia. Harvard University Press, Cambridge, MA.

5 Conceptual framework for the economic valuation of biodiversity

In the preceding chapters, biodiversity as an ecological concept (Chapter 3) and as object of interest in environmental ethics was presented (Excursus). It was shown that biodiversity is an abstract and multidimensional concept; a property of ecosystems, the *ecological* value of which results from the fact that it is highly correlated with ecosystem functioning. The overview of the environmental ethics literature on biodiversity showed that it does not have 'value on its own', which means that its value is mainly instrumental and use-related (directly or indirectly). That makes it suitable for economic analysis, as had been shown in the introductory chapter on theoretical foundations of economic valuation (Chapter 2). Chapter 4 offered an extensive overview of empirical and conceptual approaches to the economic valuation of biodiversity. Its first part offered a critical review of valuation studies which made biodiversity their *valuation object*. It was shown there that the situation in the field of economic valuation of biodiversity is precarious in many respects. Different studies use highly divergent approaches. The field is inconsistent, the results of the studies not comparable to each other. Furthermore, most biodiversity proxies used in the literature are deficient in multiple ways: they miss the target of capturing biodiversity; few studies use multiple biodiversity proxies so as to capture its multidimensionality; most value components of biodiversity, rather than translating it into well-being-influencing effects. There is a need for a coherent conceptual framework for the economic valuation of biodiversity, which would provide a basis for generating meaningful estimates of the economic value of biodiversity. The second part of Chapter 4 focused on conceptual and theoretical approaches to the economic valuation of biodiversity that can be found in the literature. It showed that uncertainty and the portfolio metaphor are central aspects of biodiversity's economic value. But there are also other value-inducing functions of biodiversity, including its influence on aesthetics and contribution to the life cycles of migratory species. Nonetheless, the conceptual arguments, too, are scattered and in need of a systematic take and unification. Moreover, surprisingly, the two literature strands, applied and conceptual, seem largely detached from each other.

This chapter will build upon the discussions in Chapters 2–4 to develop a conceptual framework for the economic valuation of biodiversity. The reason why there *should* be such a framework was indicated in the previous chapter and briefly restated above: biodiversity is a highly complex and abstract environmental public good. Current empirical approaches fail to capture its complexity and thus to provide meaningful estimates of its economic value. Many useful conceptual approaches are available but they have not yet been integrated into a consistent, unifying framework.

The conceptual framework that will be developed in this chapter provides orientation for future valuation studies as to (i) what are the sources of biodiversity's economic value; (ii) what are their implications for other environmental economic frameworks, such as total economic value (TEV); (iii) what are the specific *methodological* challenges posed by biodiversity and which valuation methods are particularly well-suited, against the background of these challenges, for this specific valuation object. The conceptual framework is meant to be precise, consistent, meaningful and informative.

Because economic valuation is inherently preference-oriented, the conceptual framework was tested in a specific setting in a focus group study with lay stakeholders. The results and implications of this study are also reported in this chapter.

The development of the framework draws from both the ecological and the ethical perspectives as well as relevant economics literature (as presented in Chapters 3 and 4 and the Excursus). The chapter consists of two major parts: a conceptual framework of the economic value of biodiversity and methodological recommendations. The purpose of the latter is to give an orientation to how the conceptual framework can be applied in valuation studies. The conceptual framework is based on a clear characterisation of the valuation object. Its main part is a discussion of various sources of biodiversity's economic value, which are presented as a consistent whole. The framework's consequences for the TEV and ESS (ecosystem services) frameworks will also be discussed, followed by presentation of the results and implications of the above-mentioned case study. Although the framework is abstract and does not solve all problems of measuring and valuing biodiversity, a number of implications can be derived for its practical implication in valuation studies, particularly regarding the question which valuation methods to use. Thus, in the second part of the chapter biodiversity will be discussed as a methodologically challenging valuation object. Based on this discussion, a specific methodological approach will be emphasised as particularly well-suited to dealing with biodiversity, namely, deliberative choice experiments. Also, in the last section of this chapter some ideas are offered on how the conceptual framework can be coupled with quantitative data.

The economic value of biodiversity

This section is an attempt to bring structure into the scattered field of biodiversity valuation (see Chapter 4) by providing an economist's view on where the value of biodiversity stems from and how it can be categorised. First, a characterisation of the valuation object biodiversity is offered, partly based on what was already said in Chapter 3. Second, the main sources of biodiversity's economic value are identified and combined to form a conceptual framework. Many of the conceptual arguments reviewed in Chapter 4 will be found in this framework, albeit in many cases in a modified form. The modifications are necessary to make the framework coherent and consistent with the insights of ecological economics, biodiversity research and environmental ethics. Third, implications will be drawn for the ESS and TEV frameworks. Fourth, a focus groups-based case study will be presented, in which the compatibility of the framework with preferences of stakeholders in a real-world context was tested.[1]

Characterisation of the valuation object

In Chapter 3 a range of definitions of biodiversity was presented. The quest for developing a conceptual framework for its economic valuation necessitates a decision on a definition that will underlie further analysis. Furthermore, any definition has implications for how biodiversity can then be translated into the language of economics. This section is devoted to discussing these issues, so as to provide the ground upon which the conceptual framework can unfold.

The general definition of diversity proposed by Stirling (2007), mentioned in Chapter 3, is a very useful starting point for defining biodiversity. It stresses that diversity is not simply variety, but also includes two further dimensions, namely, disparity and balance. In fact, applied to biodiversity this would combine the focus on relative abundances, which Baumgärtner (2007a) attributed to ecological diversity measures, and the economist's focus on dissimilarity, as exemplified in the Noah's Ark literature. In the most general sense, biodiversity can be framed as the multiplicity or richness of kinds 'in biotic and biota-encompassing categories' (Maier, 2012, pp. 76–77; see also Faith, 2017); more specifically, biodiversity has three main dimensions: taxonomic, structural and functional (Lyashevska and Farnsworth, 2012), which loosely correspond with the three diversity elements identified by Stirling (2007), since taxonomic diversity combines variety and disparity, while structural diversity is a combination of variety and balance. Functional diversity cannot be easily matched up with Stirling's concept, but it is widely argued to be an essential component of biodiversity (Cardinale et al., 2012; Farnsworth et al., 2012) and should thus be taken into account.

From this, a conclusion can be immediately drawn: biodiversity is not an entity but a property or quality of ecosystems: 'At root, diversity is an attribute of any system whose elements may be apportioned into categories' (Stirling, 2007, p. 708). In economics literature, characteristics of economic goods are often thought to be analytically as relevant as the goods themselves, which are nothing other than bundles of characteristics.[2] In the case of biodiversity, it is important to keep in mind that it is not a 'thing', it cannot be touched, smelled or seen. It is just a characteristic of ecosystems. Therefore, contrary to the term's use in many contexts, it is not equivalent to 'life on Earth' and must not be used as a synonym of 'nature', lest it lose any analytic relevance.

Bringing these insights together, we can propose the following definition, on which the arguments developed in the rest of this chapter are based:

> Biodiversity is a property of ecosystems; it is the (i) variety, (ii) balance and (iii) dissimilarity of kinds in biotic or biota-encompassing categories.

In other words, biodiversity is about the multiplicity of ecosystem components, not about their identity. As the term 'ecosystem components' suggests, the relevant spatial level of the following analysis is the ecosystem. Biodiversity can be viewed at different levels – small habitats, larger ecosystems, biomes or even the Earth as a whole. The focus here is on biodiversity of ecosystems.[3] Alas, there exists no clear-cut and unambiguous definition of ecosystems (Jax, 2006, 2010, chap. 4.3). Jax (2006, p. 240) proposed a generic definition of ecosystem as 'an assemblage of organisms of different types (species, life forms) together with their abiotic environment in space and time'. However, this definition leaves open the question of spatial-level focus, which is particularly relevant here. It is neither necessary nor possible here to provide a precise demarcation criterion, but the following framework applies for biodiversity in ecosystems at local to regional levels – a given forest or forest area, a lake or a wetland. It certainly does not apply for higher spatial levels, such as a biome or a country or a continent or the Earth. In other words, the ecosystem should be rather homogeneous in terms of structure – thus, for instance, landscape diversity is only of minor importance for this framework (although it is not completely irrelevant, as will be discussed below).

Clearly, the adoption of this definition for the purposes of the present book is an attempt to take the 'moral' out of the 'epistemic-moral hybrid' (Potthast, 2014) that is biodiversity, since there are no further restrictions such as those between, for example, 'good' natural and 'bad' artificial diversity. This is crucial for the quest to identify the economic value of biodiversity – one cannot sensibly estimate the value of something that is already defined with reference to value categories (see also Box E.1 in the Excursus on the controversial issue of nativeness). Rather, it is necessary to start with a possibly value-neutral definition of biodiversity and then to proceed by trying to find out whether it can be linked to valuable characteristics and functions of ecosystems.

Of course, the above definition is quite encompassing, as there are potentially very many 'biotic or biota-encompassing categories' to be included in biodiversity. Thus, the concept is inherently multidimensional. Within ecology, conventional one-dimensional diversity measures have been criticised for misrepresenting biodiversity (Lyashevska and Farnsworth, 2012). The cited authors acknowledge that

> [b]iodiversity, thus defined [as the amount of biological information contained by an ecosystem, see Farnsworth et al. (2012)], is too much to be directly measurable; only aspects of it may be estimated by empirical indices, which may be used for comparing diversity among systems.

Nevertheless, they argue that biodiversity needs to be measured and that it is essential to account for its multidimensionality. As an alternative to the common measures, they offer a three-dimensional biodiversity metric, which consists of the three 'axes' of structural complexity, taxonomic diversity and functional diversity and show that conventional biodiversity measures miss a significant amount of information (Lyashevska and Farnsworth, 2012). This shows that not only is 'no single component, whether genes, species, or ecosystems, [...] consistently a good indicator of overall biodiversity, as the components can vary independently' (MEA, 2005, p. 1), but one-dimensional perspectives on biodiversity miss much of the relevant information about it, too. Economic valuation of biodiversity must take this into account. As pointed out by Lyashevska and Farnsworth (see above), it is impossible to take all dimensions of biodiversity into account. Some degree of simplification is necessary. In fact, it will be argued below that some 'biotic categories' are more important than others from the point of view of economic valuation. The main message here is thus that biodiversity is not identical to, not even well correlated with, species richness, as it is often conceived.

In addition to the concept itself, biodiversity's contribution to the economic value of ecosystems is multidimensional (see next section). It was shown in Chapter 4 that many biodiversity valuation studies rely on single, rather simplistic proxies. Only a handful of studies to date used multiple proxies to account for the multidimensionality of biodiversity. From the perspective advanced in this book, this should be the proper approach to the economic valuation of biodiversity. Also, it is the sense in which Christie et al. (2006), one of the few multiple-proxies studies, used the phrase 'diversity of biodiversity' to highlight that biodiversity cannot be pinned down to one component or aspect.

The multidimensionality of biodiversity leads to challenges, both conceptual and methodological. This is one of the starting points of the methodological part of this chapter, in which methodological recommendations for biodiversity valuation will be developed. Before that, however, we have to take a closer look at the multidimensional nature of biodiversity's economic value, in an attempt to develop a coherent conceptual framework.

Sources of biodiversity's economic value

This subsection introduces and discusses the sources of biodiversity's economic value. These will then be combined to form a conceptual framework. Four value categories are distinguished in the following: insurance value, option value, spill-over value and aesthetic value.

An important preliminary remark should be made to clarify in which way the approach outlined here differs from most of those discussed in Chapter 4, especially from the empirical ones: many economic valuation studies of biodiversity have focused on components of biodiversity as objects of value, such as species or simple diversity indices. This approach might work well in valuation studies based on revealed preference methods (which, however, will likely miss important components of biodiversity's value, as will be argued later in this chapter). In stated preference methods, this is problematic, since it is not easy for laypeople to translate changes in such proxies into well-being effects.

In addition, as indicated by sociological investigations (Voigt and Wurster, 2015; Dallimer et al., 2012), laypeople's subjective understanding of 'diversity' might not reflect objective, scientific definitions of it, therefore biasing the results of studies based on valuing changes in components. It will be discussed here how the four sources of biodiversity's economic value relate to the different dimensions and components of biodiversity; this will show that from the perspective of economic valuation, biodiversity cannot be reduced to any single dimension or component.

It is important to note that biodiversity does not really contribute to human well-being directly – instead, one should rather say that it is valuable insofar as it 'promotes useful properties' (Brock and Xepapadeas, 2003). Indeed, it may well be argued that at the core of biodiversity's contribution to the economic value of ecosystems lie uncertainty and knowledge limitations (see last section of Chapter 4). Two of the four sources of biodiversity value presented below can be directly linked to uncertainty about future states of the (natural) world (insurance value) and about future preferences (option value). Thus, what is valuable is actually not biodiversity as such, but rather the properties of ecosystems which we approximate by the concept of biodiversity because we lack better understanding of the complexities of ecosystems.

Figure 5.1 summarises four sources of biodiversity's economic value that will be discussed in more detail below. These are: insurance value (*natural insurance*) and option value (*options*), which both respond to uncertainty and are related to the temporal dimension of ecosystems; spill-over value (*temporal*

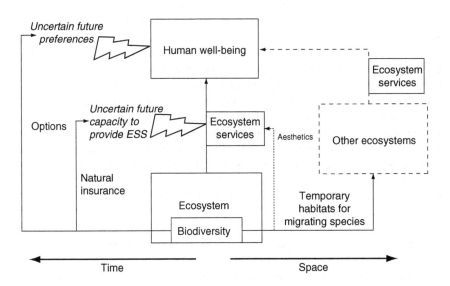

Figure 5.1 Conceptual framework of biodiversity's economic value.

Note
For explanations, see text. Modified from fig. 1 in Bartkowski (2017).

habitats for migrating species), which is related to the spatial interactions between ecosystems; and aesthetic value (*aesthetics*), which, however, will be argued below to be less relevant in the context of economic valuation because biodiversity's contribution to the overall aesthetics of a landscape cannot be easily distinguished from other factors and, in fact, need not be.

Various elements of an ecosystem provide goods and services to humans, thus influencing their well-being. Furthermore, ecosystems (and some of their elements) can have existence value, at least for some people.[4] This is nothing surprising and describes in very general terms the idea behind the ESS and TEV frameworks. However, an ecosystem has a number of properties, one of which is biodiversity, i.e. the multiplicity of dissimilar items in various biotic categories. Depending on how biodiverse the ecosystem in question is, it has additional value to society. The relevant effects of biodiversity are depicted as thin continuous arrows in Figure 5.1. In addition, the contribution of biodiversity to the aesthetic appreciation of the ecosystem in question is also depicted; however, as already noted, there are reasons for not seeing it as equally relevant as the other three value-inducing effects (see also below).

First, in accordance with the redundancy hypothesis, biodiversity provides *natural insurance* to the ecosystem itself. In and of itself, this effect is not economically relevant. It becomes relevant (as *economic insurance*) when a number of conditions are fulfilled: (i) the ecosystem under consideration must provide some goods/services or have existence value; (ii) its future capacity to provide these must be uncertain (lower thunderbolt arrow in Figure 5.1); (iii) those affected must be risk-averse. If these three conditions are fulfilled – in most cases, they are – the ecosystem's biodiversity has not only ecological, but also *economic insurance value*. It alleviates the severity of supply uncertainty (see also Chapter 4).

Two specific interpretations of insurance value are possible: first, biodiversity can be argued to promote *acute stability* (resistance or resilience) in the sense of resistance of the biodiverse ecosystem to exogenous shocks, for example, storms (Thompson et al., 2009) or climatic events such as droughts (Isbell et al., 2015). Second, when biodiversity positively influences the temporal stability of an ecosystem, this can be valuable if coupled with intergenerational equity concerns. This means that individuals may appreciate the fact that a relatively biodiverse ecosystem is more likely to be available to future generations, on top of its availability to themselves – a notion closely related to the TEV category of bequest value. However, as already mentioned above, this temporal stability is not to be understood in the sense of a non-changing state:

> Preserving productive capacity intact is not, however, an obligation to leave the world as we found it in every detail. What needs to be conserved are the opportunities of future generations to lead worthwhile lives. The fact of substitutability (in both production and consumption) implies that what we are obligated to leave behind is a generalized capacity to create well-being, not any particular thing or any particular resource. Since we do not know what

the tastes and preferences of future generations will be, and what they will do, we can talk of sustainability only in terms of conserving a capacity to produce well-being.

(Anand and Sen, 2000, p. 2035)

According to a common and influential perspective, it is the final goods and services supplied by the ecosystem that matter for economic valuation (Boyd and Banzhaf, 2007); concerns about stability may be considered a second-order problem, similar to the idea of supporting ecosystem services. However, it can well be argued that stability has value in and of itself. In fact, the idea that various sources of insurance are valuable in and of themselves can be found in other contexts, for example, climate economics and social cost of carbon literature (Kousky et al., 2011; see also van den Bergh and Botzen, 2015). Similar arguments in the area of environmental/ecological economics were provided by Baumgärtner (2007b) and Baumgärtner and Strunz (2014), among others. Thus, when valuing biodiversity, the inclusion of stability considerations is not only permissible – it is essential.

> The main point is that the natural insurance value of soil biodiversity is associated with the stabilisation of the total output value of soil biodiversity and is assumed positive when the beneficiaries of such services (the 'valuers') are risk averse.
>
> (Pascual et al., 2015, p. 15)

There is no obvious link between the insurance value of biodiversity and any specific component of it – depending on context, different components might be relevant. However, as already mentioned in Chapter 3, there are some obvious parallels between insurance value and the concepts of functional diversity and functional redundancy. Regarding the different dimensions of diversity (Stirling, 2007), insurance value obviously results from variety and disparity; but balance seems important as well – a 'functionally redundant' element of an ecosystem does not contribute much to its stability if it is very rare and thus easily lost (see Table 5.1 for a summary of the relevance of different diversity dimensions for the sources of biodiversity's economic value identified here).

Table 5.1 Relevance of diversity dimensions for sources of biodiversity's economic value

Source of value/diversity dimension	Variety	Disparity	Balance
Natural insurance	++	++	+
Options	++	++	0
Spill-over value	++	+	+
Aesthetics	++	+	0

Note
++ highly relevant, + relevant but not decisive, 0 (almost) irrelevant.

The second source of biodiversity value has a more direct effect on human well-being: the more biodiverse an ecosystem is, the more options (potential future benefits) it contains. Since our knowledge about ecosystems is inherently limited, it may be wise, according to this interpretation, to keep components of ecosystems intact (thus maintaining their diversity), even if we do not have use for them now. Here, again, uncertainty (about future preferences) and risk-aversion are constitutive. The preservation of options in an uncertain world enhances the utility of a risk-averse individual. Thus, biodiversity has *option value*. These two categories of biodiversity value, insurance and option values, have in common that they are only relevant if uncertainty about the future is taken into account. They constitute intertemporal effects. Therefore, both are higher, *ceteris paribus*, if people care about the well-being of future generations: the view of biodiversity as a carrier of option value stems from the recognition that a biodiverse ecosystem, which contains many different species and genomes, can best accommodate unanticipated desires (preferences) of both current people in the future and future people. As in the case of insurance value, this can be coupled with considerations of intergenerational equity: high levels of biodiversity now mean many different options for our grandchildren (cf. Birnbacher, 2014), who may want to extract from ecosystems technological blueprints, substances and genes which we currently have no use for.[5] An important issue regarding the option value of biodiversity, already discussed in Chapter 4 in the context of uncertainty and biodiversity, is that the probability that a given ecosystem actually does contain some prospectively useful items can hardly be known *ex ante*, as it can hardly be derived from our knowledge about similar events in the past. Thus, the estimation of option value is inherently subjective, which has important consequences for the actual estimation of the economic value of biodiversity (see below).

Option value is arguably particularly dependent on variety and disparity, in line with the focus of the Noah's Ark literature, which is essentially concerned with the preservation of future options. In this case, balance seems relatively less important – for instance, given the advancements of science and technology, in the extreme case only one specimen of a plant species is sufficient to derive from it useful substances or genetic material.

The third element of the conceptual framework depicted in Figure 5.1 is *spill-over value*. Contrary to the first two categories of biodiversity value, spill-over value operates along the spatial dimension, as it is dependent on interactions between different ecosystems.

A biodiverse ecosystem can be expected to be diverse in (micro-)habitats. Some of these habitats are essential for migratory species (e.g. salmonids, cranes, geese), whose main habitats lie outside the investigated ecosystem, but for which this ecosystem is one (potential) station in their migratory life cycle. An example of such ecosystems are the *dehesas* in the Spanish region of Extremadura, where numerous species of migratory birds from Northern Europe spend winters (Diáz et al., 1997). This is possible because of the high habitat/ landscape diversity of these agro-silvo-pastoral ecosystems. It can be argued that biodiversity in such ecosystems has spill-over effects on other ecosystems. The idea behind biodiversity's spill-over value is related to the *maintenance of life cycles of migratory species* or *nursery-service* in the TEEB classification (see Chapter 4).

Under the assumption that the relevant migratory species are economically valuable themselves, the contribution of a biodiverse ecosystem to their life cycles can be argued to contribute to the overall value of this ecosystem. Importantly, the contribution of biodiversity consists not in the fact that there is a (micro-)habitat for a specific migratory species, but that there is a *multiplicity* of habitats within one ecosystem which can (potentially) be used by such species. In a certain sense, this can be called 'efficient', as one would support a number of migratory species within one ecosystem, thus minimising the area needed for their support.[6]

Spill-over value may well be criticised as an instance of double-counting (Hamilton, 2013). This is certainly true in the context of environmental–economic accounting and large-scale cost–benefit analyses, in which the ecosystem(s) of the migratory species' origin are included as well. However, accounting, for which double-counting is a particularly problematic issue, is not the only, nor even the main, purpose of economic valuation (cf. Costanza et al., 2014). In the words of Dasgupta (2001, p. 1), '[w]e frequently value in order to evaluate. But not always. We sometimes value simply because we wish to understand a state of affairs'. For example, for communication of the importance of intact, biodiverse ecosystems to the public and policy-makers, spill-over value's importance is the following: it shows that ecosystem services, which provide direct benefits to humans and thus have use value, are embedded in a larger, highly complex dynamic system and should not be viewed atomistically or in a static way (Fromm, 2000). More generally, when the purpose is to demonstrate the economic value of a specific ecosystem, spill-overs to other ecosystems are a relevant component of this value. They should be included in examinations of the economic value of biodiversity.

It appears that spill-over value is related especially to variety and disparity within an ecosystem – for many different species to dwell, many different (micro-)habitats are needed. However, as minimally small habitats are of only limited use in this context, balance plays a role as well.

In Chapter 4, it was already argued that the fourth category of biodiversity value, resulting from its essentially variety-driven influence on the aesthetic appreciation of an ecosystem, is important from a conceptual perspective; but since biodiversity is only one of many factors influencing the ecosystem service of landscape aesthetics, it does not appear sensible to disentangle these factors. In valuation studies, it would be enough to focus on the aesthetic value of ecosystems in general, without a need to distil from it the relative contribution of biodiversity. For the sake of conceptual completeness, it should be noted that there may be distinct effects of diversity within and across taxonomic categories, so a focus solely on one aspect of a biodiversity component (say, mammal diversity) may not fully capture aesthetic value. On the other hand, the expectation appears warranted that aesthetic value has strongly diminishing returns in terms of increasing biodiversity – most likely, most people would not be able to notice changes in biodiversity beyond a certain saturation point.

In the review of existing biodiversity valuation studies in Chapter 4, four criteria were proposed for the evaluation of biodiversity proxies and also, more generally, approaches for valuing biodiversity. These criteria are fulfilled by the conceptual framework proposed here, especially if the presented sources of biodiversity value are understood as biodiversity attributes. First, biodiversity is clearly framed in terms of its influence on human well-being, not in terms of its components (criterion 3), though a link to biodiversity dimensions has been made (Table 5.1). Second, insurance value, option value and spill-over value can be attributed completely to biodiversity (criterion 2) and in Chapter 4 it was argued that biodiversity does not have further sources of value, particularly no existence value (criterion 1). Together, the presented sources of biodiversity's economic value adequately capture its multidimensional nature. Because only parts of the overall aesthetic value of an ecosystem can be attributed to biodiversity, it was argued that it is not sensible to attempt the delineation of the various aesthetics-influencing factors, so as not to violate criteria 1 and 2. At the same time, the emphasis laid on not valuing biodiversity in isolation (criterion 4), but including other aspects of a given ecosystem change, ensures that the aesthetic value of biodiversity is taken into account (as part of an overall aesthetics attribute).

The conceptual framework presented above translates the multidimensional, abstract concept of biodiversity into human well-being-relevant categories and offers a consistent, encompassing and precise picture of why biodiversity is economically valuable. It is an important basis for future economic valuation studies of biodiversity. Nevertheless, the framework is only a starting point on the road towards application in actual valuation studies. A number of further steps are made in the following sections. Before that, however, we take a closer look at implications that can be drawn from the conceptual framework described here for the ESS and TEV frameworks. Subsequently, in preparation of the second part of this chapter ('From value to valuation') on the consequences of the conceptual framework for actual valuation studies, especially regarding the choice of suitable valuation methods, a focus group-based case study will be presented, in which the compatibility of the conceptual framework with preferences of stakeholders in a real-world context was tested.

Implications for common frameworks

The conceptual framework developed in the previous subsection is not an alternative to the usual frameworks of ESS and TEV, if solely because biodiversity is only one environmental good among many. Nonetheless, it is not neutral in relationship to both these standard frameworks, as it highlights their biodiversity-related shortcomings and allows a number of conclusions to be drawn for them. The aim of this subsection is to investigate the implications of the conceptual framework of biodiversity's economic value for the ESS framework and the TEV framework. In both cases, the implications consist in extensions/modifications of these two frameworks, which are discussed accordingly.

A preliminary remark is in order: oftentimes, conceptual and applied papers on economic valuation implicitly suggest that the ESS and TEV frameworks are effectively corresponding to each other, especially when it comes to cultural ecosystem services and the non-use value branch in the TEV framework. Also, it was observed that in attempts to broaden the perspective of TEV by including 'social' or 'socio-cultural values', they are often conflated with 'cultural ecosystem services' (Scholte et al., 2015, p. 68). Consider, for example, the introductory sentence in a recent paper on bequest values: 'Perhaps the most *understudied ecosystem services* are *related to socio-cultural values* tied to nonmaterial benefits arising from human–ecosystem relationships' (Oleson et al., 2015, p. 104, emphasis added). Another example: 'locally degraded *provisioning and regulating services* may be substituted by socio-economic means, [...] but the *cultural values* of an ecosystem or a landscape are irreplaceable' (Plieninger et al., 2013, p. 118, emphasis added). Similarly, sometimes one can find the identification of existence values with ecosystem services: 'services associated with existence or bequest values' (Boyd and Banzhaf, 2007, p. 624), which is oxymoronic, as the term 'service' requires that something is 'of use' to someone. Also, the authoritative CICES classification includes 'existence' as an ecosystem service; this seems, however, to overstretch the meaning of 'service' quite substantially. Accordingly, identifying 'bequest values' or 'altruistic values' with ecosystem services (or, for that matter, biodiversity) is permissible, for there still is a 'user', who just happens to be someone other than the 'valuer'. Yet the concept of 'existence value' is explicitly detached from any kind of use and cannot thus be attached to an ecosystem service (see also the related discussion in the Excursus). These are matters that cannot be further pursued here, but it should be kept in mind that biodiversity's roles in the two frameworks, too, by no means perfectly correspond to each other.

As already mentioned in Chapter 2, in their influential paper on the relationship between biodiversity and ecosystem services, Mace et al. (2012) propose a 'multi-layered' perspective on biodiversity as: regulator of ecosystem services, a final ecosystem service and a good. Their starting point is similar to the argument of this book, as they criticise the usual focus either solely on biodiversity's influence on ecosystem functioning or without any notion of it. Thus, their perspective is actually partly compatible with the conceptual framework advanced here, but the terminology chosen is rather misguided. Especially, it appears not to be sensible to frame biodiversity as a (final) ecosystem service. Ultimately, ecosystem services can be identified with specific elements of or processes in ecosystems. Conversely, biodiversity is rather an abstract concept, a property of ecosystems. It cannot be 'consumed' in any direct or indirect way like ecosystem services, even though it does provide benefits to humanity. Thus, in a certain sense, biodiversity underpins the provision of ecosystem services in a way similar to supporting ecosystem services in the MEA classification.

The main difference between most conventional versions of the ESS framework, especially the cascade model, and what was presented here is that biodiversity contributes to human well-being (i.e. it provides benefits) in ways that are dependent on ecosystem services but nevertheless constitute additional benefits – mainly in that it provides insurance and is the carrier of options. Furthermore, biodiversity contributes to aesthetics, which is considered as underlying a number of cultural ecosystem services (Haines-Young and Potschin, 2013). In this sense, biodiversity is located beyond the ESS cascade (see Figure 5.2). The question is, thus, whether biodiversity really fits especially the cascade model, because the latter consists of links between objects and processes, while biodiversity is only a (multidimensional) property of one of these objects.

However, in a more general sense (beyond the cascade model), biodiversity's contribution to human well-being, particularly via its function as insurance, is highly dependent on ecosystem services – only if humans derive benefits from a given ecosystem (either from its own or its elements' existence or from the services it provides), they may benefit from biodiversity 'insuring' the provision of these benefits. Also, when biodiversity is understood as a pool of options, these options can be viewed as yet-unrealised ecosystem services. This suggests that the relationship between biodiversity and ecosystem services is rather complex and cannot be easily expressed in a simple model such as the cascade. From this, the conclusion can be drawn that the cascade is not well-suited to depict the relevance of biodiversity for ecosystem functioning and human well-being; if biodiversity is to be included, one option would be to complement the cascade by including our conceptual framework's depiction (Figure 5.1); the cascade can be seen as specifying the link between the 'ecosystem' and 'human well-being' boxes there.

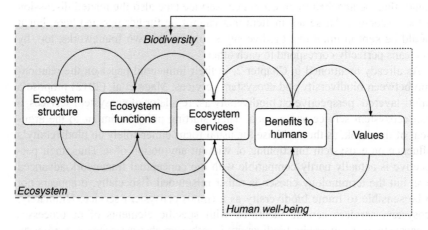

Figure 5.2 ESS cascade with biodiversity.

Note
Biodiversity is symbolised by the pattern of the left box ('ecosystem'). The thick dashed arrow symbolises the benefits provided by biodiversity to human well-being without the mediation of ecosystem services.

Turning now to the total economic value (TEV) framework: it is the single most influential framework used in the area of economic valuation of environmental goods. So, it is interesting to think about how the biodiversity values suggested above fit this framework.

TEV in its most common form consists of three main value categories: use values, non-use values and option value. In earlier publications, if insurance value was included in TEV, it happened as a category additional to the 'output value' of an ecosystem, which corresponds to the TEV as usually defined (Pascual et al., 2015). Conversely, in Pascual et al. (2010), insurance value was identified with resilience and critical natural capital (CNC). However, there is a difference between these two notions. As discussed above, resilience and stability can be linked to biodiversity. One can have more or less stability and resilience, and it is straightforward, given that most people are risk-averse (Dohmen et al., 2011; Holt and Laury, 2002), that they would be willing to pay for changes in an ecosystem's stability and/or resilience (cf. Baumgärtner and Strunz, 2014). Conversely, CNC *ex definitione* precludes the application of economic valuation because it is defined as the essential, non-substitutable 'minimum' stock of natural capital (Ehrlich and Goulder, 2007; Farley, 2008), while economic value is inherently based on substitutability. Thus, the 'insurance value' of CNC is of a different kind than the insurance value of biodiversity; it cannot be expressed in terms of willingness-to-pay.

So, how can biodiversity's contribution to the economic value of an ecosystem be properly included in the TEV framework? To do that, TEV has to be restructured and extended – two dimensions have to be added. An extension along a temporal axis helps to include insurance value (and make better place for option value, which is often in a kind of limbo somewhere between use and non-use values in many versions of the framework), while spill-over value necessitates the addition of a spatial dimension. Both extensions are depicted in Figure 5.3.

To integrate the two dimensions, two additional levels are added to the usual TEV scheme: first, *local values* and *external values* are distinguished (spatial dimension); second, we have *certain-world values* and *uncertain-world values* (temporal dimension). In Figure 5.3, values attributable to biodiversity are highlighted as shaded boxes.

Including the spatial dimension necessitates the distinction between local values, i.e. values occurring to the ecosystem in question itself, and external values, i.e. spill-overs to other ecosystems. Usually, the TEV has no notion of inter-ecosystem value spill-overs – the notions of altruistic value and existence value only take preference-based effects between locations (since they are based on the idea that the *valuer* is located elsewhere than the *object of value*). External values, on the other hand, amount to contributions of one ecosystem to the value of another, where it can be distinguished between the biodiversity-related spill-over value and other, non-biodiversity-related value spill-overs, such as the contribution of an ecosystem to the value of a particular 'visiting' migrating species (in contrast to *multiple* contributions to the value of *multiple* migrating

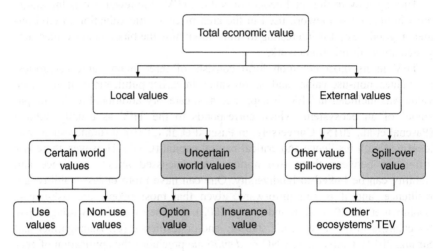

Figure 5.3 TEV with biodiversity.

Note
Biodiversity-related values are highlighted by patterns. Modified from fig. 2 in Bartkowski (2017).

species, i.e. spill-over value). As has been argued above, only in some contexts does the estimation of these values not amount to double-counting (namely, when only a single ecosystem's value is considered), which might explain its absence from conceptual frameworks of economic value. Nonetheless, spill-over remains relevant in these contexts in which double-counting is not a problem, and might be viewed as a kind of *value export* from the ecosystem under consideration to other ecosystem(s). Spill-over value of the biodiversity in an ecosystem consists in its contribution to the TEV of other ecosystems.

Let us now turn to the temporal dimension. It is rooted in the idea that uncertainty 'creates' value – both insurance and option value derive from the fact that there is irreducible uncertainty about the future (see also Chapter 4). Without this uncertainty, these values would be non-existent. In Figure 5.3, a proposal for how to account for this is presented. The basic idea is related to Pascual et al.'s (2015, fig. 3), the difference being that in Figure 5.3, option value and insurance value are put together under the heading of *uncertain-world values*, i.e. values which result from uncertainty about the future, whereas use and non-use values are *certain-world values*. From what was said above, it is obvious that biodiversity's contribution to the TEV of an ecosystem is mainly via uncertain-world values – both of the latter's components can be directly attributed to biodiversity.

Within the new uncertain-world values category, demarcation criteria are necessary to distinguish between option and insurance value. A basic criterion was proposed when the two value categories were discussed above: as defined here, option value responds to demand uncertainty (i.e. uncertainty regarding future preferences and needs), whereas insurance value derives from supply uncertainty (i.e. uncertainty regarding the future ability of ecosystems to provide services).[7] Another possible criterion would be the already discussed difference between risk, ambiguity and ignorance, where risk implies known probabilities/ probability distributions of a set of known possible events (the 'world of classical statistics'); ambiguity implies that probability distributions are unknown, but the set of possible events is known (the 'world of Bayesian statistics'); and ignorance implies that nothing is known about possible future events ('anything can happen'). Insurance value can be associated with risk and ambiguity – while future development of ecosystems cannot be known with certainty, it can at least be described as a set of scenarios, even if no probabilities can be attributed to these scenarios (cf. Peterson et al., 2003). Conversely, at least if we look far into the future, preferences can be argued to be completely unknown – a case of ignorance. Thus, option value is, at least to some extent, the result of ignorance. Of course, the difference between the two is at best gradual, not clear-cut. Furthermore, if option value would really result from pure ignorance, there would be no way of estimating it – every estimation implies some, however vague, beliefs about whether the ecosystem in question might contain anything relevant for the future. Thus, ambiguity under a Bayesian interpretation would allow for estimation (see Chapter 4). A third demarcation criterion is closeness to ecological concepts. While insurance value is inspired by the biodiversity–ecosystem functioning (BEF) research and the notion of functional redundancy, thus finding much resonance with ecologists (e.g. Farnsworth et al., 2015), option value is clearly a predominantly economic concept. However, this distinction is closely related to the supply uncertainty–demand uncertainty axis discussed above. Altogether, the supply–demand criterion appears to be the most encompassing, easily comprehensible and clear-cut.

Even though insurance value is viewed here as an additional TEV category, it differs from the other three categories in an important sense: it is dependent on the other categories, i.e. in a way, secondary. The higher the non-insurance value of an ecosystem, the higher the insurance value of its biodiversity. In an extreme case, if an ecosystem has no use, option and non-use value at all, *it cannot have insurance value*. This is obvious, as insurance is not needed if there is nothing of value to be insured.

As was argued before, there seems to be no reason why biodiversity should have existence value. Altruistic value, on the other hand, is not dependent on any additional characteristics of the environmental good at hand, but only on the presence of other-regarding preferences in economic actors' utility functions. Thus, it is obvious that biodiversity can well have altruistic value as it is commonly defined. It is not highlighted in Figure 5.3 because it is not a biodiversity-specific value category (the same holds for aesthetic value; see Chapter 4).

Empirical verification

To test the suitability of the conceptual framework developed above, a case study was conducted. The framework had been developed on the basis of literature analysis and is of a rather inductive or bottom-up nature. However, the framework's ultimate goal is to advance the estimation of biodiversity's *economic* value or, rather, its contribution to the economic value of ecosystems. Economic valuation, as was repeatedly mentioned in Chapter 2, is inherently preference-oriented. Thus, even though the framework might have an intellectual appeal in being logically consistent and adequately capturing the contribution of biodiversity to human well-being in a conceptual sense, it is worth little if it cannot be linked to the actual appreciation of biodiversity by people in concrete settings. To assess its worth as an economic concept, one must confront it with actual people in an actual socio-ecological setting. This was the overarching reason for conducting the case study presented here.

The fact that the case study is qualitative, which is not necessarily typical for economic research, is due to the insight that this is the best way to test the suitability of the conceptual framework in the sense envisioned here. In fact, at least for economic valuation studies based on stated preference approaches, qualitative focus groups are a crucial element in the refining and pre-testing processes that lead towards the actual study (e.g. Bakhtiari et al., 2014; Champ et al., 2004, p. 86; Hoyos, 2010). As this book is predominantly conceptual, the goal is not to find out the exact willingness-to-pay for a change in biodiversity in a specific ecosystem – rather, it is to offer an orientation as to how this should be properly done.

In what follows, first some related work from existing literature will be linked to the conceptual framework developed here; then, the case study setting will be presented. The focus group approach will also be very briefly introduced, before the results of the study can be presented and discussed.

The framework of biodiversity's economic value presented in the preceding sections can be analysed against the background of some qualitative empirical studies which can be found in the biodiversity (valuation) literature. For instance, it finds some empirical support in a study conducted by Bakhtiari et al. (2014). Their goal was to identify 'measurable attributes of biodiversity for a CE [discrete choice experiment] that align with perception of lay people and are relevant to management' (p. 28). In their qualitative, bottom-up study based on interviews and focus groups, conducted in Denmark, they found that laypeople identify the value of biodiversity with aesthetics, stability due to a variety of different species and, seldom, option value (see also Table 5.2). The authors also point out that species numbers and the functionality of biodiversity were deeply interconnected in the understanding of the participants in their study. Also, they point out emphatically that 'using species numbers as an attribute of a CE study would not cover the true value the general public has for biodiversity' (p. 33) and, similarly, 'using specific species, charismatic or not, is probably not a good way to describe biodiversity as it does not cover the entire concept – if the aim is to define biodiversity' (p. 34). This is very much in line with the arguments developed in the present book.

This study obviously provides some empirical evidence in support of the biodiversity value framework developed in the previous chapter. The value

Table 5.2 Attributes of biodiversity value in Bakhtiari et al. (2014)

Attributes of forest biodiversity value	Relative frequency (%)	Correspondence with conceptual framework
Naturalness	98	Not biodiversity
Variety of species	96	Component of biodiversity
Insurance/resilience/stability	96	Insurance value
Peace and quietness	96	Not biodiversity
Aesthetics	58	Aesthetic value
Charismatic species	49	Not biodiversity
Education	35	Not biodiversity
Adventure/exciting experience	29	Not biodiversity
Potential medicinal and genetic use	5	Option value

categories *aesthetic, option* and *insurance value* can be clearly identified in the responses Bakhtiari et al. (2014) collected in their study. However, there are also differences between their findings and the conceptual framework developed here. For instance, 'naturalness' was the most frequently named biodiversity-related attribute in their study, while 'peace and quietness', 'charismatic species', 'education' and 'adventure/exciting experience' also appeared repeatedly. According to the understanding of biodiversity advanced in this book, these attributes have little to nothing to do with biodiversity.

Another study which is of interest from the perspective of an empirical assessment of the conceptual framework proposed here is the older but quite extensive valuation study conducted by Christie et al. (2004, 2006), already highlighted as best practice in Chapter 4. Here, the focus groups that the Christie team used for preparation of their valuation study are of particular interest. Contrary to Bakhtiari et al. (2014), whose study can be described as essentially bottom-up since they did not suggest to their respondents any particular interpretation of biodiversity, Christie et al. (2006) took a similar route as that pursued in the present book – on the basis of a review of ecological literature (Christie et al., 2004) they proposed a conceptual framework, which the focus groups were based on. This framework identified a number of 'biodiversity concepts', divided into 'ecological concepts' and 'anthropocentric concepts'. The former were further subdivided by the authors in 'habitat quality' (including keystone species, umbrella species and flagship species) and 'ecosystem processes' (ecosystem function and ecosystem health), the latter in 'rare, unfamiliar species of wildlife' (rare species and endangered species) and 'familiar species of wildlife' (charismatic species, cuteness, familiar species, locally important species). What strikes first is that Christie et al. based their analysis on a much broader and vaguer understanding of biodiversity than is the case here. In the focus groups, the authors found that laypeople can handle biodiversity concepts if these are presented in simple language; they also found that people pay much more attention to the achievement of biodiversity outcomes than to the ways they are achieved – a finding that is at odds both with the results of a later study which aimed at refining the Christie approach (Czajkowski et al., 2009) and with what was found in the focus groups conducted within our project (see below).

Even though the general approach of the Christie et al. study is very similar to the approach pursued in the present book and theirs is likely the most comprehensive study on the economic valuation of biodiversity available, the findings of their focus groups are of limited relevance for the framework advanced here. In fact, apart from the finding that laypeople can handle biodiversity concepts when these are presented in a simplified way, most other insights are too specific to their own conceptual framework which, as already mentioned, is at odds with the perspective advanced in this book.

Another potentially insightful study, though with a non-valuation focus, was conducted by Buijs et al. (2008), who looked at public representations of biodiversity. They investigated the perception by both laypeople and conservation practitioners of biodiversity's benefits and functions. These include: biodiversity as the basis of human life; biodiversity as the source of 'balance' in nature (related to the notion of insurance value developed here); aesthetics; creation of a 'sense of place' (in the sense of 'typical' compositions of species and habitats); economic values (i.e. the direct and indirect influence of biodiversity on forestry, fisheries etc.). Clearly, there is some overlap with the conceptual framework developed here and with the results from the Bakhtiari et al. study. However, due to the focus of the study (to reveal 'the reasons for the acceptance of, and protest against, biodiversity-related measures'; Buijs et al., 2008, p. 77), the interpretation of biodiversity was much broader than in the present book. It can be argued that this study's results offer some tentative support for the conceptual framework developed here, as there is overlap with what Buijs et al. found regarding perceptions by the public of what makes biodiversity valuable. Yet the evidence provided by them is not sufficient to draw any far-reaching conclusions about the suitability of the conceptual framework developed here.

As emphasised by Meinard and Quétier (2014), the common assumption among biodiversity researchers that 'biodiversity is simply the diversity of living things, and that everyone knows what diversity and living things mean' (p. 705) is mistaken. In the area of economic valuation, committing this mistake can be particularly severe in consequences. Therefore, there is a need to close the 'science–society communication gap'. In the case of the present book, it means that there is a need to check whether the conceptual framework advanced here has any relevance to the broader society. The study by Christie et al. (2004, 2006) shows the way how this might be approached and that laypeople have the capacity to handle biodiversity concepts. However, since their own conceptual framework is misguided from the point of view of this book's argument, no *specific* inferences can be drawn from their study. Similarly, Buijs et al.'s (2008) results, while interesting in their own respect, are the offspring of a different scientific motivation and thus only limitedly helpful in the context of the present volume. Conversely, Bakhtiari et al.'s (2014) bottom-up study provides some important support for the conceptual framework of this book – but since it was conducted independently, the support is only tentative. We now turn to a qualitative focus groups study that aimed at applying the conceptual framework in an ecosystem-specific setting.

The case study area was the Biosphere Reserve Vessertal–Thuringian Forest (Vessertal Reserve or simply Vessertal in what follows). It is located in and around the valley of Vesser, a small (10.5 km) river belonging to the Weser river basin, located in the southern part of the Thuringian Forest in Germany. The Reserve covers an area of around 17,000 ha and reaches partly into the Thuringian Highland. The Reserve was established in 1979. In 2011, a public consultation process was initiated with the aim to enlarge the Reserve to 32,000 ha, so as to meet UNESCO guidelines demanding that a Man and Biosphere Reserve should cover an area of at least 30,000 ha. By 2015, when the study reported here was conducted, the enlargement process had not been finished yet, although public consultations had already taken place. To date, only 3.7 per cent of the Reserve's forest area (3.3 per cent of total area) comprises its *core areas*, which are not used at all and allowed to develop naturally. Another 12.8 (11.4) per cent are *buffer zones*, which are managed in a 'seminatural' way. The remaining 83.5 (85.3) per cent are *transition areas* where both forestry and agriculture take place (http://biosphaerenreservat-vessertal.de (retrieved on 6 May 2015)).[8]

The rationale for choosing the Vessertal Reserve to test the suitability of the conceptual framework discussed in this book was the choice of this Biosphere Reserve for the implementation of the German *National Strategy on Biological Diversity* (Deutsche Bundesregierung, 2007; Die Linke et al., 2014; MLFUN, 2011).[9] The idea for the test of the conceptual framework was to use a context of ecosystem *change*, and the goal of the *Strategy* and the measures proposed is to *enhance* the state of biodiversity in Germany; in Vessertal, particularly large biodiversity effects can be expected. According to a publication of the Thuringian Environmental and Geological Agency (Thüringer Landesanstalt für Umwelt und Geologie) on the *Potential Natural Vegetation in Thuringia* (Bushart and Suck, 2008), the area of the Vessertal Reserve would be naturally covered by beech-dominated mixed forests. Meanwhile, according to the Reserve's administration (http://biosphaerenreservat-vessertal.de (retrieved on 6 May 2015)), 89 per cent of the Vessertal area is covered by forests. The dominant tree species is clearly spruce (*Picea abies*) with more than 75 per cent of all trees, followed by beech (*Fagus sylvatica*) with around 20 per cent. Other tree species are much less common and include maple (*Acer pseudoplatanus*), larch (*Larix decidua*), birch (*Betula pendula*), rowan (*Sorbus aucuparia*), Douglas fir (*Pseudotsuga menziesii*), pine (*Pinus sylvestris*) and ash (*Fraxinus excelsior*) (Treß and Erdtmann, 2006).

The starting point for the focus group discussions were proposals to set aside additional areas within the Biosphere Reserve (Succow and Sperber, 2012). The aim is to achieve an ecological situation closer to what is considered 'natural' in this area, given its morphological and microclimatic conditions. According to Bushart and Suck (2008), the Vessertal area would naturally be covered by beech-based mixed forests: in the montane parts beech–fir forest with understorey dominated by white woodrush (*Luzula luzuloides*) and wood millet (*Milium effusum*); in high montane parts beech–fir–spruce forest with *Calamagrostis villosa* in the understorey, partly also spruce-dominated bog forest. While today around 60 per cent of the forest area is covered by pure stands of spruce and only 20 per cent by beech-dominated forests, their shares would naturally be around 20 per cent and 40 per cent, respectively. Generally, mixed forest stands would account for around 40 per cent of the Reserve's area, rather than today's 10–15 per cent (TMLNU, 2003). A development towards beech-dominated mixed forests would have significant biodiversity effects, even beyond the obvious fact that a (semi-) natural mixed forest is more species-rich than a pure stand of whichever species. Although they are usually not considered particularly biodiverse, beech forests are in fact marked by a high diversity of especially deadwood-related species (Meyer and Schmidt, 2008). Generally, old-stand forests (which would be achieved by setting aside areas within Vessertal to allow a natural development towards beech forests) are well-known to be rich in terms of biodiversity, especially functional diversity (e.g. Spake et al., 2015). On the other hand, beech forest's response to climate change is uncertain and may be negative (Sutmöller et al., 2008), climate change being an important factor in the future development of biodiversity in Germany (Essl and Rabitsch, 2013). All in all, however, it appears safe to assume that the proposed measures would increase biodiversity levels in the Biosphere Reserve in the long term. As already mentioned, this offers a useful context for the conducting of the case study.

This background was used as a starting point for a focus group case study in the Vessertal Reserve. The reasons for choosing focus groups to test the conceptual framework developed here are twofold. First, focus groups have the important advantage over individual interviews in that they emphasise discussions and interactions between different people, which are conducive of handling difficult topics people are unfamiliar with. Biodiversity and its value certainly are such a topic. Second, focus groups are an accepted means of preparing and conceptually pre-testing economic valuation studies – exactly the purpose of their use within the present volume.

There are three main research questions which the study is supposed to provide an answer to, each of which includes more specific sub-questions. Their specificity increases in the order in which they are listed below:

1   What does the presented change in the Vessertal ecosystem mean for the participants?

    a   What (implicit) values are involved?
    b   Are biodiversity or related effects mentioned?

2   What meaning do the changes in biodiversity have that would be triggered by setting parts of Vessertal aside?

    a   What (implicit) values of biodiversity are involved?

3   Is the conceptual framework suitable to capture biodiversity value?

    a   Is it comprehensible for laypeople?
    b   Can it be 'applied' to Vessertal?
    c   Does it capture relevant values of biodiversity?

Of course, these questions cannot be expected to be answered directly in the group discussions. Rather, they have to be derived from a properly prepared and structured discussion setting. Due to the structure of the study, the discussion was most likely to provide answers to question 1, while to attain meaningful responses to questions 2 and 3 a questionnaire was needed.

The study consisted of three focus groups conducted between 16 and 18 June 2015. It was decided to conduct two focus groups within the Biosphere Reserve (in the villages of Schmiedefeld am Rennsteig and Frauenwald), where the population is directly affected by the planned changes. In addition, a third focus group was conducted in Ilmenau, a nearby medium-sized town (approx. 30,000 inhabitants). Participants from there could be expected to know Vessertal but not be affected in any direct way by changes in its protection status. For all three groups, participants were selected so as to ensure the representation of most age cohorts and approximate gender parity. A market research bureau was commissioned to enlist participants by phone. Politicians and employees of forestry offices and the Biosphere Reserve's administration were excluded because it was feared that they would dominate the discussions by representing the interests of their employers.

The context for the study was the already-mentioned responsibility of Thuringia to set aside 25,000 ha of its forests. Specifically, the proposal outlined in Succow and Sperber (2012) was used so as to present a more or less realistic scenario that would make clear to participants in the study that biodiversity and other important characteristics and functions of forests cannot be had all at once (for instance, there is a clear conflict between wood production and nature conservation). Thus, they were encouraged to think about trade-offs, which are the foundation of economic value.

The focus groups consisted of three main elements. First, two questionnaires were used to collect information about the participants before they were introduced to the study's context and engaged in discussions with others (questionnaire 1) and to elicit their individual insights from the discussion sessions (questionnaire 2).[10] Questionnaire 1, which included socio-economic questions and questions considering individual forest use, was distributed in the beginning, directly after the arrival of the participants. Questionnaire 2 was distributed at the end of the meetings to capture the relative importance of biodiversity from the point of view of the participants after they had discussed the issue. Second, there were two inputs provided by the moderator. The first one was in the beginning and provided an introduction to the problem. This set the ground for the participants and enabled them to retrieve or form general opinions on the problem at stake. The second input, which followed the first discussion round, was meant to introduce participants to the concept of biodiversity and to the conceptual framework developed here in a way comprehensible for laypeople. It was presented after the first discussion session so as not to overly pre-frame it and enable discussion of non-biodiversity issues. Third, there were two discussion blocks following each of the inputs. The first discussion block was additionally preceded by an exercise inspired by the so-called Nominal Group Technique (NGT) (Delbecq et al., 1975; Horton, 1980): participants were asked to write down the most important consequences of the discussed environmental change from their perspective. These points were then used as a starting point for the first discussion session. Note that in actual, fully fledged NGT exercises, usually no discussion takes place – participants exchange arguments in written form and the moderator is the only one who actually speaks. The NGT is an attempt to overcome the problem common in discussion group settings that some people who are shy or unsure do not express their (true) thoughts/preferences. However, since no actual discussion takes place, NGT is viewed critically by many researchers (cf. Stewart and Shamdasani, 1990). Therefore, it was decided to use an element of NGT to ease the initiation of the discussion, but to proceed then in the usual focus group mode. The discussion blocks were moderated only insofar as the moderator responded to questions and made sure that discussions were not overly dominated by single individuals and that participants did not digress.

The main source of the study's results were the questionnaires and the NGT exercises. The discussion sessions were transcribed and analysed using MaxQDA software, but they provided only supporting information.

As already mentioned, two questionnaires were used in the focus groups, a general one in the beginning, and one focusing on the relative appreciation of bio-diversity at the end of each meeting. Regarding socio-cultural data, the overall sample was rather homogenous. Mean age of the participants was 52 years (youngest: 20; oldest: 82; median: 54). There were slightly more women than men involved (23 against 19; one participant did not respond to the question). Basic demographic statistics and the distribution of accomplished levels of education can be found in Table 5.3. As can be seen, the groups were dominated by participants with higher degrees of education. Of the 43 people involved, 38 had lived in the Thuringian Forest for more than 10 years at the time of study. Fifteen persons indicated that they visit a forest several times a week; 22 do this several times a month; only five reported doing it less frequently. Everyone who responded to that question indicated that they know about the Biosphere Reserve Vessertal–Thuringian Forest. Some 35 had visited it more than once; only two people indicated that they never had entered the Reserve (three more were unsure).

Table 5.3 Basic statistics for each group (absolute numbers)

	Ilmenau	Schmiedefeld	Frauenwald
Participants	13	15	15
Age	51	50	55
Female/male	7/6	7/7	9/6
Education			
Higher education	4	6	5
Higher education entrance qualification (Abitur)	3	3	3
10-year secondary school (Regelschule or Polytechnische Oberschule)	6	5	4
9-year secondary school (Hauptschule)	0	0	2
Others	0	1	1

Some interesting findings from the first questionnaire can be found in Table 5.4, which gives the relative frequency of 'yes' responses to the closed-ended question 'How do you use the forest?' The options were 'watching animals', 'gathering wild fruits' (berries and mushrooms), 'hunting', 'walking', 'gathering wood'. Also, there was a possibility to add further use categories. 'Cycling' was the most frequent one here with nine mentions altogether. It can be seen from Table 5.4 that there is a difference in use patterns between Ilmenau, which is a city, and Schmiedefeld and Frauenwald, which are villages. The inhabitants of the two villages extract resources from the forest much more frequently than urban dwellers do ('gathering wild fruits' and 'gathering wood').

More important, however, than the results of the first questionnaire, which are only meant to provide an overview of the participants in the focus groups, are the results of the second questionnaire. These are presented in Tables 5.5–5.8. All four questions in this questionnaire were based on Likert scale evaluations.

Table 5.5 shows the relative frequencies of different answers to the question 'How important do you find the following functions of the forest?' Responses are ordered according to the relative frequency of positive ratings ('rather important' or '(very) important'). The most positively rated forest functions[11] are water regulation and air purification, followed by CO_2 sequestration and erosion prevention, all of which are regulating ecosystem services. Biodiversity follows them in terms of appreciation by the groups' participants. Only after these rather abstract functions do those appear that can be associated with provisioning and cultural ecosystem services. Additionally, some participants used the option to name further important functions: 'tourism' was named five times (but rated on the Likert scale only twice). For our purposes it is relevant that biodiversity's relative appreciation appears to be rather high, even though regulating ecosystem services achieved higher ratings.

Questions 2–4 of the second questionnaire were specifically concerned with appreciation of biodiversity. Questions 2 and 3 both aimed at checking the relevance participants attached to the conceptual framework developed in the present

Table 5.4 Activities undertaken in the forest by groups (relative shares)

Activity	Ilmenau	Schmiedefeld	Frauenwald
Walking, hiking, jogging	1.00	1.00	0.93
Gathering wild fruits	0.38	0.79	1.00
Watching animals	0.54	0.29	0.67
Gathering wood	0.15	0.50	0.53
Hunting	0.00	0.00	0.20
Cycling	0.46	0.21	0.00
Skiing	0.08	0.00	0.00
Horse riding	0.00	0.00	0.07

Notes
The figures are relative shares of participants who engage in a given activity; italics indicate activities added by the participants under 'others'.

Table 5.5 Appreciation of different functions of forest by the participants

	Unimportant (1)	Rather unimportant (2)	So-so (3)	Rather important (4)	(Very) important (5)	Ø
Air quality	0	0	0	4	36	4.90
CO$_2$ sequestration	0	0	1	3	33	4.86
Water quality	0	0	0	8	29	4.78
Erosion prevention	0	1	1	9	25	4.61
Biodiversity	0	1	2	11	26	4.55
Aesthetics	0	1	4	14	19	4.34
Quiet	0	0	8	10	19	4.30
Wood	0	1	8	20	10	4.00
Gathering wild fruits	0	5	4	16	16	4.05
Hunting	1	2	12	14	8	3.70

book. In Table 5.6 the responses to the question 'How important do you find the following aspects of biodiversity?' are presented, by means of which the perceived importance of the biodiversity values that were presented to the participants during the meetings was investigated. Biodiversity's influence on stability (i.e. its insurance value according to the conceptual framework) is the most important value category according to the participants, followed by spill-over value (habitat diversity), option value and aesthetics. However, the latter two were much less appreciated. 'Options' were rated fewer times than the others, which might mean that despite directions as to where the terms come from (by referring to a handout provided earlier during the discussion sessions), some participants could not recollect what was meant by 'Options'.

Table 5.7 presents responses to the question 'How relevant do you find the following aspects of biodiversity for the Vessertal area?', which was meant to make the idea of the value of biodiversity more concrete by encouraging the participants to translate it to a specific area they are familiar with. The ranking of relative importance changed only slightly as compared with the more general question (aesthetics having gained relatively, so as to 'surpass' option value). There is a moderate correlation between the responses to questions 2 and 3 of the second questionnaire (the Pearson correlation coefficient is 0.66 with p-value $2.2*e^{-16}$). It seems that the relevance of the various sources of biodiversity value for the Vessertal area was assessed lower than their general importance, as can be seen by comparing the last columns of Tables 5.6 and 5.7.

The relative gain of the aesthetics component might be due to the fact that the visual transformation of the ecosystem following the change presented in the groups would be rather dramatic, away from spruce monoculture-dominated forest to a beech-dominated mixed forest. However, this is just speculation.

Table 5.6 Perceived importance of biodiversity values

	Unimportant (1)	Rather unimportant (2)	So-so (3)	Rather important (4)	(Very) important (5)	Ø
Stability	0	0	0	9	29	4.76
Habitat	0	1	1	8	29	4.67
Options	0	1	9	12	12	4.03
Aesthetics	0	4	10	11	14	3.90

Table 5.7 Perceived relevance of biodiversity values for Vessertal area

	Unimportant (1)	Rather unimportant (2)	So-so (3)	Rather important (4)	(Very) important (5)	Ø
Stability	0	1	1	13	24	4.54
Habitat	0	1	2	12	24	4.51
Aesthetics	0	2	7	9	21	4.26
Options	0	4	6	16	9	3.86

The last question of the second questionnaire concerned the motivations participants had for their appreciation of biodiversity. As can be seen in Table 5.8, the overwhelming majority thought of biodiversity value mainly in terms of the interests of future generations. Self-interested motives (measured through agreement with the sentence 'Biological diversity is important for me mainly when it is useful for myself') met with the least agreement of the four motivation categories used. Interestingly, many participants responded that they value biodiversity independently of its usefulness for anyone, i.e. for its own sake. This is in conflict with the argument developed in the Excursus, where it was argued that biodiversity cannot sensibly have existence value (see below).

Briefly summing up, biodiversity scored relatively high in the assessment of the relative importance of various forest functions; stability (insurance value) and habitat (spill-over value) were considered more important and relevant than aesthetics (aesthetic value) and options (option value). The primary motivation for valuing biodiversity is the consideration of future generations, followed by its sheer existence, its usefulness to others and usefulness for oneself.

The discussion sessions started with an NGT-like exercise, where participants were asked, after having been introduced to the Vessertal scenario, to write down the two most important aspects of the proposed change from their own perspective. The results, grouped into four categories and divided into positive and negative within each, are presented in Figure 5.4.

As can be seen, most arguments contra the proposed changes in the Vessertal area concerned limitations to private use (walking, gathering wood, mushrooms, berries) by the inhabitants of the area. Accordingly, most of these aspects were named in Schmiedefeld and Frauenwald (eight mentions each), very few in Ilmenau (two). Pro arguments mostly had to do with ecological consequences of the proposed changes, which is understandable, as these are the main rationale behind the 5 per cent goal of the *National Biodiversity Strategy*. Here, too, there was a clear discrepancy between Ilmenau (12 mentions) and Schmiedefeld/Frauenwald (5/6). Generally, in Ilmenau positive arguments dominated (22 vs 6), while in Schmiedefeld and Frauenwald the picture was more balanced (12 vs 17 and 12 vs 12, respectively).

Biodiversity, obviously, played a minor role in the initial assessment of the proposed changes. Participants focused much more on more immediate and

Table 5.8 Motivations for the appreciation of biodiversity

	Strongly disagree (1)	*Disagree (2)*	*Neither agree nor disagree (3)*	*Agree (4)*	*Strongly agree (5)*	*Ø*
Future generations	0	0	1	5	33	4.82
Existence	2	3	4	7	21	4.14
Altruism	2	1	7	16	12	3.92
Self-interest	2	5	10	7	17	3.78

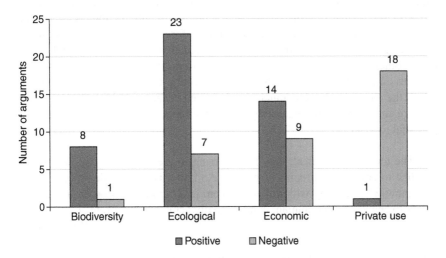

Figure 5.4 Arguments pro and contra proposed changes in Vessertal.

Note
Biodiversity: arguments regarding species diversity; Ecological: arguments regarding consequences for flora and fauna, 'naturalness', implications of lack of 'maintenance' etc.; Economic: arguments involving forestry or tourism; Private use: arguments involving consequences for individual activities in the forest (walking, gathering wood, mushrooms etc.).

'tangible' issues, especially changes in the structure of the forest, tourism and private use. This trend continued in the discussion rounds in each group. Especially in Schmiedefeld and Frauenwald it was difficult to steer the discussion away from private use and tourism towards other issues. In the following, the most important points from the discussions will be summarised, including exemplary quotations.[12]

In all three groups, participants voiced concerns about the implications of the planned changes in protection status for the life of the local population. Above all, restrictions on private use, such as wood collection, collection of berries and mushrooms, walking beyond paths etc., were considered highly problematic by the participants:

> many people nowadays built fireplaces because of the exploding gas and electricity prices, they installed wood-fired heating units, they equipped themselves with chainsaws and the full panoply; are they still allowed to go to the forest then, to gather firewood, because that's why they did it.
>
> (Ilmenau)

> Many people go to the forest three times a day; they walk here and there, to their favourite spots and all [...] All this is not allowed any more!
>
> (Frauenwald)

Moreover, the restrictions were considered disproportionate given the goals of the proposed changes. Some participants pointed to contradictions between, for example, subsidies provided by the government for the installation of wood-fired heating units on the one hand and the proposed restrictions to wood collection on the other. Accordingly, in the discussions no positive effects of the proposed changes on private use were identified. For 'economic' use, i.e. tourism and forestry, the arguments were much more mixed. Many participants expressed concern that restrictions regarding hiking, walking and skiing might scare off potential tourists:

> The tourists come here, they like walking in the forest, maybe they would like to collect mushrooms or berries. And all this is forbidden then. I don't know whether they will still come then. [...] Shouldn't it be an interaction between nature and human, that you really achieve a compromise.
>
> (Frauenwald)

Conversely, some participants, both in Ilmenau ('outside perspective') and in the two villages within the Reserve, argued that increased levels of protection might be beneficial for the region – in similar ways as in regions with national parks:

> It is a marketing argument, too. Like it is with national parks. Tourism works with these national parks, too.
>
> (Ilmenau)

The time frames involved in the proposed changes (it was repeatedly stressed by the moderators that the ecosystems would need decades to reach the status envisaged in the *Biodiversity Strategies*) were mentioned a few times, with different interpretations. On the one hand, it was pointed out that the effectiveness of the measures (given their long-term goals) is uncertain, while the current generation would have to bear the costs:

> this will take decades and centuries.
>
> (Schmiedefeld)

On the other hand, other participants interpreted the long-term vision as something positive, in terms of responsibility towards future generations:

> Future generations might be thankful to us for this.
>
> (Frauenwald)

> This short[-term] thinking, can I gather my firewood or how long will it last for myself; you have to think beyond that...
>
> (Frauenwald)

As one participant in the Ilmenau group summed up the issue:

I don't know whether we will ever arrive there, but it could be positive in the long term, if we say, here we will have untouched nature one day, you have to take a look at that. But in the short term there will be difficulties, I think.

(Ilmenau)

Interestingly, it was questioned repeatedly by the participants whether the proposed changes in protection status would be beneficial for ecological reasons. The reasons given for why they might be detrimental were: an unspecified 'UNESCO study' showing that species diversity would go down by 90 per cent as a result of total protection;[13] fears of bark beetle (*Scolytinae*) calamities in an unmanaged, spruce-dominated forest (here, however, other participants countered that increased tree diversity would actually reduce the danger of bark beetle infestation); some participants voiced concerns that the planned changes towards no management would reduce landscape diversity since the many meadows characteristic of the Vessertal area would likely disappear:

Mountain meadows. [...] we should be proud that by now there are still very many mountain meadows, which are used as pastures, where the cattle and horses are in the summer and the grass is eaten; otherwise it would become totally overgrown.

(Schmiedefeld)

The latter point is particularly interesting since it reflects a general contention of virtually all participants in the three groups: they at least rhetorically embraced the idea of increasing the level of protection of the forest ecosystems in the Vessertal area and welcomed the perspective of increasing biodiversity:

This ecological aspect, this is what I can support out of my conviction.

(Schmiedefeld)

Furthermore, I'd say, what is depicted here [on a handout] is finding my unconditional support. You're preaching to the choir here.

(Frauenwald)

However, they were highly sceptical of the means chosen to bring about these biodiversity increases. Rather, they envisaged sustainable use of the forest as a much more sensible strategy. Two distinct justifications were given for that: first, as in the meadows and bark beetle examples, complete restrictions of use/management were viewed as potentially detrimental and inefficient. Second, the focus group participants contested the idea that total protection is necessary to achieve high levels of biodiversity and actually worth it – a trade-off between (sustainable) local use and biodiversity levels achieved through the proposed measures was identified:

We are talking all the time about forestry use on the one hand and ecological diversity on the other hand. Does it really contradict each other?

(Schmiedefeld)

I think, it works better if we don't leave nature alone, but if we deal with it reasonably.

(Frauenwald)

It is important to note that sustainable use was called for in Frauenwald and Schmiedefeld only. Participants in Ilmenau did not criticise the choice of measures to achieve high levels of biodiversity.

The last points are more directly of relevance for the conceptual framework. One participant distinguished between 'native' and 'non-native' biodiversity:

However, in my opinion there are restrictions to species diversity as well, of course. I would like to name only a few examples; it is because of the international tourism, also because we travel abroad, you bring some small plant or seed with you, which then spreads here and which has extremely negative consequences.

(Schmiedefeld)

Two of the four value categories proposed in the conceptual framework were explicitly commented upon. With regard to insurance value a link was drawn to recent extreme weather events:

We saw after Kyrill [a 2007 storm event] what the consequences are of these monocultures.

(Ilmenau)

Somewhat provoked by the moderator who questioned the relevance of option value in the Vessertal area, it was pointed out by one participant that one never knows what will be found there in the future. Other, older participants recollected that there are plants in the Vessertal area which are used for medical purposes, thus concluding that others could be found in the future:

The Vessertal and surroundings have always been used for medicinal purposes.

(Schmiedefeld)

What can be learned from this case study for the conceptual perspective developed in this book? The case study was conducted with the aim to provide answers to three research questions:

1   What does the presented change in the Vessertal ecosystem mean for the participants?

2   What meaning do the changes in biodiversity have which would be trig-
     gered by setting aside part of Vessertal?
3   Is the conceptual framework suitable to capture biodiversity value?

The overarching question was, of course, question 3, the former two effectively
feeding into it and providing context. The three focus groups did in fact provide
answers to the research questions, albeit the question of the conceptual framework's suitability can be answered only tentatively on the basis of the study's
results. This is so for two reasons. First, as should be apparent from the summary
above, discussion of the conceptual framework was overshadowed, at least in
Frauenwald and Schmiedefeld, by debates about limitations to private and commercial use of the Vessertal forests that would result from the proposed changes
in the area's protection status. Second, as is always the case with focus group
studies, the conclusions drawn from this case study can be generalised only to a
very limited extent. Other stakeholders might have different views and the suitability of the framework might be different in other ecosystems. Nonetheless,
some generalisation appears warranted since the framework itself is quite general
and was presented as such to the groups' participants. Also, there is no ad hoc
reason to assume that the inhabitants of the Vessertal area are different in any
relevant way from people elsewhere.

Ad 1: Regarding the first research question, there is a difference between
the general picture in the two villages in the Biosphere Reserve and the group
in Ilmenau. While the latter evaluated the proposed changes in the Vessertal
area rather positively (despite being aware that people living in the Reserve
would likely have reservations), the former were highly sceptical of them. The
fear of significant reductions in their ability to use the forest and to live off it
(in terms of tourism) was highly present in both Frauenwald and Schmiedefeld. On the other hand, virtually all participants embraced the goals of the
discussed changes – i.e. increases in diversity and 'naturalness' of the forest.
The bone of contention was rather the (perceived) drastic restrictions for
inhabitants. So, generally, a change away from the now persisting spruce
monoculture would be welcome. However, the participants would rather have
this goal achieved through a switch towards sustainable forest use – in line
with the idea of UNESCO Biosphere Reserves, one must add – rather than
total protection as envisioned in the *National Biodiversity Strategy*. Thus, it is
important to note that stakeholders do differentiate between different policy
strategies aiming at the same conservation goal. In fact, this is in line with the
findings in Czajkowski et al.'s (2009) forest biodiversity valuation study,
where they found that 'how environmental changes were provided (whether
by an extension of national park status or not) turned out to be [...] significant'
(p. 2915). The fact that participants in the focus groups obviously found biodiversity valuable but at the same time opposed radical protection plans could
be interpreted as reflecting the fact that a significant part of biodiversity value,
namely its insurance value, is highly contingent upon use of the ecosystem in
question – there must be something worthy of insuring.

Interestingly, there was a significant discrepancy between the results of the questionnaires, where regulating ecosystem services and biodiversity were assessed as more important than provisioning services (i.e. private use), and the discussions, where use-related issues were dominant. This discrepancy also does not disappear when we ignore the questionnaires from Ilmenau. It is not easy to interpret this result, but one possible explanation would be some kind of loss aversion (Kahneman and Tversky, 1979): the discussions were about changes which would lead to a *loss* in terms of use opportunities against a *gain* in the actually more valuable ecosystem regulating services. Another possibility would be that participants assessed the expected negative changes (use) as more severe than the expected positive changes in terms of ecological functioning. This can possibly be coupled with a divergence in the evaluation of events with different temporal dimensions: changes in use opportunities would come immediately, while ecological changes would take several years or even decades to unfold. Moreover, the former are far less abstract than the latter. Last but not least, it is possible that those who focused more on use issues were more actively participating in the discussions. Alas, these are only speculations, as the available data and observations during the discussions do not allow for any definite explanation of the discrepancy.

Ad 2: With respect to the second research question, i.e. how participants perceived the changes in biodiversity which would likely result from the proposed changes in protection status, it turned out that especially the inhabitants of the Vessertal area have quite a differentiated perspective on the issue. On the one hand, they expressed support for the idea of making the forests more diverse, moving away from the historically contingent spruce monoculture. On the other hand, they pointed to potential losses in terms of biodiversity that might result from the proposed changes, particularly with regard to meadows, which are a very important element of the Vessertal landscape. Thus, the participants showed that they are able to distinguish between policy goals and suitable means in their area. Regarding justifications of the embracing of biodiversity maintenance and increase, it seemed that aesthetic considerations played a major role. Other arguments came into discussion only after being introduced by the moderator.

Ad 3: The most important research question regarded the suitability of the conceptual framework, as well as the possibility to translate it into terms understandable to laypeople. As it turned out, the four sources of biodiversity value (stability enhancement, options, spill-overs and aesthetics) were understood by most participants. While the discussions provided hints that participants were able to relate the value components to the Vessertal area, most relevant information derives from the questionnaires. As indicated in the above summary of results, insurance value and spill-over value were deemed both relatively more important and more relevant to the Vessertal area than the other two sources of biodiversity value. As for the relatively low importance and relevance attached to option value, this could be interpreted as reflecting the rather low potential of the relatively well-known ecosystems of Middle Europe (such as Vessertal), where the probability of finding anything useful in the future is comparatively low – it is much higher in less well-known ecosystems, especially in the tropics.

Generally, the results of the case study seem to support the hypothesis that the conceptual framework developed here is both understandable for laypeople and compatible with their preferences. To the degree of generalisation allowed by the nature of the focus group study and the kind of research questions investigated, the suitability of the conceptual framework can be seen as confirmed. However, one specific result of the case study is problematic: according to the answers to the last question of the second questionnaire ('Why is biodiversity important to you?'), many participants value biodiversity for its own sake, which is in conflict with the theoretical arguments reviewed in the Excursus. It was argued there that there is no reason why biodiversity could have existence or intrinsic value. This dissonance is potentially problematic since economic valuation is based on preference utilitarianism, i.e. it is up to the valuing stakeholders what and why they value. The conceptual framework is supposed to 'anticipate' the preferences people may have and to provide a basis for informing them about the environmental good, which they are generally not familiar with. What to do about that?

It is important to keep in mind that the argument about the existence value of biodiversity is rather abstract and dependent on a clear understanding of what biodiversity is and what it is not. Also, it is not uncontroversial. Although it was explained to the participants of the focus groups what understanding of biodiversity is underlying the analysis here, it cannot be assumed with certainty that all participants were entirely clear about that matter (especially given that 'biodiversity' is often understood much more broadly in public discussions, on which their pre-understanding was likely based). Furthermore, it is not perfectly certain whether participants interpreted the Likert question in the way it was intended. The statement to be evaluated read 'Biodiversity is important irrelevant of whether it is useful for anybody'. This could be interpreted as implying direct use only and not necessarily excluding such indirect influences on human well-being as those exhibited by biodiversity. Moreover, participants of the groups were not confronted with the arguments speaking against ascribing existence value to biodiversity, as this would have gone beyond the scope admitted by time and cognitive constraints.

Nonetheless, it is unlikely that it would be possible in an actual valuation study to go so deep into so specific and demanding a question as whether biodiversity can have value on its own. This certainly makes the application of conventional economic valuation methods questionable and provides an argument in favour of deliberative monetary valuation, in line with the arguments developed in Lienhoop et al. (2015). But, ultimately, the dissonance between the theoretical argument developed here and the subjective perception of participants in future biodiversity valuation studies may well be inevitable to some extent. These considerations lead us to the issue of valuation methodology, which is the topic of the next section.

From value to valuation

In previous sections, a conceptual framework *of the economic value of biodiversity* was developed. For this framework to become a conceptual framework *for the economic valuation of biodiversity*, we have to think about how this special valuation object should best be approached in valuation studies. The following section is concerned with this issue. First, biodiversity will be analysed as a challenging valuation object and its particularities will be elaborated. Also, it will be shown how different valuation methods respond to these challenges posed by biodiversity. Based on that, an approach will be discussed in more detail which fits the requirement profile of biodiversity particularly well: a combination of discrete choice experiments (CE) with deliberative monetary valuation (DMV), also called *deliberative choice experiments* (Lienhoop and Völker, 2016; Völker and Lienhoop, 2016). In the last section of this chapter, some tentative recommendations are expressed about how the conceptual framework can be coupled with (quantitative) data, so as to make its application in deliberative choice experiments viable.

Biodiversity as methodological challenge

Biodiversity is an unusual environmental good and thus poses particular challenges to valuation (the identification of the challenges is based on the discussion in previous chapters). These are, specifically: (i) the non-market nature of components of biodiversity value (especially in the case of insurance value); (ii) high levels of uncertainty involved in the relationship between biodiversity and human well-being and, relatedly, the multidimensionality of the concept; (iii) its abstractness and complexity. These can be used as criteria for a stepwise identification of suitable valuation methods. We build here upon the brief introduction of valuation methods in Chapter 2; however, more information about the potential of these methods is included here, as the points discussed go in their specificity beyond the basics presented there. The assessment of the potential of three broad classes of methods (production function, revealed preference and stated preference methods) to account for these challenges is depicted in Table 5.9. Note that cost-based methods are excluded because, first, they are problematic from a welfare theoretic point of view (see Chapter 2); second, the fact that they were not used at all in biodiversity valuation studies (Chapter 4) reinforces the impression that they are not suitable for this valuation object.

Table 5.9 Suitability of valuation methods for valuing biodiversity

	Production function	*Revealed preferences*	*Stated preferences*
Non-market aspects	–	++	++
Uncertainty			
Subjectivity	+ (BP)	–	+
Two-level	+	++ (HP)	++ (CE)
Abstractness	–	–	++ (DMV)

Notes
Assessment based on standard literature. If a specific method within a class is particularly well-suited to tackle a given challenge, it is named in brackets (and the assessment applies to this method only). For explanations, see main text.

Ad (i): The first challenging biodiversity characteristic that can be used to identify methods suited for the economic valuation of biodiversity is related especially to the notion of insurance value. As understood in the present book, this value results from the influence biodiversity has on ecosystem stability and resilience, thus 'insuring' the delivery of ecosystem goods and services. Accordingly, it was argued in the literature that biodiversity's economic value can be estimated by means of production function and related methods (Farnsworth et al., 2015), and related approaches specifically targeting the insurance value of biodiversity were developed and applied (Baumgärtner, 2007b; Finger and Buchmann, 2015; Henselek et al., 2016). However, such approaches can only be sensibly used to estimate the insurance value of biodiversity towards *marketed* ecosystem goods and services, effectively excluding all others. For instance, the insurance value of biodiversity in Vessertal does not much depend on marketed ecosystem services provided by the forests there; as indicated by the data summarised in Table 5.5, the stakeholders in this case appreciate non-provisioning, non-marketed ecosystem services much more. In this and similar cases, application of production function methods would result in a serious underestimation in many cases. Conversely, revealed preference methods and stated preference methods are better suited to deal with this issue. Assuming that stakeholders know about the insuring effect of biodiversity (on this, see below), they can be assumed to express their appreciation of this insurance of locally enjoyable non-marketed ecosystem services by moving into the vicinity of ecosystems exhibiting high levels of biodiversity. This could be potentially captured by means of hedonic pricing analysis. However, the insurance of globally or supra-locally relevant ecosystem services (such as carbon sequestration) is unlikely to have an influence upon choices of place of living. Here, stated preference methods have the advantage of not being dependent on any actual market behaviour.

Ad (ii): Biodiversity's economic value is inherently linked to issues of uncertainty about the future. This characteristic offers another 'filtering' criterion for choosing methods suitable for the economic valuation of biodiversity. First, deep uncertainty (i.e. ambiguity or ignorance; see Chapter 4) is involved: especially in the case of option value, but also for insurance value, relevant probability distributions are not necessarily known. As a result of this, the economic value of biodiversity is based on inherently subjective judgements of stakeholders – judgements which, in many cases, cannot be linked to any observed behaviour in (surrogate) markets other than, possibly, markets for bioprospecting (BP). This is another argument in favour of stated preference methods, though bioprospecting contracts could be used as a proxy here, at least for some ecosystems. Furthermore, as was pointed out in the discussion of the underlying BEF research, it is not *entirely* clear if and how biodiversity has an influence on ecosystem functioning: the exact relationship between biodiversity and ecosystem functioning (in terms of stability, resilience or other related concepts) is still controversial and contested. From the perspective of economic valuation, this amounts to a *two-level uncertainty*: first, it is uncertain whether a given land-use change will in fact result in a specific change in biodiversity – this type of uncertainty is common in valuation studies in general and there exist approaches to deal with it (e.g. Lundhede et al., 2015; Torres et al., 2017); second, it is uncertain whether and how the change in biodiversity will affect ecosystem functioning, which is not easily comparable to the situation regarding other environmental goods. For instance, when the economic value of an endangered species is to be estimated, respondents in stated preference surveys are asked for their willingness-to-pay for a change between two states of the world: the status quo and a world in which the abundance of the species in question is significantly raised. This can then be directly compared with the costs of a suitable protection programme. Conversely, since biodiversity is the property of an ecosystem, changes in it cannot be sensibly valued in isolation – rather, they can only be valued as a result of a specific land-use change. Then, the above-mentioned two-level uncertainty emerges. This uncertainty also has to be handled when biodiversity's economic value is to be estimated; furthermore, it is closely related to the fact that biodiversity and its value are multidimensional and different parts of it are differently affected by uncertainty – for instance, option value is more affected by the subjectivity issue, while insurance value is affected by two-level uncertainty. Discrete choice experiments (CE) offer an opportunity to handle these issues. This valuation method makes it possible to assess the valuation weights people attach to different attributes of a good (e.g. the influence of biodiversity on ecosystem functioning), instead of simply valuing the good as such, as done, for example, in conventional contingent valuation (CV) studies. Due to the type of econometric models CE is based on, it is inevitable anyway that what is valued are not 'realistic' scenarios but more or less arbitrary combinations of attribute levels – while potentially problematic due to the hypothetical nature of the choices participants are asked to make, this means that uncertainty can be handled comparatively well in CE studies. Also, uncertainty can be included more explicitly in CE surveys (namely, as a qualitative or quantitative attribute) and it was argued that it is important in stated preference surveys to '(1) assess, whenever relevant, respondents' prior belief in policy outcome uncertainties and ([2]) incorporate when possible the degree of uncertainty into the valuation exercise, even if only in qualitative terms' (Lundhede et al., 2015, p. 314). Moreover, by combination of a number of biodiversity attributes with other ecosystem characteristics, it is possible to account for both the multidimensionality of biodiversity – that it is at the same time 'insurance', the carrier of future options, a provider of temporary habitats – and the fact that the concept is meaningless when detached from an actual ecosystem. In fact, this intuition is confirmed by the observation that most *embedded* biodiversity valuation studies (i.e. those in which biodiversity is not the only valuation object) apply CE (see Chapter 4). However, other methods can also produce weights of different factors/attributes of value. Particularly, hedonic pricing (HP) and some types of production function methods (PF) allow for distinguishing between the relative contributions of different factors to the overall value of an environmental good. None of them, however, can provide an answer to the problem of ambiguity and ignorance that can at least partially be accounted for in stated preference studies. Moreover, while they can capture biodiversity as one attribute among many, and possibly also identify the relative contributions of the different dimensions of biodiversity, they cannot distinguish between the different value sources of biodiversity, as those cannot be pinned down to single measurable dimensions of biodiversity (see above).

Ad (iii): A particularly challenging issue in the context of economic valuation of biodiversity is that people are rather unfamiliar with the abstract good biodiversity, as shown in a number of different studies and polls in different countries (Bakhtiari et al., 2014; Buijs et al., 2008; DEFRA, 2007; UEBT, 2013). They cannot be expected to have predefined preferences for this special environmental good. As a consequence, valuation methods which are based on observed choices of people, i.e. revealed preference methods, have a serious disadvantage – for biodiversity to influence people's choices such as where to live (HP) or which area to visit during vacations (travel cost method) it must be assumed that those people are aware of the importance of biodiversity. This is a bold assumption. Therefore, stated preference methods, which usually involve the provision of information about an environmental good before the WTP for it is elicited, appear more suitable for biodiversity. Of course, production function methods, being supply-oriented, do not depend on the knowledge of consumers. However, they suffer from other limitations, especially their inability to capture the insuring effect of biodiversity on non-marketed ecosystem services (see above); therefore, the case for stated preference methods in biodiversity valuation appears particularly strong. Furthermore, it can be argued that biodiversity is even 'worse' than so-called *experience goods* (e.g. Czajkowski et al., 2015), which pose a challenge to economic valuation because consumers learn about their preferences towards these goods in the act of consuming them. Biodiversity can be seen as an even more extreme case, as there is no obvious way of 'consuming' it, so other ways of learning about one's preferences are necessary. In addition, ecosystems in general are complex and it takes years of full-time scientific training to understand them properly. As has been argued throughout this book, biodiversity is an especially complex and abstract concept (Meinard and Grill, 2011). Lack of knowledge of/experience with biodiversity and the concept's abstractness not only suggest that revealed preference methods may not be helpful (since they can only be used to derive preferences people hold for things they know are valuable), but even that conventional stated preference methods may not be sufficient. Here, DMV could be a viable option, as this approach has been developed to tackle such limitations involving limited knowledge and familiarity with environmental goods. Because it is a novel approach, it will be discussed in more detail in the next subsection, with a focus on its relevance for the economic valuation of biodiversity.

According to the criteria emphasised here, it seems that stated preference methods are much better suited for the economic valuation of biodiversity than other methods, which rely on observed data. Furthermore, a combination of CE with DMV seems particularly attractive because, as shown in Table 5.9, CE is particularly well-suited to handle non-market effects, uncertainty and multidimensionality, while DMV offers a powerful tool for dealing with complexity and abstractness. The combination of both, termed *deliberative choice experiments* elsewhere (Lienhoop and Völker, 2016; Völker and Lienhoop, 2016),[14] is more thoroughly discussed in the next section.

Deliberative monetary valuation of biodiversity

It was argued above that DMV has the potential to solve possibly the single most important methodological issue in estimating the economic value of biodiversity, which is the difficulty that respondents in stated preference studies have with such complex and abstract environmental goods as biodiversity as well as the general unfamiliarity of people with biodiversity and its relevance for human well-being. In combination with CE, DMV offers a very potent approach for the economic valuation of biodiversity.

DMV is a rather new approach. We will therefore take a closer look at its origin and its recent role in advancing the theory of economic valuation, before we turn to its potential in the context of biodiversity valuation, particularly in combination with CE. The general introduction of DMV draws heavily upon Lienhoop et al. (2015) and Bartkowski and Lienhoop (2016). Following this discussion, we will also take a look at the limitations of CE and DMV, as their understanding is important to properly assess the potential of this approach for the economic valuation of biodiversity.

The application of deliberative methods in economic valuation, usually as an extension of standard stated preference methods, is a relatively new phenomenon. The underlying theory of deliberative democracy, however, has quite long a history, with theoretic roots reaching back at least to John Stuart Mill's understanding of democracy as 'government by discussion' (Mill, 1859; see Bohman and Rehg, 1997). More recent sources of inspiration can be found particularly in the writings of John Rawls (1971), Jürgen Habermas (1981) or Amartya Sen (2010).

The theory of deliberative democracy emerged in the twentieth century as a new approach to representation in a democratic society (O'Neill, 2001). In the wake of the Second World War the idea of deliberation as a central ingredient of a democratic order attracted some attention, which has been interpreted as a critique of the predominant instrumental and individualistic perspectives on political processes (Elster, 1997; Smith and Wales, 2000). Deliberative democracy or, as it is also called, *discursive ethics* differs largely from other moral theories in that it is explicitly procedural, i.e. it lacks a predefinition of values (O'Hara, 1996), thus being a 'second-order theory' (Lo, 2011). Early theorists were mainly concerned with the description of an ideal democracy based on deliberation, the main features being freedom and equality of participation, the dominant role of reason and argument, and consensus (Cohen, 1997; Habermas, 1981).[15] With time, the ideas of deliberative democracy have been put into practice. Many deliberative institutions were developed and tested in different contexts. The most common include focus groups, citizens' juries, citizens' panels, planning cells, consensus conferences and deliberative opinion polls (Smith, 2005). Differences between these varied approaches include the number of participants, selection mechanism, decision rule, length and intensity (Lienhoop et al., 2015). This reflects the use of deliberative institutions in different contexts and in different roles: they can be involved in and feed into political processes with various degrees of bindingness (Goodin and Dryzek, 2006). Many deliberative institutions were launched by civil society organisations (Smith, 2005), but in some cases at least the initiators were public authorities, as in the case of the Danish consensus conferences (Joss, 1998) or the British citizens' councils. These deliberative institutions have been an inspiration for environmental economists wanting to overcome some of the limitations of economic valuation methods (Bunse et al., 2015).

Accordingly, one of the main areas of application of deliberative democratic theory in recent years has been environmental policy and economics. According to O'Hara (1996), the strengths of deliberative approaches in this context are their capacity to deal with the complexity and interconnectedness of ecosystems, their potential to address uncertainty and risk, and to account for the contextual factors in valuation processes (note the parallels to the above discussion of biodiversity-specific challenges for valuation). Many of the early attempts to promote deliberative democracy by putting its theoretical concepts into practice took place in the context of environmental planning (Burgess et al., 1988a, 1988b; Gregory, 2000; Pelletier et al., 1999; Renn and Webler, 1992). With time, the issue gained increasing interest from economists; in particular, the question whether deliberative methods could be an alternative to or an extension of the common economic valuation methods and environmental cost–benefit analysis became prominent (Bunse et al., 2015). Here, too, a number of different approaches emerged, which give different answers to the general question of where in the spectrum between classic deliberative institutions, such as citizens' juries, and traditional economic valuation methods, such as contingent valuation, the right mixture of their respective strengths is located (Bunse et al., 2015; Lienhoop et al., 2015; Lo and Spash, 2013).

DMV can be seen as an attempt to incorporate insights from psychology, behavioural economics, political science and ethics in economic valuation. While usually still relying on questionnaire-based stated preferences methods such as CV or CE, DMV includes deliberation as an important component of the process of preference formation.[16] Focus groups, which are also a deliberative institution, have been present in economic valuation studies for some years already – there, basic issues concerning relevant ecosystem components, understanding and knowledge of stakeholders etc. are typically clarified. However, the final value elicitation still mostly takes place by means of face-to-face or telephone interviews, self-conducted mail-based and, increasingly, web-based questionnaires. Such approaches are based on a number of problematic assumptions (some of which will be discussed below). The interposition of focus groups, while helpful and sensible, does not offer a solution to most of them.

As already mentioned, there is no agreement regarding how much deliberation and how much of traditional economic methods is a proper proportion. Some scholars argue against the elicitation of individual preferences and in favour of deliberative institutions which are very similar to those known from political sciences (Brown et al., 1995; Kenter et al., 2011; Wilson and Howarth, 2002). If their proposals include any monetary values at all, these are to be elicited collectively, based on either consensus or majority voting. Others argue, in line with Elster (1983, p. 38), that both collective and individual preferences are important, so questionnaire-based stated preferences methods offer a possible device for elicitation of preferences shaped by deliberation (Lo and Spash, 2013). Still others view deliberation mainly as a way to overcome issues of incomplete or lacking preferences (Gregory, 2000; MacMillan et al., 2002), paying little or no attention to political–ethical considerations that are used to justify deliberative institutions.

The most common deliberative valuation methods are known as deliberative workshops or Market Stall. They can be viewed as a combination of deliberative elements (guided group discussions) with 'traditional' methods of stated preference elicitation, either via CV or CE (see Box 5.1). In studies applying these methods (e.g. Álvarez-Farizo et al., 2007; Christie et al., 2006; Lienhoop and MacMillan, 2007; Völker and Lienhoop, 2016), the procedure is more or less uniform: first, the environmental change of interest is presented to participants in small groups of 8–12 people (the number of groups, however, varies considerably between the studies). They are encouraged to discuss the issue for, in most cases, 1–2 hours. Eventually, the actual valuation exercise takes place, by means of a CV or CE questionnaire.

Box 5.1 Theory and application of CE

Although they had been applied before in the area of environmental valuation, discrete choice experiments (CE) came into acclaim particularly due to the publication of Adamowicz et al. (1998), who made a strong argument for using this class of valuation methods to estimate non-use values of environmental public goods. Since then, CE's popularity in valuation studies has grown very quickly (Adamowicz, 2004; Mahieu et al., 2014).

In the most basic sense, the theoretical foundation of CE can be found in Lancaster's (1971) consumer theory. In his theory, consumers do not derive utility, as is usually assumed, from the consumption of goods, but from those goods' characteristics (attributes). Thus, consumer demand and, accordingly, valuation as WTP is based on a good's attributes.

With respect to modelling, CE are based on Random Utility Theory (RUT) (Marschak, 1960; McFadden, 1974). In empirical studies of choice (stated or revealed), only a part of the relevant characteristics of economic actors and attributes of goods can be observed. These influence subjective utility and thus choice decisions, but there is some unobservable influence as well. In RUT it is assumed that these unobservable variables are random. Using various statistical identification models (depending on different assumptions about the nature of the random term) the probabilities of a person making the observed choice given a statistical model with observable features of this person and the good in question as explanatory variables can be inferred.

RUT assumes, quite straightforwardly, that individual n chooses a specific alternative i (a good, a bundle of goods etc.) if and only if she derives more utility from this alternative than from any other available alternative belonging to the choice set S:

$$U_{in} > U_{jn}, \forall j \neq i \text{ and } i, j \in S \tag{5.1}$$

Of course, in empirical settings, the researcher is not able to directly observe U_{in}. She can only observe a part of it, based on the observation of various characteristics of the alternative and of the individual – this is called the systematic or representative utility component, V_{in}. A random (from the researcher's perspective), non-observable component of utility, e_{in}, connects V_{in} to U_{in}:

$$U_{in} = V_{in} + e_{in} \tag{5.2}$$

Combining equations (5.1) and (5.2), one gets:

$$V_{in} - V_{jn} > e_{jn} - e_{in} \tag{5.3}$$

Since the researcher is not able to observe the random utility components, she must recur to the calculation of the probability that the left-hand side of equation (5.3) is indeed larger than its right-hand side, based on a specific assumption regarding the probability distribution of e.

$$P_n(i) = \Pr(U_{in} > U_{jn}) = \Pr(V_{in} - V_{jn} > e_{jn} - e_{in}), \forall i \neq j \tag{5.4}$$

Equation (5.4) can be further reformulated by reference to an indicator function I, which equals 1 when the expression in parentheses is true and 0 otherwise:

$$P_n(i) = \int_e (V_{in} - V_{jn} > e_{jn} - e_{in}) f(e_n) de_n \tag{5.5}$$

This transformation makes the theory tractable in empirical discrete choice models.

Discrete choice models are a class of models that are specifications of equations (5.4) and (5.5) above. They are based on the additional assumption that the alternatives from the choice set S can be characterised by a number of attributes. These attributes can be used as variables to estimate the systematic component of utility V, while the model specification is the result of the researcher making an assumption about the nature of the random utility component e.

The basic discrete choice model, which is based on the most rigid assumptions from all such models, is the conditional logit (CL) model. It assumes that the error terms/random utility components e are independently identically distributed (i.i.d.) Gumbel variables. This basic model can be formulated as follows:

$$P_n(i) = \frac{\exp(V_{in})}{\sum_{j \in S} \exp(V_{jn})} \qquad (5.6)$$

The systematic component of utility V is assumed to be a linear additive function of the independent variables (attributes of the good in question and characteristics of the choosing individual) X_{ikn}, where K is the number of coefficients (β):

$$V_{in} = \beta_0 + \sum_{k=1}^{K-1} \beta_k X_{ikn} \qquad (5.7)$$

There exist a number of further models that relax the assumptions of CL. The most common models are nested logit, probit and mixed logit. Depending on the context, different models can be used.

The application of CE typically consists of four steps (see also Lancsar and Louviere, 2008):

1   Identification of relevant attributes of the good that is to be valued, including their levels (for instance, forest might be the good, carbon sequestration an attribute with levels expressed in terms of tonnes of CO_2; if the good is bio-diversity, one attribute might be its influence on the probability of regime shifts in the ecosystem, expressed as percentages). The relevant attributes, levels and their description are mostly determined through analysis of literature, in focus groups and/or through pre-testing (Jeanloz et al., 2016).

2   Determination of the experimental design, i.e. the 'combination of attributes and levels used to construct the alternatives included in the choice sets' (Hoyos, 2010, p. 1596). Here a number of issues play a role, including the number of alternatives per choice task (where each alternative is described in terms of the attributes identified beforehand), whether the alternatives are to be labelled, which statistical model is appropriate. Since mostly there exist far more combinations of attributes than can be used in an actual study, statistical procedures are applied to create a *fractional design*, which contains only a part of attribute combinations but allows for unbiased statistical inference. The main options are orthogonal main-effects design or various so-called efficient designs.

3   Conducting of choice experiment: participants are asked to make a choice between a number of alternatives (usually 2–4) presented on so-called *choice cards* (or *choice sets*). In most cases, each participant is confronted with multiple choice cards (sequential CE).

4   Statistical analysis and estimation of marginal WTPs for changes in the attributes on the basis of choice cards (see above).

For more details on the theory and application of CE, see Hensher et al. (2005), Louviere et al. (2000) and Train (2009). Aizaki et al. (2015) offer an introduction to the application of discrete choice modelling in the statistical software R (R Core Team, 2015). Hoyos (2010) is an excellent overview about state-of-the-art application of CE in environmental valuation.

In the context of economic valuation of biodiversity the potential of DMV to overcome certain cognitive issues is central. While their potential to address ethical challenges of conventional economic valuation is of high importance in general, this is not central for the present thesis. See Lo and Spash (2013), Kenter et al. (2015), Bartkowski and Lienhoop (2017, 2016) or a recent Special Issue in *Ecosystem Services* (Kenter, 2016; Kenter et al., 2016) for publications on this aspect.

As was mentioned above, economic valuation of ecosystem goods and services faces the difficulty that laypeople often do not possess enough information for the assumption of pre-formed, rational preferences to be justified. Biodiversity is a particularly severe case, as it is inherently complex, multidimensional and abstract. Also, it is inherently linked to uncertainty, which is generally a source of problems for economic valuation. Moreover, laypeople are often unfamiliar with biodiversity and do not (cannot) have meaningful experience with it. Therefore, it is essential to facilitate preference formation in valuation exercises.

The facilitation of the formation of informed preferences has been one of the main motivations for the inclusion of deliberative elements in economic valuation studies (Christie et al., 2006; Dietz et al., 2009; MacMillan et al., 2006). There exist other approaches, for example, providing respondents with more visual and/or verbal information, possibly using the possibilities offered by Internet-based surveys (Lindhjem and Navrud, 2011). However, Sandorf et al. (2016) recently showed that CE administered via the Internet produce significantly more status quo responses than deliberative workshops, indicating that Internet respondents do not take enough time to form preferences. Moreover, it was shown by Kenyon and others, who compared traditional contingent valuation with citizens' juries, that visual and verbal information presented individually may not be enough for respondents to form preferences – conversely, deliberation seems to help overcome cognitive obstacles (Kenyon et al., 2001; Kenyon and Nevin, 2001; see also Brouwer et al., 1999). Also, it was shown in previous research that deliberation has the potential to reduce protest votes (Szabó, 2011) and to increase the stability of choices (Lienhoop and Völker, 2016), which can be viewed as indicating that deliberation facilitates the formation of more well-informed preferences.

One potential problem in public good contexts, including stated preference methods, is strategic behaviour (Schläpfer, 2016), i.e. people making choices/reporting WTP that does not reflect their true preferences but is dictated by their hope to influence the survey in a specific manner. This can have a disturbing effect on the elicitation of economic values. Yet, Elster (1983, p. 36) argued that deliberation can solve the problem of strategic behaviour because it is based on rational discussion and makes the stakes clear to the participants. In the language of game theory, deliberation has the potential to move a previously non-cooperative public good game closer to cooperation, where strategic behaviour is not a pronounced issue (for more on the issue of strategic behaviour, see next subsection).

It was argued repeatedly that deliberation allows for the consideration of multiple criteria and thus eases the limits to monetary valuation posed by system complexity and value plurality (Frame and O'Connor, 2011; see also Stern et al., 1996). Deliberation makes it easier to deal with uncertainty, which is especially prevalent in the interactions between ecological and socio-economic systems. As was already pointed out above, the ecological and economic importance of biodiversity has very much to do with uncertainty.

Overall, DMV offers ways and means to handle some of the challenges posed by the valuation object biodiversity. Especially, deliberation significantly supports the process of preference formation, which is utterly necessary given biodiversity's complexity and abstractness. This is especially so because biodiversity can hardly be viewed as an instance of experience goods, for which preference formation approaches are being developed within the conventional valuation field (e.g. Czajkowski et al., 2015). However, deliberation does not offer a response to all challenges posed by biodiversity – see Table 5.9. Therefore, a proper preference elicitation approach has to be chosen with these challenges in mind. As was already argued above, CE appears to be fitting the needed profile quite well (Box 5.1). This is the reason why the combination of DMV and CE, i.e. deliberative choice experiments, appears to be particularly well-suited to handle biodiversity.

Of course, all that glitters is not gold. While deliberative choice experiments appear to have a large potential in responding to the challenges biodiversity poses for economic valuation, this approach has limitations of its own. To properly assess its potential, one should be aware of these limitations. They are discussed in the next subsection.

Limitations of deliberative choice experiments

To start with, deliberative choice experiments can still be seen as an instance of stated preference methods. And these face a number of limitations and challenges that deliberation alone cannot resolve (though it can offer part-solutions in some cases).

The main advantage of stated preference methods is at the same time their main limitation – they are hypothetical, not bound by observed behaviour of stakeholders in an environmental problem. While this means that they are particularly flexible, it also means that the responses cannot be taken at face value. For instance, it was argued that respondents in stated preference surveys do not express their specific *preferences*, but rather more general *attitudes* (Kahneman et al., 1999). Contrary to the assumptions of standard economic theory, these attitudes and preferences need not be always concerned with the self-regarding welfare of the respondents, but can include farther-reaching considerations (Aldred, 1994; Kenyon and Nevin, 2001; Sen, 1977; Spash et al., 2009) – an issue already discussed in Chapter 2. Also, such general attitudes are a source of responses of the kind described by Kahneman and Knetsch (1992) as 'purchase of moral satisfaction' or the related concept of *warm glow* (Andreoni, 1990), which are behaviours not really reflecting individual preferences that economic valuation is to elicit, but some more general and imprecise conceptions of 'doing the right thing'. However, this problem disappears when we give up the pretence to elicit 'true preferences':

> But if contingent valuation is simply conceived as a procedure used to let consumers express the economic importance they bestow on the good or the attribute studied, there is no reason to filter out expressive or ethical manifestations. [...] The very act of expressing a preference participates in its formation by way of allowing articulating it. Contingent valuation, conceived as an expressive medium, is one way to give to consumers the opportunity to express, and thereby form and refine, their preferences for the good or attribute to be valued.
>
>   (Meinard and Grill, 2011, p. 1709)

In other words, economics may have an overly rigid view of what is to count as human preference (see also Aldred, 1994). The prevalence of attitudes, not preferences, strengthens the point that there is a need for institutions that make possible and facilitate preference formation if we want to obtain meaningful estimates of economic values of ecosystems. Also, modifications of the underlying economic theory might be in order (Bartkowski and Lienhoop, 2016).

Another important 'psychological' issue, which was already mentioned above, can be summarised under the label of *strategic behaviour*. Early on in the history of stated preference methods, they were indirectly criticised by the luminary of modern economics, Paul Samuelson, who pointed out that the hypothetical nature of survey-based valuation techniques dooms them to failure – public good contexts invite those involved to engage in strategic behaviour, and the hypothetical markets constructed in stated preference methods make the problem even more severe (Samuelson, 1954). Why should people answer honestly how much an environmental public good is worth to them, if (i) they do not bear the consequences of their choices and (ii) they can hope that others will provide the good even if they do not contribute (free-riding)? This critique has, however, lost some of its power due to the results from various experiments in which it was shown that free-riding is not as pervasive a phenomenon as economic theory would predict (Chaudhuri, 2010; Horowitz et al., 2013; Ledyard, 1997). Also, there is growing evidence that *hypothetical bias*, a similar problem resulting from the hypothetical nature of the responses to stated preference surveys, is a much less pronounced problem than often believed and that it can be well accounted for by means of proper elicitation design (Interis, 2014).

Last but not least, stated preference methods are prone to a number of 'heuristics and biases', which have been intensely studied in recent decades by cognitive psychologists and behavioural economists (see Kahneman, 2012; Kahneman and Tversky, 2000). These include framing effects, embedding effect, insensitivity to scope, anchoring and loss aversion, among many others. Their severity and thus relevance for stated preference methods is debated (Sugden, 2005). Many of them can be handled by means of proper survey design but the respective approaches are still being developed and refined. One should bear in mind, however, that actual 'real-world behaviour' of people is equally prone to these cognitive biases, so they are not so much a stated preference-specific problem.

The problems discussed above are related to stated preference methods in general. Some of them can be handled by proper design, for example, hypothetical bias; others are a by-product of excessive expectations placed on the results of economic valuation, which should not be viewed as a precise, objective, end-of-story tool. In what follows, we will focus on problems that are specific to CE and DMV.

The application of CE faces three main challenges. First, the main limitation is that there is a trade-off between (i) the cognitive capacity of respondents/danger of cognitive overstrain; (ii) the statistical quality of the results, which is dependent on the sample (determined not only by the number of participants, but also by the number of choice tasks per person); and (iii) the number of attributes per alternative and levels per attribute – the more attributes/levels, the larger must be the sample. The inclusion of large numbers of attributes/levels not only increases the sample necessary for statistical inference, but also places large cognitive burdens on respondents, who might respond by recurring to choice heuristics. Mostly, the researcher faces 'hard choices', having to reconcile the three factors where there is no one-size-fits-all optimal approach. To some extent, deliberation can help here, as it has the potential to reduce the general level of cognitive demand; however, as here the main problem is the mode of preference elicitation, its help can be only limited.

Second, the commonly applied sequential CE (where respondents are confronted with multiple-choice cards) is not *incentive compatible* or *consequential*. Incentive compatibility is given when respondents have the feeling that their individual choices/contributions matter for the end result of the survey. Because of the type of econometric models CE is based on, what is valued are not 'realistic' scenarios but more or less arbitrary combinations of attribute levels, which often 'contradict' each other or the common sense. The practical relevance of this problem is debated and may be much less pronounced than economic theory would suggest (cf. Interis, 2014). Nevertheless, the danger of negative effects of incentive incompatibility (notably, hypothetical bias) should be borne in mind when CE are applied (Carson et al., 1999; Rakotonarivo et al., 2016). One possibility of overcoming this problem would be to go for single CE (one choice card per respondent), which, however, would increase the required number of respondents. This is a trade-off of a more 'budgetary' nature, which is nevertheless highly relevant in actual applications.[17] It can be argued, however, that deliberation can reduce the negative consequences of inconsequentiality in a similar way as it seems to reduce proneness to hypothetical bias (see Sandorf et al., 2016).

Third, a more pragmatic-practical limitation in the application of CE is that very often the choice of attributes and attribute levels is not based on ecological modelling, but dictated by the needs of experimental design. This is also partly due to the difficulty that scenarios from ecological models are not easily and directly transferrable to CE attributes. This has led to calls for a more transparent and structured process of attribute choice (Jeanloz et al., 2016). In the next sub-section, this thread will be taken up again.

Even though DMV offers solutions to many difficulties related to economic valuation in general and to biodiversity valuation in particular, it also faces a number of limitations, both conceptual and practical. First, a central limitation of DMV is that it is still a relatively young and developing approach which does not yet have a consistent theoretical basis (see Bunse et al., 2015). Particularly, its rationality assumptions are controversial. On the one hand, there is the economic concept of rationality (*homo oeconomicus*), on which conventional stated preference surveys are implicitly based.[18] From this perspective DMV is problematic because it rejects the premise that preferences for environmental public goods are predefined and independent of social processes. Also, DMV is often criticised by conventional economists since 'economic value is at its core derivative of individual (economic) preferences – not "citizen" of "group" opinions which could probably be useful for evaluation of policies but not necessarily valuation'.[19] On the other hand, DMV is also sometimes criticised by those who emphasise concepts such as *reflexive rationality* or *communicative rationality*, and for whom DMV is still too close to the conventional neoclassical economic paradigm (Lo and Spash, 2013). To resolve this conundrum, attempts were made to propose consistent theoretical foundations for DMV – for instance, Lo (2013) argues that it can be based on the Habermasian notion of communicative rationality, while Bartkowski and Lienhoop (2016) provide a different perspective by invoking Amartya Sen's rationality approach (e.g. Sen, 2010). However, these are very recent developments and it remains to be seen how the theory of DMV will develop further.

Second, to be effective and successful in promoting preference formation, the number of participants in deliberative workshops must be limited to around 10–15 per group. Obviously, a single group cannot possibly come even close to achieving statistical representativeness. This problem is usually coped with by conducting a number of workshops, so as to increase the overall number of participants, thus making statistical analysis and at least some limited generalisation of results possible. In practice, however, most DMV studies have used very small samples, usually under 100 participants (see Lienhoop and Völker, 2016, n. ii), which is a consequence of the high costs and effort that have to be put into such a study (see below). While some authors suggested that 'political representativeness', which can be achieved by encouraging impartiality among participants, might suffice (Gregory et al., 2012, pp. 64–65; see also Meinard et al., 2017), it is not clear whether DMV can move that far away from economic theory without sacrificing theoretical consistency (see above). Accordingly, it was recommended to apply DMV mainly on local and regional levels (Lienhoop et al., 2015).[20]

Third, stated preference surveys are generally a rather expensive enterprise. DMV stands out in this respect. Valuation studies that make use of deliberative approaches are not only very expensive in monetary terms, as one needs trained personnel, financial incentives for participants, supporting materials and infra-structure for the discussion sessions etc.; they are also very time-consuming in terms of preparation, carrying out and analysis (as there is an additional layer of data, i.e. video-taped or audio-recorded discussions). However, it should be borne in mind that due to the complexity and abstractness of the valuation object biodiversity, the alternative to DMV is not a postally administered stated prefer-ence survey, but rather more 'resource-intensive' options, particularly the already-mentioned Internet-based surveys or, possibly, computer-supported in-person interviews. In the former case, there is the already-mentioned downside of hypothetical bias (Sandorf et al., 2016); in the latter, administration costs are unlikely to be much lower than for DMV.

According to the analysis provided here, the combination of DMV and CE not only seems to respond comparatively well to the challenges posed by the valuation object biodiversity, the two approaches also correct to some extent for the downsides of each other – for instance, DMV can be expected to reduce the severity of hypothetical bias, to which CE is prone. Of course, there are more general limitations of the reach of economic valuation which deliberative choice experiments are not better suited to tackle than conventional methods. These include the existence and identification of critical natural capital (CNC) (Farley, 2008), decisions involving sacred goods (Temper and Martínez-Alier, 2013) or 'taboo trade-offs' (Daw et al., 2015; Stikvoort et al., 2016) or the issue of distri-butional impacts of analysed policies and equity weighting (Anthoff et al., 2009; Dasgupta et al., 1972, chap. 3.2). These issues point to general limitations of the application and interpretation of economic valuation, which were mentioned in Chapter 2 of the present book. Most of them do not apply so much for biodiver-sity. Thus, the verdict still holds that, given the specificities of biodiversity, deliberative choice experiments appear to be the method with the highest potential.

Coupling the conceptual framework with quantitative data

Above, it was argued at length that *deliberative choice experiments* are a method particularly well-suited for the economic valuation of biodiversity. However, for the conceptual framework to be applied in an actual valuation study, it is still necessary to (i) translate the framework into CE attributes understandable to lay-people (on this, see the discussion of the case study above) and (ii) to couple these with objective, possibly quantitative data. The latter issue is briefly dis-cussed in this subsection.

It is often emphasised in the context of economic valuation that '[t]he kinds of activities in each policy alternative must be described in sufficient detail to provide a basis for analysis' (Freeman, 2004, p. 7). While this does not neces-sarily mean that quantification is indispensable, quantitative attributes increase the interpretability and objectivity of the analysis. Qualitative attributes are sometimes inevitable, but they should still be precise, transparent and easily interpretable.

With regard to the conceptual framework developed in this book, this poses a special problem: since it was argued here that it is not sensible to base biodiversity valuation on simple biodiversity indices (first, because these do not normally capture all biodiversity; second, because they are not meaningful from the point of view of respondents in stated preference surveys), it must be based on qualitatively framed value categories. Of course, at least some of them can be expressed in quantitative terms – for instance, insurance value can be expressed in terms of the probability of a major flip in the state of the ecosystem, option value as the probability of finding useful items in the future. Spill-over value could be translated into a CE attribute as the number of migrating species that can be potentially carried by the ecosystem. Aesthetic value cannot be easily quantified, which, however, is a lesser problem: first, it was already argued here that distinguishing between biodiversity's influence on aesthetics and other factors can be very difficult anyway and is not really necessary or sensible. Second, there exist a number of valuation studies which used photographs to express changes in aesthetics (e.g. Lienhoop and Völker, 2016; Polak and Shashar, 2013; Tagliafierro et al., 2016).

The main problem, however, is that it is anything but straightforward to translate a specific (potential) ecosystem change into its effects on biodiversity levels and their effects on the value categories. This can be viewed as a two-stage problem, which is closely related to the issue of two-level uncertainty discussed above: first, quantitative data are needed about the effects of land-use changes on biodiversity; second, these effects have to be translated into changes in option potential, insurance and spill-over potential. With regard to the first level, some attempts have been made to develop suitable approaches within the research on environmental–economic accounting, i.e. the enrichment of conventional national accounts with information on ecosystems. For instance, a recent report of UNEP's Biodiversity Accounting initiative suggests ways of incorporating species richness and ecosystem diversity in satellite accounts (UNEP-WCMC, 2015). Alas, the usefulness of these from the point of view of the present book is rather limited, species richness being arguably a rather information-poor measure (Lyashevska and Farnsworth, 2012) and ecosystem diversity going beyond the focus of our conceptual framework (which aims at conceptualising the economic value of changes in biodiversity *within* a given ecosystem). A particularly interesting approach to the measurement of biodiversity, which could be used as a basis for its economic valuation along the lines sketched in this book, was proposed by Farnsworth and colleagues (Farnsworth et al., 2015, 2012; Lyashevska and Farnsworth, 2012): they argue that biodiversity can be well approximated by combining three *orthogonal dimensions* of it, namely, taxonomic/phylogenetic, structural and functional diversity. This approach, which is quite encompassing when compared with common biodiversity metrics (Lyashevska and Farnsworth, 2012), offers an as yet theoretical possibility to base the multiple dimensions of the conceptual framework developed here on a quantitative footing. The actual calculation of biodiversity measures of the kind proposed by Farnsworth and colleagues is likely to face serious data-availability problems; conversely, when the focus is on the different dimensions of biodiversity's economic value – which cannot, as was argued above, be reduced to species richness or the variety dimension in general – there seems to be no other way than to work with rather complex biodiversity measures.

Generally, however, the problem of the translation of environmental changes in resulting biodiversity changes appears to be the smaller issue and can be done by means of models (e.g. Fung et al., 2015; Lautenbach et al., 2017; Lyashevska and Farnsworth, 2012). The much more demanding task is the next step from changes in biodiversity to changes in its effect on stability, options and spill-over, especially the former two. It is conceivable, however, to base the option and insurance effects of biodiversity changes on statistical information from other, possibly similar cases, i.e. to infer the relevant probabilities (discovery of some useful items in the ecosystem and a flip in the state of that ecosystem, respectively) from historical observation of other, similar ecosystems. Also, again, various ecological models can be helpful here (e.g. Grace et al., 2016).

Obviously, these suggestions are very tentative since the primary focus of the present book is on conceptual issues, application being of secondary interest and a subject for future research. Furthermore and more importantly, the coupling of the conceptual framework with empirical data should essentially be a context-specific, interdisciplinary exercise, based on active cooperation between economists and biologists.[21] This section thus gives only general orientation on the issue. Another point should be made, though, regarding the relative importance of first-level vs second-level uncertainty and the relationship *ecosystem change → biodiversity change → value*. As was already suggested above, the second level seems to be much more problematic than the first. Fortunately, its importance varies between applications of economic valuation. Mainly, it is highly important in CBA and similar applications, where precision and realistic scenarios are crucial. Conversely, when communication and demonstration of the value of specific ecosystems is in focus, precision demands are lower and the second level's importance diminishes. Thus, the conceptual framework can be applied even though a satisfactory solution to the second-level problem has yet to be found.

Summary

The starting point for the present book was the diagnosis that (i) we are experiencing unprecedented rates of biodiversity loss, (ii) biodiversity is a potentially valuable ecosystem property from the economic point of view, (iii) currently, there is no established framework for estimating its value (a point reinforced by the literature review presented in Chapter 4), (iv) such a framework is urgently needed if biodiversity values estimated in economic valuation studies are to have meaningful information content and be consistent. This chapter offers a therapy to the diagnosed ills by proposing a consistent, unifying conceptual framework for the economic valuation of biodiversity. The framework is based on a definition of biodiversity as the *diversity of kinds in biotic or biota-encompassing categories* and a firm emphasis on its multidimensionality. Building upon the extensive discussion of available literature in Chapter 4, we identified four sources of biodiversity's economic value, and found that insurance value, option value and spill-over value are directly attributable to biodiversity, which also contributes to the aesthetic appreciation of ecosystems. The four value categories were then combined in a conceptual framework (Figure 5.1). The framework emphasises the role of uncertainty and spatial interconnections between ecosystems as underlying biodiversity's economic value.

The next step was then to look at the implications the framework proposed here has for the common frameworks of TEV and ESS. It was found that both are not particularly well-suited to incorporate biodiversity, which necessitates extensions and modifications. Suitable proposals were developed accordingly.

An important step in the process of developing the conceptual framework was its empirical verification. The approach chosen to do this was a focus group study, conducted in a German UNESCO Biosphere Reserve. A planned extension of set-aside areas within the Reserve was used as the environmental change context against which participants in the focus groups discussed their general perceptions of forest ecosystems and their relative appreciation of biodiversity. The main aim of this exercise was to find out whether the conceptual framework is compatible with the preferences of stakeholders in a real-world context. The results are not entirely conclusive but they indicate that (i) the conceptual framework includes relevant dimensions of biodiversity value, (ii) these are understandable for laypeople and (iii) they can be translated into a specific context of environmental change. Biodiversity scored relatively high in importance as compared with other forest functions (including various provisioning, regulating and cultural ecosystem services); the biodiversity value categories proposed in the conceptual framework were evaluated as relevant both generally and in the specific context of the Reserve. A somewhat problematic finding is related to the motivations participants named for their appreciation of biodiversity: in contrast to the conceptual arguments presented in the Excursus, many participants stated that they value biodiversity not only because of its usefulness to themselves, others and future generations, but also without any usefulness considerations. Nonetheless, the overall results of the focus group study indicate that the conceptual framework for the economic valuation of biodiversity proposed in the present book has the potential to be applied in fully fledged valuation studies, which is the reason why it was developed.

To move the conceptual framework of biodiversity's economic value closer to application in actual valuation studies, we conducted an analysis of the methodological challenges posed by this specific valuation object. The challenges identified were used as criteria for the choice of suitable valuation methods. The resulting recommendation – to apply *deliberative choice experiments* – was then fleshed out in a thorough presentation and discussion of the two components of this methodological approach, especially the less well-known and still developing deliberative monetary valuation. Furthermore, some tentative proposals were made for how the conceptual framework can be coupled with measurable, empirical data.

Notes

1 Much of the discussion here is based on Bartkowski (2017).
2 One approach based on the notion of goods' characteristics is Lancaster's (1971) theory of consumer demand, which will be touched upon further below in the context of discrete choice experiments. Another strand of economic theory which makes use of the characteristics notion is new institutional economics, particularly property rights theory. I am thankful to Erik Gawel for pointing this out to me.
3 Another option would be to focus on landscapes (see Bastian et al., 2014). In fact, the understanding of *ecosystem* that underlies the present thesis is quite close to how *landscapes* are usually perceived. The ultimate difficulty, however, is that neither term is unambiguous and both depend to a large extent on subjective evaluations and site-specific demarcation criteria. I stick to the term *ecosystem* in the following, the reference to the landscape concept serving mainly as a *caveat lector*.
4 Note that some classifications of ecosystem services, including CICES, view existence value as an ecosystem service. This seems to overstretch the meaning of the word 'service', as the latter implies a minimum of instrumental usefulness, while the concept of existence value explicitly negates any instrumental considerations (see, e.g., Aldred, 1994).
5 This interpretation of option value of biodiversity is a part-response to a criticism of neoclassical environmental economics and the preference utilitarian foundation of economic valuation expressed by Scholtes (2007, 2010), whose concept of *environmental dominance* emphasises the problem that our current use of ecosystems has repercussions for the freedom of choice of future generations; he thus seeks concepts which would help justify and alleviate our environmental dominance. Preserving future options would be one possible approach.
6 Note that this 'efficiency' is a value-inducing effect only when it is linked to spillovers to other ecosystems. Of course, a diverse ecosystem is also home to a number of potentially useful local species, thus contributing to the provision of a large bundle of ecosystem services. However, this 'within-efficiency' is unlikely to have additional value beyond the sum of the values of those ecosystem services. Furthermore, the thus induced diversity of species using the diverse (micro-)habitats is itself part of the ecosystem's biodiversity.
7 Note, however, that some operationalisations of option value have focused on supply uncertainty and are thus closer to the notion of insurance value as understood here (e.g. Bishop, 1982).
8 For definitions of the zoning schemes in UNESCO Man and Biosphere Reserves, see www.unesco.org/new/en/natural-sciences/environment/ecological-sciences/biosphere-reserves/main-characteristics/zoning-schemes (retrieved on 24 April 2015).
9 The *National Strategy on Biological Diversity* of the German federal government sketches the government's plans regarding protection of biological diversity in the country. One of the specific goals of the *Strategy* is to increase the forest area where 'natural development' takes place (understood as areas not used for forestry and/or agriculture) to 5 per cent of overall forest area by 2020 (by 2015, around 2.6 per cent had been achieved). Every federal state is supposed to contribute to achieving this goal. Thuringia specifies the goals of the *National Strategy* in its own *Strategy on the Preservation of Biological Diversity*, adopted in 2011, with the goal to reach 25,000 ha of set-aside forests in the federal state by 2029.
10 All materials used in the focus groups study are available from the author upon request.
11 The term *function* is used here in a rather general meaning, not in the strict sense of *ecosystem functions*. Actually, the question here was 'How important do you find the following *functions/characteristics* of the forest?'

12 All quotations were translated into English by the author. Some corrections of grammar etc. were unavoidable; also, some incomprehensible passages were left out.
13 '[There was] an investigation, also by the UNESCO, that such a core zone, developments like those you present here, that are envisioned here, reduce biodiversity by around 90 per cent' (Frauenwald).
14 The term *deliberative choice experiments* was first used by Kenter et al. (2011). However, their approach differs from the one advanced here, as they elicited collective preferences, while the deliberative choice experiments discussed here (and applied by Lienhoop and Völker, 2016) are based on individual preference elicitation (but collective preference *formation*).
15 Especially the latter point, a traditional ingredient of deliberative democracy, was criticised by many commentators (Elster, 1983, chap. I.5; Gaus, 1997; Lo and Spash, 2013; O'Neill, 2001; Sen, 2010). It was argued that consensus is not always feasible or sensible, as the related costs of reaching a decision might well be higher than the gains of the decision itself (Buchanan and Tullock, 1962, chap. 7). In modern philosophy, much emphasis is put on plurality (Dryzek, 2013; Sen, 2010), which also undermines the absolute call for unanimity (see also Bartkowski and Lienhoop, 2016).
16 In addition to *preference formation* (e.g. Sagoff, 1998; Vatn, 2004), one finds similar terms in the literature, such as *preference learning* (e.g. Shogren et al., 2000), *preference construction* (MacMillan et al., 2006) and *preference discovery* (Braga and Starmer, 2005). For the purposes of the discussion here they can be taken as synonymous.
17 Another potential problem, which, however, is still difficult to interpret, was studied by van Zanten et al. (2016), who showed that the price attribute has statistically significant influence on the relative 'strength' of other, non-monetary attributes. Since non-attendance to the price attribute appears to be quite common (Scarpa et al., 2009; van Zanten et al., 2016), this has implications for the validity of results of CE studies.
18 For illuminating discussions of rationality assumptions in economic theory, see chap. 3 in Reiss (2013) and, for an epistemological perspective, chap. 15 in Blaug (1992).
19 This quotation is a comment by an anonymous referee of the first submitted version of Bartkowski et al. (2015).
20 Note, however, that this problem is differently pronounced depending on whether the elicitation method is CV or CE – in the latter, it is usual to let respondents give answers to a number of choice tasks, so that the size of the sample can be increased by either increasing the number of participants (costly) or increasing the number of choice tasks per person (potentially problematic due to cognitive limits).
21 For a similarly inspired approach in the area of landscape valuation, see Tagliafierro et al. (2016).

References

Adamowicz, W.L., 2004. What's it worth? An examination of historical trends and future directions in environmental valuation. Aust. J. Agric. Resour. Econ. 48, 419–443.
Adamowicz, W.L., Boxall, P.C., Williams, M., Louviere, J., 1998. Stated preference approaches for measuring passive use values: Choice experiments and contingent valuation. Am. J. Agric. Econ. 80, 64–75.
Aizaki, H., Nakatani, T., Sato, K., 2015. Stated preference methods using R, Chapman & Hall/CRC the R series. CRC Press, Boca Raton.
Aldred, J., 1994. Existence value, welfare and altruism. Environ. Values 3, 381–402.
Álvarez-Farizo, B., Hanley, N., Barberán, R., Lázaro, A., 2007. Choice modeling at the 'market stall': Individual versus collective interest in environmental valuation. Ecol. Econ. 60, 743–751.

Anand, S., Sen, A., 2000. Human development and economic sustainability. World Dev. 28, 2029–2049.

Andreoni, J., 1990. Impure altruism and donations to public goods: A theory of warm-glow giving. Econ. J. 100, 464–477.

Anthoff, D., Hepburn, C., Tol, R.S.J., 2009. Equity weighting and the marginal damage costs of climate change. Ecol. Econ. 68, 836–849.

Bakhtiari, F., Jacobsen, J.B., Strange, N., Helles, F., 2014. Revealing lay people's perceptions of forest biodiversity value components and their application in valuation method. Glob. Ecol. Conserv. 1, 27–42.

Bartkowski, B., 2017. Are diverse ecosystems more valuable? Biodiversity values as result of uncertainty and spatial interactions in ecosystem service provision. Ecosyst. Serv. 24, 50–57.

Bartkowski, B., Lienhoop, N., 2016. Beyond rationality, towards reasonableness: Deliberative monetary valuation and Amartya Sen's approach to rationality. Presented at the AES 2016, Warwick.

Bartkowski, B., Lienhoop, N., 2017. Democracy and valuation: A reply to Schläpfer (2016). Ecol. Econ. 131, 557–560.

Bartkowski, B., Lienhoop, N., Hansjürgens, B., 2015. Capturing the complexity of biodiversity: A critical review of economic valuation studies of biological diversity. Ecol. Econ. 113, 1–14.

Bastian, O., Grunewald, K., Syrbe, R.-U., Walz, U., Wende, W., 2014. Landscape services: The concept and its practical relevance. Landsc. Ecol. 29, 1463–1479.

Baumgärtner, S., 2007a. Why the measurement of species diversity requires prior value judgements. In: Kontoleon, A., Pascual, U., Swanson, T.M. (Eds), Biodiversity economics. Cambridge University Press, Cambridge; New York, pp. 293–310.

Baumgärtner, S., 2007b. The insurance value of biodiversity in the provision of ecosystem services. Nat. Resour. Model. 20, 87–127.

Baumgärtner, S., Strunz, S., 2014. The economic insurance value of ecosystem resilience. Ecol. Econ. 101, 21–32.

Birnbacher, D., 2014. Biodiversity and the 'substitution problem'. In: Lanzerath, D., Friele, M. (Eds), Concepts and values in biodiversity. Routledge, London; New York, pp. 39–54.

Bishop, R.C., 1982. Option value: An exposition and extension. Land Econ. 58, 1–15.

Blaug, M., 1992. The methodology of economics: Or how economists explain, 2nd edn. Cambridge University Press, Cambridge; New York.

Bohman, J., Rehg, W. (Eds), 1997. Deliberative democracy: Essays on reason and politics. MIT Press, Cambridge, MA.

Boyd, J., Banzhaf, S., 2007. What are ecosystem services? The need for standardized environmental accounting units. Ecol. Econ. 63, 616–626.

Braga, J., Starmer, C., 2005. Preference anomalies, preference elicitation and the discovered preference hypothesis. Environ. Resour. Econ. 32, 55–89.

Brock, W.A., Xepapadeas, A., 2003. Valuing biodiversity from an economic perspective: A unified economic, ecological, and genetic approach. Am. Econ. Rev. 93, 1597–1614.

Brouwer, R., Powe, N., Turner, R.K., Bateman, I.J., Langford, I.H., 1999. Public attitudes to contingent valuation and public consultation. Environ. Values 8, 325–347.

Brown, T.C., Peterson, G.L., Tonn, B.E., 1995. The Values Jury to aid natural resource decisions. Land Econ. 71, 250–260.

Buchanan, J.M., Tullock, G., 1962. The calculus of consent: Logical foundations of constitutional democracy. University of Michigan Press, Ann Arbor.

Buijs, A.E., Fischer, A., Rink, D., Young, J.C., 2008. Looking beyond superficial knowledge gaps: Understanding public representations of biodiversity. Int. J. Biodivers. Sci. Manag. 4, 65–80.

Bunse, L., Rendon, O., Luque, S., 2015. What can deliberative approaches bring to the monetary valuation of ecosystem services? A literature review. Ecosyst. Serv. 14, 88–97.

Burgess, J., Limb, M., Harrison, C.M., 1988a. Exploring environmental values through the medium of small groups: 1. Theory and practice. Environ. Plan. A 20, 309–326.

Burgess, J., Limb, M., Harrison, C.M., 1988b. Exploring environmental values through the medium of small groups: 2. Illustrations of a group at work. Environ. Plan. A 20, 457–476.

Bushart, M., Suck, R., 2008. Potentielle natürliche Vegetation Thüringens (No. 78), Schriftenreihe der TLUG. Thüringer Landesanstalt für Umwelt und Geologie, Jena.

Cardinale, B.J., Duffy, J.E., Gonzalez, A., Hooper, D.U., Perrings, C., Venail, P., Narwani, A., Mace, G.M., Tilman, D., Wardle, D.A., Kinzig, A.P., Daily, G.C., Loreau, M., Grace, J.B., Larigauderie, A., Srivastava, D.S., Naeem, S., 2012. Biodiversity loss and its impact on humanity. Nature 486, 59–67.

Carson, R.T., Flores, N.E., Mitchell, R.C., 1999. The theory and measurement of passive-use value. In: Bateman, I., Willis, K.G. (Eds), Valuing environmental preferences: Theory and practice of the contingent valuation method in the US, EU, and developing countries. Oxford University Press, Oxford; New York, pp. 97–130.

Champ, P.A., Boyle, K.J., Brown, T.C. (Eds), 2004. A primer on nonmarket valuation, reprint. edn., The economics of non-market goods and resources. Kluwer Acad. Publ, Dordrecht.

Chaudhuri, A., 2010. Sustaining cooperation in laboratory public goods experiments: A selective survey of the literature. Exp. Econ. 14, 47–83.

Christie, M., Hanley, N., Warren, J., Murphy, K., Wright, R., Hyde, T., 2006. Valuing the diversity of biodiversity. Ecol. Econ. 58, 304–317.

Christie, M., Warren, J., Hanley, N., Murphy, K., Wright, R., 2004. Developing measures for valuing changes in biodiversity: Final report. DEFRA, London.

Cohen, J., 1997. Deliberation and democratic legitimacy. In: Bohman, J., Rehg, W. (Eds), Deliberative democracy: Essays on reason and politics. MIT Press, Cambridge, MA, pp. 67–91.

Costanza, R., de Groot, R., Sutton, P., van der Ploeg, S., Anderson, S.J., Kubiszewski, I., Farber, S., Turner, R.K., 2014. Changes in the global value of ecosystem services. Glob. Environ. Change 26, 152–158.

Czajkowski, M., Buszko-Briggs, M., Hanley, N., 2009. Valuing changes in forest biodiversity. Ecol. Econ. 68, 2910–2917.

Czajkowski, M., Hanley, N., LaRiviere, J., 2015. The effects of experience on preferences: Theory and empirics for environmental public goods. Am. J. Agric. Econ. 97, 333–351.

Dallimer, M., Irvine, K.N., Skinner, A.M.J., Davies, Z.G., Rouquette, J.R., Maltby, L.L., Warren, P.H., Armsworth, P.R., Gaston, K.J., 2012. Biodiversity and the feel-good factor: Understanding associations between self-reported human well-being and species richness. BioScience 62, 47–55.

Dasgupta, P., 2001. Human well-being and the natural environment. Oxford University Press, Oxford; New York.

Dasgupta, P., Sen, A., Marglin, S., 1972. Guidelines for project evaluation, Project Formulation and Evaluation Series. United Nations, New York.

Daw, T.M., Coulthard, S., Cheung, W.W.L., Brown, K., Abunge, C., Galafassi, D., Peterson, G.D., McClanahan, T.R., Omukoto, J.O., Munyi, L., 2015. Evaluating taboo trade-offs in ecosystems services and human well-being. Proc. Natl. Acad. Sci. 112, 6949–6954.

DEFRA, 2007. Report, questionnaire and data tables following Survey of Public Attitudes and Behaviours towards the Environment: 2007. DEFRA, London.

Delbecq, A.L., Ven, A.H.V. de, Gustafson, D.H., 1975. Group techniques for program planning: A guide to nominal group and Delphi processes. Scott, Foresman, Glenview, IL.

Deutsche Bundesregierung, 2007. Nationale Strategie zur biologischen Vielfalt. Bundesministerium für Umwelt, Naturschutz und Reaktorsicherheit, Berlin.

Diáz, M., Campos, P., Pulido, F.J., 1997. The Spanish dehesas: A diversity in land-use and wildlife. In: Pain, D., Pienkowski, M. (Eds), Farming and birds in Europe: The Common Agricultural Policy and its implications for bird conservation. Academic Press, London, pp. 178–209.

Die Linke, SPD, Bündnis 90/Die Grünen, 2014. Thüringen gemeinsam voranbringen – demokratisch, sozial, ökologisch: Koalitionsvertrag zwischen den Parteien Die Linke, SPD, Bündnis 90/Die Grünen für die 6. Wahlperiode des Thüringer Landtags. Erfurt.

Dietz, T., Stern, P.C., Dan, A., 2009. How deliberation affects stated willingness to pay for mitigation of carbon dioxide emissions: An experiment. Land Econ. 85, 329–347.

Dohmen, T., Falk, A., Huffman, D., Sunde, U., Schupp, J., Wagner, G.G., 2011. Individual risk attitudes: Measurement, determinants, and behavioral consequences. J. Eur. Econ. Assoc. 9, 522–550.

Dryzek, J.S., 2013. The deliberative democrat's idea of justice. Eur. J. Polit. Theory 12, 329–346.

Ehrlich, P.R., Goulder, L.H., 2007. Is current consumption excessive? A general framework and some indications for the United States. Conserv. Biol. 21, 1145–1154.

Elster, J., 1983. Sour grapes: Studies in the subversion of rationality. Cambridge University Press, Cambridge; New York.

Elster, J., 1997. The market and the forum: Three varieties of political theory. In: Bohman, J., Rehg, W. (Eds), Deliberative democracy: Essays on reason and politics. MIT Press, Cambridge, MA, pp. 3–33.

Essl, F., Rabitsch, W. (Eds), 2013. Biodiversität und Klimawandel: Auswirkungen und Handlungsoptionen für den Naturschutz in Mitteleuropa. Springer Spektrum, Berlin Heidelberg.

Faith, D.P., 2017. A general model for biodiversity and its value. In: Garson, J., Plutynski, A., Sarkar, S. (Eds), The Routledge handbook of philosophy of biodiversity. Routledge, New York.

Farley, J., 2008. The role of prices in conserving critical natural capital. Conserv. Biol. 22, 1399–1408.

Farnsworth, K.D., Adenuga, A.H., de Groot, R.S., 2015. The complexity of biodiversity: A biological perspective on economic valuation. Ecol. Econ. 120, 350–354.

Farnsworth, K.D., Lyashevska, O., Fung, T., 2012. Functional complexity: The source of value in biodiversity. Ecol. Complex. 11, 46–52.

Finger, R., Buchmann, N., 2015. An ecological economic assessment of risk-reducing effects of species diversity in managed grasslands. Ecol. Econ. 110, 89–97.

Frame, B., O'Connor, M., 2011. Integrating valuation and deliberation: The purposes of sustainability assessment. Environ. Sci. Policy 14, 1–10.

Freeman, A.M., 2004. Economic valuation: What and why. In: Champ, P.A., Boyle, K.J., Brown, T.C. (Eds), A primer on nonmarket valuation. Kluwer Acad. Publ, Dordrecht, pp. 1–25.

Fromm, O., 2000. Ecological structure and functions of biodiversity as elements of its total economic value. Environ. Resour. Econ. 16, 303–328.

Fung, T., Farnsworth, K.D., Reid, D.G., Rossberg, A.G., 2015. Impact of biodiversity loss on production in complex marine food webs mitigated by prey-release. Nat. Commun. 6.

Gaus, G.F., 1997. Reason, justification, and consensus: Why democracy can't have it all. In: Bohman, J., Rehg, W. (Eds), Deliberative democracy: Essays on reason and politics. MIT Press, Cambridge, MA, pp. 205–242.

Goodin, R.E., Dryzek, J.S., 2006. Deliberative impacts: The macro-political uptake of mini-publics. Polit. Soc. 34, 219–244.

Grace, J.B., Anderson, T.M., Seabloom, E.W., Borer, E.T., Adler, P.B., Harpole, W.S., Hautier, Y., Hillebrand, H., Lind, E.M., Pärtel, M., Bakker, J.D., Buckley, Y.M., Crawley, M.J., Damschen, E.I., Davies, K.F., Fay, P.A., Firn, J., Gruner, D.S., Hector, A., Knops, J.M.H., MacDougall, A.S., Melbourne, B.A., Morgan, J.W., Orrock, J.L., Prober, S.M., Smith, M.D., 2016. Integrative modelling reveals mechanisms linking productivity and plant species richness. Nature 529, 390–393.

Gregory, R., 2000. Using stakeholder values to make smarter environmental decisions. Environ. Sci. Policy Sustain. Dev. 42, 34–44.

Gregory, R., Failing, L., Harstone, M., Long, G., McDaniels, T., Ohlson, D., 2012. Structured decision making: A practical guide to environmental management choices. Wiley-Blackwell, Chichester; Hoboken, NJ.

Habermas, J., 1981. Theorie des kommunikativen Handelns. Suhrkamp, Frankfurt am Main.

Haines-Young, R., Potschin, M., 2013. Common International Classification of Ecosystem Services (CICES): Consultation of version 4, August–December 2012 (EEA Framework Contract No. EEA/IEA/09/003). University of Nottingham, Nottingham.

Hamilton, K., 2013. Biodiversity and national accounting (No. WPS 6441). World Bank, Washington, DC.

Henselek, Y., Klein, A.-M., Baumgärtner, S., 2016. The economic insurance value of wild pollinators in almond orchards in California. Presented at the 18th Annual BIOECON Conference, Cambridge.

Hensher, D.A., Rose, J.M., Greene, W.H., 2005. Applied choice analysis: A primer. Cambridge University Press, Cambridge; New York.

Holt, C.A., Laury, S.K., 2002. Risk aversion and incentive effects. Am. Econ. Rev. 92, 1644–1655.

Horowitz, J.K., McConnell, K.E., Murphy, J.J., 2013. Behavioral foundations of environmental economics and valuation. In: List, J.A., Price, M.K. (Eds), Handbook on experimental economics and the environment. Edward Elgar, Cheltenham, pp. 115–156.

Horton, J.N., 1980. Nominal group technique. Anaesthesia 35, 811–814.

Hoyos, D., 2010. The state of the art of environmental valuation with discrete choice experiments. Ecol. Econ. 69, 1595–1603.

Interis, M.G., 2014. A challange to three widely held ideas in environmental valuation. J. Agric. Appl. Econ. 46, 347–356.

Isbell, F., Craven, D., Connolly, J., Loreau, M., Schmid, B., Beierkuhnlein, C., Bezemer, T.M., Bonin, C., Bruelheide, H., de Luca, E., Ebeling, A., Griffin, J.N., Guo, Q., Hautier, Y., Hector, A., Jentsch, A., Kreyling, J., Lanta, V., Manning, P., Meyer, S.T., Mori, A.S., Naeem, S., Niklaus, P.A., Polley, H.W., Reich, P.B., Roscher, C., Seabloom, E.W., Smith, M.D., Thakur, M.P., Tilman, D., Tracy, B.F., van der Putten, W.H., van Ruijven, J., Weigelt, A., Weisser, W.W., Wilsey, B., Eisenhauer, N., 2015. Biodiversity increases the resistance of ecosystem productivity to climate extremes. Nature 526, 574–577.

Jax, K., 2006. Ecological units: Definitions and application. Q. Rev. Biol. 81, 237–258.

Jax, K., 2010. Ecosystem functioning. Cambridge University Press, Cambridge; New York.

Jeanloz, S., Lizin, S., Beenaerts, N., Brouwer, R., Van Passel, S., Witters, N., 2016. Towards a more structured selection process for attributes and levels in choice experiments: A study in a Belgian protected area. Ecosyst. Serv. 18, 45–57.

Joss, S., 1998. Danish consensus conferences as a model of participatory technology assessment: An impact study of consensus conferences on Danish Parliament and Danish public debate. Sci. Public Policy 25, 2–22.

Kahneman, D., 2012. Thinking, fast and slow. Penguin, London.

Kahneman, D., Knetsch, J.L., 1992. Valuing public goods: The purchase of moral satisfaction. J. Environ. Econ. Manag. 22, 57–70.

Kahneman, D., Tversky, A., 1979. Prospect theory: An analysis of decision under risk. Econometrica 47, 263–291.

Kahneman, D., Tversky, A. (Eds), 2000. Choices, values, and frames. Cambridge University Press, New York; Cambridge.

Kahneman, D., Ritov, I., Schkade, D.A., 1999. Economic preferences or attitude expressions? An analysis of dollar responses to public issues. J. Risk Uncertain. 19, 203–235.

Kenter, J.O., 2016. Editorial: Shared, plural and cultural values. Ecosyst. Serv.

Kenter, J.O., Bryce, R., Christie, M., Cooper, N., Hockley, N., Irvine, K.N., Fazey, I., O'Brien, L., Orchard-Webb, J., Ravenscroft, N., Raymond, C.M., Reed, M.S., Tett, P., Watson, V., 2016. Shared values and deliberative valuation: Future directions. Ecosyst. Serv.

Kenter, J.O., Hyde, T., Christie, M., Fazey, I., 2011. The importance of deliberation in valuing ecosystem services in developing countries: Evidence from the Solomon Islands. Glob. Environ. Change 21, 505–521.

Kenter, J.O., O'Brien, L., Hockley, N., Ravenscroft, N., Fazey, I., Irvine, K.N., Reed, M.S., Christie, M., Brady, E., Bryce, R., Church, A., Cooper, N., Davies, A., Evely, A., Everard, M., Fish, R., Fisher, J.A., Jobstvogt, N., Molloy, C., Orchard-Webb, J., Ranger, S., Ryan, M., Watson, V., Williams, S., 2015. What are shared and social values of ecosystems? Ecol. Econ. 111, 86–99.

Kenyon, W., Nevin, C., 2001. The use of economic and participatory approaches to assess forest development: A case study in the Ettrick Valley. For. Policy Econ. 3, 69–80.

Kenyon, W., Hanley, N., Nevin, C., 2001. Citizens' juries: An aid to environmental valuation? Environ. Plan. C Gov. Policy 19, 557–566.

Kousky, C., Kopp, R.E., Cooke, R.M., 2011. Risk premia and the social cost of carbon: A review. Econ. Open-Access Open-Assess. E-J. 5, 1.

Lancaster, K., 1971. Consumer demand: A new approach. Columbia University Press, New York.

Lancsar, E., Louviere, J., 2008. Conducting discrete choice experiments to inform healthcare decision making. PharmacoEconomics 26, 661–677.

Lautenbach, S., Jungandreas, A., Blanke, J., Lehsten, V., Mühlner, S., Kühn, I., Volk, M., 2017. Trade-offs between plant species richness and carbon storage in the context of afforestation: Examples from afforestation scenarios in the Mulde Basin, Germany. Ecol. Indic. 73, 139–155.

Ledyard, J.O., 1997. Public goods: A survey of experimental research. In: Kagel, J.H., Roth, A.E. (Eds), The handbook of experimental economics. Princeton University Press, Princeton, pp. 111–194.

Lienhoop, N., MacMillan, D.C., 2007. Valuing wilderness in Iceland: Estimation of WTA and WTP using the market stall approach to contingent valuation. Land Use Policy 24, 289–295.

Lienhoop, N., Völker, M., 2016. Preference refinement in deliberative choice experiments. Land Econ. 92, 555–557. doi:10.3368/le.92.3.555.

Lienhoop, N., Bartkowski, B., Hansjürgens, B., 2015. Informing biodiversity policy: The role of economic valuation, deliberative institutions and deliberative monetary valuation. Environ. Sci. Policy 54, 522–532.

Lindhjem, H., Navrud, S., 2011. Are Internet surveys an alternative to face-to-face interviews in contingent valuation? Ecol. Econ. 70, 1628–1637.

Lo, A.Y., 2011. Analysis and democracy: The antecedents of the deliberative approach of ecosystems valuation. Environ. Plan. C Gov. Policy 29, 958–974.

Lo, A.Y., 2013. Agreeing to pay under value disagreement: Reconceptualizing preference transformation in terms of pluralism with evidence from small-group deliberations on climate change. Ecol. Econ. 87, 84–94.

Lo, A.Y., Spash, C.L., 2013. Deliberative Monetary Valuation: In search of a democratic and value plural approach to environmental policy. J. Econ. Surv. 27, 768–789.

Louviere, J.J., Hensher, D.A., Swait, J.D., 2000. Stated choice methods: Analysis and application. Cambridge University Press, Cambridge; New York.

Lundhede, T., Jacobsen, J.B., Hanley, N., Strange, N., Thorsen, B.J., 2015. Incorporating outcome uncertainty and prior outcome beliefs in stated preferences. Land Econ. 91, 296–316.

Lyashevska, O., Farnsworth, K.D., 2012. How many dimensions of biodiversity do we need? Ecol. Indic. 18, 485–492.

Mace, G.M., Norris, K., Fitter, A.H., 2012. Biodiversity and ecosystem services: A multi-layered relationship. Trends Ecol. Evol. 27, 19–26.

McFadden, D., 1974. Conditional logit analysis of qualitative choice behavior. In: Zarembka, P. (Ed.), Frontiers in econometrics. Academic Press, New York.

MacMillan, D.C., Hanley, N., Lienhoop, N., 2006. Contingent valuation: Environmental polling or preference engine? Ecol. Econ. 60, 299–307.

MacMillan, D.C., Philip, L., Hanley, N., Alvarez-Farizo, B., 2002. Valuing the non-market benefits of wild goose conservation: A comparison of interview and group based approaches. Ecol. Econ. 43, 49–59.

Mahieu, P.-A., Andersson, H., Beaumais, O., Crastes, R., Wolff, F.-C., 2014. Is choice experiment becoming more popular than contingent valuation? A systematic review in agriculture, environment and health (Working Paper No. 2014.12). FAERE – French Association of Environmental and Resource Economists.

Maier, D.S., 2012. What's so good about biodiversity? A call for better reasoning about nature's value. Springer, Dordrecht; New York.

Marschak, J., 1960. Binary choice constraints on random utility indications. In: Arrow, K.J., Karlin, S., Suppes, P. (Eds), Stanford Symposium on Mathematical Methods in the Social Sciences. Stanford University Press, Stanford, pp. 312–329.

MEA, 2005. Ecosystems and human well-being: General synthesis. World Resources Institute, Washington, DC.

Meinard, Y., Grill, P., 2011. The economic valuation of biodiversity as an abstract good. Ecol. Econ. 70, 1707–1714.

Meinard, Y., Quétier, F., 2014. Experiencing biodiversity as a bridge over the science–society communication gap. Conserv. Biol. 28, 705–712.

Meinard, Y., Remy, A., Schmid, B., 2017. Measuring impartial preference for biodiversity. Ecol. Econ. 132, 45–54.

Meyer, P., Schmidt, M., 2008. Aspekte der Biodiversität von Buchenwäldern – Konsequenzen für eine naturnahe Bewirtschaftung. In: Nordwestdeutsche Forstliche

Versuchsanstalt (Ed.), Ergebnisse angewandter Forschung zur Buche, Beiträge aus der Nordwestdeutschen Forstlichen Versuchsanstalt. Universitätsverlag Göttingen, Göttingen, pp. 159–192.

Mill, J.S., 1859. On liberty. J.W. Parker & Son, London.

MLFUN, 2011. Thüringer Strategie zur Erhaltung der biologischen Vielfalt. Ministerium für Landwirtschaft, Forsten, Umwelt und Naturschutz, Erfurt.

O'Hara, S.U., 1996. Discursive ethics in ecosystems valuation and environmental policy. Ecol. Econ. 16, 95–107.

Oleson, K.L.L., Barnes, M., Brander, L.M., Oliver, T.A., van Beek, I., Zafindrasil-ivonona, B., van Beukering, P., 2015. Cultural bequest values for ecosystem service flows among indigenous fishers: A discrete choice experiment validated with mixed methods. Ecol. Econ. 114, 104–116.

O'Neill, J., 2001. Representing people, representing nature, representing the world. Environ. Plan. C Gov. Policy 19, 483–500.

Pascual, U., Muradian, R., Brander, L., Gómez-Baggethun, E., Martín-López, B., Verma, M., 2010. The economics of valuing ecosystem services and biodiversity. In: Kumar, P. (Ed.), The economics of ecosystems and biodiversity: Ecological and economic foundations. Routledge, London; New York, pp. 183–256.

Pascual, U., Termansen, M., Hedlund, K., Brussaard, L., Faber, J.H., Foudi, S., Lemanceau, P., Jørgensen, S.L., 2015. On the value of soil biodiversity and ecosystem services. Ecosyst. Serv. 15, 11–18.

Pelletier, D., Kraak, V., McCullum, C., Uusitalo, U., Rich, R., 1999. The shaping of collective values through deliberative democracy: An empirical study from New York's North Country. Policy Sci. 32, 103–131.

Peterson, G.D., Cumming, G.S., Carpenter, S.R., 2003. Scenario planning: A tool for conservation in an uncertain world. Conserv. Biol. 17, 358–366.

Plieninger, T., Dijks, S., Oteros-Rozas, E., Bieling, C., 2013. Assessing, mapping, and quantifying cultural ecosystem services at community level. Land Use Policy 33, 118–129.

Polak, O., Shashar, N., 2013. Economic value of biological attributes of artificial coral reefs. ICES J. Mar. Sci. 70, 904–912.

Potthast, T., 2014. The values of biodiversity: Philosophical considerations connecting theory and practice. In: Lanzerath, D., Friele, M. (Eds), Concepts and values in biodiversity. Routledge, London; New York, pp. 132–146.

Rakotonarivo, O.S., Schaafsma, M., Hockley, N., 2016. A systematic review of the reliability and validity of discrete choice experiments in valuing non-market environmental goods. J. Environ. Manage. 183, Part 1, 98–109.

Rawls, J., 1971. A theory of justice. Belknap Press of Harvard University Press, Cambridge, MA.

R Core Team, 2015. R: A language and environment for statistical computing. R Foundation for Statistical Computing, Vienna.

Reiss, J., 2013. Philosophy of economics: A contemporary introduction. Routledge, New York.

Renn, O., Webler, T., 1992. Anticipating conflicts: Public participation in managing the solid waste crisis. GAIA – Ecol. Perspect. Sci. Soc. 1, 84–94.

Sagoff, M., 1998. Aggregation and deliberation in valuing environmental public goods: A look beyond contingent pricing. Ecol. Econ. 24, 213–230.

Samuelson, P.A., 1954. The pure theory of public expenditure. Rev. Econ. Stat. 36, 387–389.

Sandorf, E.D., Aanesen, M., Navrud, S., 2016. Valuing unfamiliar and complex environmental goods: A comparison of valuation workshops and internet panel surveys with videos. Ecol. Econ. 129, 50–61.

Scarpa, R., Gilbride, T.J., Campbell, D., Hensher, D.A., 2009. Modelling attribute non-attendance in choice experiments for rural landscape valuation. Eur. Rev. Agric. Econ. 36, 151–174.

Schläpfer, F., 2016. Democratic valuation (DV): Using majority voting principles to value public services. Ecol. Econ. 122, 36–42.

Scholte, S.S.K., van Teeffelen, A.J.A., Verburg, P.H., 2015. Integrating socio-cultural perspectives into ecosystem service valuation: A review of concepts and methods. Ecol. Econ. 114, 67–78.

Scholtes, F., 2007. Umweltherrschaft und Freiheit: Naturbewertung im Anschluss an Amartya K. Sen, Edition panta rei. transcript-Verl, Bielefeld.

Scholtes, F., 2010. Whose sustainability? Environmental domination and Sen's capability approach. Oxf. Dev. Stud. 38, 289–307.

Sen, A., 1977. Rational fools: A critique of the behavioural foundations of economic theory. Philos. Public Aff. 6, 317–344.

Sen, A., 2010. The idea of justice. Penguin, London.

Shogren, J.F., List, J.A., Hayes, D.J., 2000. Preference learning in consecutive experimental auctions. Am. J. Agric. Econ. 82, 1016–1021.

Smith, G., 2005. Beyond the ballot: 57 democratic innovations from around the world. Power Inquiry, London.

Smith, G., Wales, C., 2000. Citizens' juries and deliberative democracy. Polit. Stud. 48, 51–65.

Spake, R., Ezard, T.H.G., Martin, P.A., Newton, A.C., Doncaster, C.P., 2015. A meta-analysis of functional group responses to forest recovery outside of the tropics. Conserv. Biol. 29, 1695–1703.

Spash, C.L., Urama, K., Burton, R., Kenyon, W., Shannon, P., Hill, G., 2009. Motives behind willingness to pay for improving biodiversity in a water ecosystem: Economics, ethics and social psychology. Ecol. Econ. 68, 955–964.

Stern, P.C., Feinberg, H.V., Ahearne, J., Burke, T., Chess, C., Davis, B., Defur, P., Harris, J., Harwell, M., Jasanoff, S.S., Lamb, J., North, D.W., Shrader-Frechette, K., Slovic, P., Small, M., Vaughan, E., Wilson, J., Zeise, L., Connick, S., Webler, T., Thomas, M.E., 1996. Understanding risk: Informing decisions in a democratic society. National Academy Press, Washington, DC.

Stewart, D.W., Shamdasani, P.N., 1990. Focus groups: Theory and practice. Sage Publications, Newbury Park.

Stikvoort, B., Lindahl, T., Daw, T.M., 2016. Thou shalt not sell nature: How taboo trade-offs can make us act pro-environmentally, to clear our conscience. Ecol. Econ. 129, 252–259.

Stirling, A., 2007. A general framework for analysing diversity in science, technology and society. J. R. Soc. Interface 4, 707–719.

Succow, M., Sperber, G., 2012. Urwälder in Thüringen. NABU und BUND.

Sugden, R., 2005. Anomalies and stated preference techniques: A framework for a discussion of coping strategies. Environ. Resour. Econ. 32, 1–12.

Sutmöller, J., Spellmann, H., Fiebiger, C., Albert, M., 2008. Der Klimawandel und seine Auswirkungen auf die Buchenwälder in Deutschland. In: Nordwestdeutsche Forstliche Versuchsanstalt (Ed.), Ergebnisse Angewandter Forschung Zur Buche, Beiträge Aus Der Nordwestdeutschen Forstlichen Versuchsanstalt. Universitätsverlag Göttingen, Göttingen, pp. 135–158.

Szabó, Z., 2011. Reducing protest responses by deliberative monetary valuation: Improving the validity of biodiversity valuation. Ecol. Econ. 72, 37–44.

Tagliafierro, C., Boeri, M., Longo, A., Hutchinson, W.G., 2016. Stated preference methods and landscape ecology indicators: An example of transdisciplinarity in landscape economic valuation. Ecol. Econ. 127, 11–22.

Temper, L., Martínez-Alier, J., 2013. The god of the mountain and Godavarman: Net Present Value, indigenous territorial rights and sacredness in a bauxite mining conflict in India. Ecol. Econ. 96, 79–87.

Thompson, I., Mackey, B., McNulty, S., Mosseler, A., 2009. Forest resilience, biodiversity, and climate change: A synthesis of the biodiversity/resilience/stability relationship in forest ecosystems (No. 43), CBD Technical Series. Secretariat of the Convention on Biological Diversity, Montreal.

TMLNU, 2003. Bericht zur Überprüfung des UNESCO-Biosphärenreservates 'Vessertal – Thüringer Wald'. Thüringer Ministerium für Landwirtschaft, Naturschutz und Umwelt, Erfurt.

Torres, C., Faccioli, M., Riera Font, A., 2017. Waiting or acting now? The effect on willingness-to-pay of delivering inherent uncertainty information in choice experiments. Ecol. Econ. 131, 231–240.

Train, K., 2009. Discrete choice methods with simulation, 2nd edn. Cambridge University Press, Cambridge; New York.

Treß, J., Erdtmann, J., 2006. Rahmenkonzept zur Entwicklung und zum Schutz des Biosphärenreservats Vessertal-Thüringer Wald. Verwaltung Biosphärenreservat Vessertal-Thüringer Wald, Schmiedefeld a. R.

UEBT, 2013. Biodiversity Barometer 2013.

UNEP-WCMC, 2015. Experimental Biodiversity Accounting as a component of the System of Environmental-Economic Accounting Experimental Ecosystem Accounting (SEEA-EEA) (Supporting document to Advancing the SEEA Experimental Ecosystem Accounting project). United Nations, New York.

van den Bergh, J.C.J.M., Botzen, W.J.W., 2015. Monetary valuation of the social cost of CO2 emissions: A critical survey. Ecol. Econ. 114, 33–46.

van Zanten, B.T., Koetse, M.J., Verburg, P.H., 2016. Economic valuation at all cost? The role of the price attribute in a landscape preference study. Ecosyst. Serv. 22B, 289–296.

Vatn, A., 2004. Environmental valuation and rationality. Land Econ. 80, 1–18.

Voigt, A., Wurster, D., 2015. Does diversity matter? The experience of urban nature's diversity: Case study and cultural concept. Ecosyst. Serv. 12, 200–208.

Völker, M., Lienhoop, N., 2016. Exploring group dynamics in deliberative choice experiments. Ecol. Econ. 123, 57–67.

Wilson, M.A., Howarth, R.B., 2002. Discourse-based valuation of ecosystem services: Establishing fair outcomes through group deliberation. Ecol. Econ. 41, 431–443.

6   A look back and a look ahead

Economic Valuation of Biodiversity: An Interdisciplinary Conceptual Perspective. This has been both the book's title and its programme. The idea was not to fill a vacuum: there already exists much literature on the value of biodiversity, from ecological, ethical and economic perspectives. The rationale from the beginning was, above all, to sort, filter and unify the dispersed arguments about biodiversity's economic value, and combine them in a unifying conceptual framework for the economic valuation of biodiversity. Such a framework is an essential basis for future biodiversity valuation studies if they are to provide meaningful information about how biodiversity is valued in comparison to other environmental and non-environmental goods.

We started the journey towards the conceptual framework in Chapter 2, where the welfare theoretic foundations of economic valuation were presented, so as to clarify what economic valuation is about. The common valuation frameworks of ecosystem services (ESS) and total economic value (TEV) were also presented there, because the conceptual framework could hardly be developed in complete detachment from these highly influential concepts; last but not least, common valuation methods were presented with a brief overview of their relative strengths and weaknesses, as preparation for the development of biodiversity-specific methodological recommendations further on.

The basis of every conceptual framework is definitional: what are the objects of interest? In the case of biodiversity, there exists a large number of competing definitions, which often focus on different aspects of it. Chapter 3 illuminated this and offered a comprehensive account of different attempts to define and measure biodiversity. On this basis, a biodiversity definition underlying the present thesis could be then formulated in Chapter 5. The next question regarding the *ecological* concept of biodiversity was its function within ecosystems, its *ecological* value in a manner of speaking. As it turned out, it mainly stems from biodiversity's influence on ecosystem functioning, particularly via a mechanism called *functional redundancy*. Building upon this, central arguments regarding biodiversity's *economic* value could then be developed in Chapter 5.

But Chapter 3 stayed within the confines of ecology in the attempt to clarify what biodiversity is and why it *may* be valuable. To make the perspective broader, we made an Excursus to briefly introduce the environmental ethics perspective. The focus there was on two issues: the ethical basis of economic valuation and the question of whether biodiversity can have value on its own (in economic terms: *existence value*). The clear verdict on the latter was: it cannot.

Chapter 4 amounted to a critical survey of existing literature on the economic value of biodiversity. In its first part, we focused on the empirics: a review of existing biodiversity valuation studies. It showed that the problem with existing valuation studies is that they use very diverging and often flawed approaches to approximate the complex valuation object biodiversity; in most cases, they do not capture the economic value of biodiversity, but rather either only the value of some of its components or, even worse, of other things, such as habitats or particular species. Also, due to very different approaches, the results of these studies are hardly consistent and comparable with each other. This reinforced the initially stated rationale for developing a consistent, unifying conceptual framework for the economic valuation of biodiversity. In the second part of Chapter 4, we focused on conceptual works on the economic value of biodiversity. It turned out that there exists much interesting literature on that, but the relevant literature strands are only limitedly related to each other. Particularly influential were the Noah's Ark literature and the related 'biodiversity as portfolio' perspective. In any case, uncertainty seems key in the economic perspective on biodiversity, so that was an important aspect of Chapter 4 in preparation of the conceptual framework.

As already indicated by the frequent reference to it, the central part of the book was Chapter 5. In this chapter, all the threads from previous chapters were combined so as to develop a consistent, unifying conceptual framework for the economic valuation of biodiversity. The aim was to close the research gap identified in the Introduction and reinforced in Chapter 4, which results from the observation that 'there is certainly not yet an established framework for valuing biological variety' (Nijkamp et al., 2008, p. 218). Of course, only time will tell whether the conceptual framework developed here will become *established*. However, the present book did accomplish the following necessary (even if not sufficient) conditions for closing the gap:

1   Based on an extensive analysis of the relevant literature, an understanding of biodiversity was offered that is (i) precise, thus not stretching the term beyond its definition, as is often done in both public and scientific discussions; (ii) encompassing, i.e. not restricted to one or a handful of specific biodiversity dimensions (such as, e.g., species diversity or functional diversity); and (iii) as objective as possible, thus minimising the extent of the 'moral' in the 'epistemic-moral hybrid' (Potthast, 2014). On the basis of this definition, the reasons why biodiversity is valuable and how it contributes to human well-being could be analysed. The definition finally arrived upon framed biodiversity as the (i) variety, (ii) balance and (iii) dissimilarity of kinds in biotic or biota-encompassing categories. The definition already implicitly stresses the multidimensionality of biodiversity, which is crucial to take into account when conceptualising its economic value.

2   A taxonomy of the sources of biodiversity's economic value was proposed, which is the core of the conceptual framework. Special care was given to the (positive) task of identifying all relevant categories of biodiversity value and excluding value categories which are sometimes ascribed to biodiversity but which are not applicable to it (negative task). This taxonomy of values has a firm basis in ecological, economic and ethical literatures and can inform future biodiversity valuation studies. The portfolio metaphor discussed in Chapter 4 allows distinguishing between two main components of biodiversity's economic value, which are both heavily tied to the uncertainty that surrounds the future of human and eco-systems: these are *natural insurance* and *pool of options*. While insurance value can be seen as a response to uncertainty regarding the ecosystem's future capacity to provide known/ expected goods and services (as well as utility derived directly from the ecosystem's very existence), option value is a response to uncertainty regarding the unknown future needs and preferences towards elements of an ecosystem. For the former, risk and ambiguity are relevant concepts, while for the latter ambiguity and ignorance are more applicable. The two, it was argued in Chapter 5, are the main reasons why biodiversity is valuable. But there are two more reasons: first, when the economic value of a given ecosystem is to be demonstrated, its biodiversity can be viewed as providing (potential) *spill-overs* to other ecosystems; since biodiverse ecosystems are rich in (micro-)habitats, *multiple* migrating species can 'use' them within their migratory life cycles. The fact that multiple migrating species can be supported within a given ecosystem is a value that can be attributed to biodiversity. Of course, similarly to insurance value, which is contingent upon the ecosystem in question being *statically* valuable, spill-over value is contingent upon the migrating species supported having economic value on their own. Second, biodiversity is in a comparatively more obvious but analytically less relevant way a factor in the *aesthetic appreciation* of ecosystems and landscapes. However, it appears neither feasible nor necessary to disentangle the contribution of various factors (including biodiversity) to aesthetics. So, this category of biodiversity value is mainly of theoretical interest. Beyond those four value categories, biodiversity seems to have no further value (arguments to the contrary, especially regarding existence value, were analysed in the Excursus and in Chapter 4).

3   This framework of biodiversity's economic value was then used to draw implications for both theory and empirics. With regard to theory, it was shown that to better accommodate biodiversity and its value, the common TEV framework should be extended by more explicitly introducing the temporal and spatial dimensions of ecosystem value. Also, more tentative implications were formulated for the ESS framework, mainly by pointing out that biodiversity is linked to it in numerous ways, but is not really a part of it (especially not in its cascade-model formulation).

4   In order to investigate the compatibility of the conceptual framework with the preferences of stakeholders in a real-world context, the framework had

been subjected to a qualitative empirical test, namely, a focus group study conducted in a German Biosphere Reserve. The results of the study, while tentative because of the small sample and limited generalisability of the case, suggest that the conceptual framework contains relevant values of bio-diversity and that these can be understood by laypeople. Both insights are important for future biodiversity valuation studies. Furthermore, some additional issues were identified in the study, particularly the reluctance of participants to accept restrictive protection status as a means to increase bio-diversity levels in their area.

5   Taking a step further towards the application of the conceptual framework in valuation studies, the taxonomy of values was used to formulate meth-odological challenges that are specific to the economic valuation object biodiversity: (i) the non-market nature of components of biodiversity value; (ii) high levels of uncertainty involved in the multidimensional relationship between biodiversity and human well-being; and (iii) its abstractness and complexity. These challenges were framed as criteria for choosing the most appropriate method (mix) to be applied in economic valuation studies of biodiversity. They were used to stepwise narrow down the field of economic valuation methods until one particular (com-bination of) method(s) was identified as particularly suitable for biodiver-sity: deliberative choice experiments. This rather new approach was then discussed in more detail, with a special focus on its potential to capture the economic value of biodiversity.

6   Furthermore, to move the conceptual framework even closer to application, some (tentative) suggestions were made, on the basis of the literature included in Chapter 3, as to how to couple the conceptual framework with measurable, empirical data. This is necessary to ensure high quality, com-prehensibility and comparability of results of biodiversity valuation studies. However, in the end this task should be tackled in a context-specific, inter-disciplinary manner as cooperation between economists and ecologists.

Thus far the achievements of the book from the subjective point of view of its author. However, this positive affirmation of the book's contribution can only be properly put into perspective by identifying (potential) limitations and suggest-ing directions for future research. We now turn to these issues.

Caveats and open questions

During the process of working on the present book, the question emerged repeat-edly whether the economic valuation of biodiversity is feasible and sensible at all. As has been emphasised throughout the book, biodiversity is an extremely complex and abstract, multidimensional environmental public good. It can hardly be captured in its entirety, especially in valuation contexts, which neces-sitate a significant degree of simplification and idealisation. So, is it nonetheless a good idea to estimate the economic value of biodiversity?

To give a truly satisfactory answer to this question, one would have to provide an answer to the more fundamental question about the sensibleness (in terms of quality of information provision, influence on decision-making processes, interactions with other 'valuation languages' and lines of argument in conservation contexts etc.) of economic valuation in general.[1] However, as was pointed out in the Introduction, this is beyond the scope of the present book. Rather, a general usefulness and sensibleness of economic valuation is a premise or an assumption upon which the argument developed here is built. This, however, does not mean that the question regarding the usefulness and sensibleness of economic valuation of *biodiversity* cannot be answered at all. A partial answer can be given by comparing biodiversity (against the background of the conceptual framework developed in Chapter 5) with other, more common valuation objects. Of course, such a comparison cannot but be inherently qualitative and subjective. Nevertheless, it is important, even indispensable, if the overall quality of the argument of this book is to be assessed.

Biodiversity is a relatively 'thankless' valuation object. The demands it poses in terms of conceptualisation, operationalisation, measurement and valuation methodology are probably higher than for most other environmental public goods which usually serve as valuation objects, with the possible exception of cultural ecosystem services (see, e.g., Chan et al., 2012; Paracchini et al., 2014; Winthrop, 2014). However, I hope that this book could show that the economic valuation of biodiversity is not a hopeless task after all. The conceptual framework developed here is certainly not easy to handle in actual valuation contexts and must be developed further in this direction, but it provides a sound enough basis for valuation studies wishing to estimate the economic value of the diversity of living things. If applied properly and carefully, it should not be substantially more problematic than usual valuation approaches devoted to more 'mundane' environmental public goods.

Nonetheless, as was shown in the review of valuation studies in Chapter 4, most biodiversity valuation studies conducted to date failed to 'capture the complexity of biodiversity' (Bartkowski et al., 2015). This can be interpreted in two ways: either, the requirements posed by the valuation object biodiversity are too high and cannot be fulfilled. This, however, would seem overly pessimistic. Even though no study, not even those identified as best practice, stood up to the criteria formulated in the present book, it seems that a few failed just because of different interpretations of the valuation object (particularly Christie et al., 2006; Czajkowski et al., 2009), not because of some objective impossibility. Or, the other, more optimistic interpretation, the problem is the lack of a consistent 'framework for valuing biological variety' (Nijkamp et al., 2008). Starting from this latter interpretation, the present book's aim was to develop such a consistent framework for the economic valuation of biodiversity. As indicated in the previous section, this aim was met.

Within the conceptual framework, four sources of biodiversity's economic value were identified: it can be conceived, in line with the results of biodiversity–ecosystem functioning (BEF) research, as insurance of ecosystems; as carrier of future options; as provider of spill-overs to other ecosystems; and as a component of ecosystem aesthetics. It was argued repeatedly that the two former notions – insurance and option values – are likely the main components of the economic value of biodiversity. In fact, biodiversity's insurance value may be the most important generally. However, its very 'existence' is dependent on the findings of the BEF research – if the redundancy hypothesis in particular and the positive relationship between biodiversity levels and ecosystem functioning in general are wrong, then biodiversity has no insurance value. Against this background, it is important to keep in mind that while these relationships are a consensus position within the ecological research community (see Cardinale et al., 2012; Isbell et al., 2015; Jax, 2010), they are not entirely uncontroversial and uncontested (see Chapter 3). However, criticism mostly targets the generalisability of the findings accumulated to date; at least in some cases, for specific ecosystems or settings, the BEF relationship can be taken as certain (as far as certainty in scientific matters goes). In fact, it can be argued that this only means that there is a need for interdisciplinary research – the economic valuation of biodiversity in any given ecosystem has to be informed by ecological research about this very ecosystem (or at least this specific ecosystem type). Furthermore, this shows the need for valuation approaches that allow for handling uncertainty in key parameters – a criterion that was used in Chapter 5 to identify methods that are particularly well-suited for the economic valuation of biodiversity.

On the basis of conceptual arguments, partly inspired by the relevant literature on environmental ethics, two possible and often-discussed value categories were discarded as incompatible with biodiversity: existence value and dis-value (Excursus and Chapter 4). As was shown later on, most parts of the conceptual framework find at least tentative support in empirical studies which aimed at identifying the reasons why people think biodiversity is valuable. The qualitative focus groups case study conducted specifically for this purpose also provides support for the conceptual framework. This is important because economic valuation is inherently preference-oriented, which means that, at the end of the day, it is the preferences of stakeholders which count. Conceptual frameworks such as the one developed here can only help clarify and structure the relevant arguments. This means, however, that there are some problems to be handled, as the correspondence between the value categories of the conceptual framework and what was found, especially, by Bakhtiari et al. (2014) and within the author's own case study is not perfect. One has to differentiate here: that laypeople seem to understand biodiversity more broadly, for instance by combining it with such concepts as wilderness or naturalness, is relatively less problematic. The separation of these concepts can be achieved, for example, by properly introducing stakeholders to the problem at stake and by including distinct attributes for each concept. A bigger problem, already touched upon in the previous chapter, is the finding that at least some people seem to assign existence value to biodiversity. Alas, there appears to be no simple solution to this problem. It may well be insoluble. The question is then: how severe is it? It is a matter of subjective judgement, but it could be proposed that this is a problem that can be ignored to a large extent. First, the decision to adopt a preference-oriented perspective means that one accepts the risk of including inconsistent and 'irrational' preferences. Deliberation can help to reduce particularly obvious instances of these and identify those which cannot be reduced, but the general problem is paramount to economic valuation. Second, it was argued here that preferences for changes in biodiversity should be elicited by means of discrete choice experiments, where the researcher has the opportunity to specify quite clearly which attributes are relevant for her purposes and which are not. Thus, while the consideration of biodiversity's existence value cannot be avoided altogether, its influence on people's choices can be significantly reduced by the choice of suitable biodiversity attributes.

This leads us to another important message of the present book, namely that the conceptual framework can be best applied in deliberative choice experiments. This, again, is to some extent a matter of subjective judgement – favouring this particular method is the result of a decision regarding which criteria are relevant.[2] Others come to different conclusions. For instance, Farnsworth et al. (2015) reject the application of stated preference methods in biodiversity valuation because of a general scepticism towards their supposedly 'unscientific' subjective nature. Indeed, this method class is controversial – it has many advantages, but it also has serious downsides, which were discussed in Chapter 5. Many arguments developed in this book are based on the contention that the advantages dominate, at least if stated preference methods are applied with care and if their results are not misinterpreted. For instance, because they provide a number, they are often seen as precise, which is wrong – a brief look at a few typical stated-preference-based valuation studies reveals that they only offer an idea about orders of magnitude, while the specific numbers depend highly on statistical approaches, experimental design or sampling. Furthermore, people's preferences are often not precise themselves. All this has to be kept in mind when stated preference methods are applied. If it is kept in mind, however, they can be very useful. Another issue consists in the fact that the particular interpretation of the uncertainty that underlies much of biodiversity's economic value could be challenged – in formal treatments, it is often assumed that option value and insurance value can be coupled with known probability distributions, which was doubted here. But if they can, the case for applying stated preference methods gets weaker. Similarly, the question whether people need deliberative settings to form preferences for biodiversity and whether deliberation is actually helpful, cannot be answered with authority, as these are questions that are very difficult to test empirically (for some results, see Christie et al., 2006; Lienhoop and Völker, 2016; MacMillan et al., 2006).

A related question also concerns the methodological part of the present book. When deliberative monetary valuation (DMV) was introduced as being particularly well-suited for the economic valuation of biodiversity, the focus was on 'cognitive' issues such as dynamic preference formation. However, this 'preference economisation' (Lo and Spash, 2013) is only one side of the DMV coin, the other being 'preference moralisation', which means the attempts to make economic valuation more 'democratic'[3] and less driven by the 'consumer perspective' than conventional approaches. In the context of biodiversity the argument was made that economic valuation should be understood as an 'expressive device' (Meinard and Grill, 2011, p. 1709). There remain, however, open questions, such as what is the status, in the biodiversity context and generally, of ideas such as *social values* (Hansjürgens et al., 2017; Kenter, 2016; Kenter et al., 2015). These are important issues deserving further investigation.

The empirical case study presented in Chapter 5 had the aim, among others, to assess whether the conceptual framework developed in this book is applicable in actual valuation settings. The qualitative results suggest that it is – participants in the focus groups seemed to be capable of understanding the laypeople-friendly version of the conceptual framework that they were confronted with. Also, the investigation showed that the value categories are both meeting the views of the stakeholders regarding biodiversity value, and that they are considered relevant in this particular setting. Nonetheless, to fully demonstrate the practical value of the conceptual framework one would have to apply it in a fully fledged valuation study. Its applicability remains a hypothesis to be tested. For this, the main tenets of the overall argument developed in the present book would have to be taken up and developed further where necessary. This book provides a conceptual framework with a proposal for its translation to laypeople's terms, an informed recommendation regarding the valuation approach to be used and some more tentative suggestions regarding the coupling with quantitative data (in addition to the overall recommendation, mentioned above in the discussion, to conceive of a biodiversity valuation study as an interdisciplinary project, where ideas and information from economics and ecology have to be combined). Application of these ideas is still needed.

In addition to the above-mentioned caveats regarding the interpretation of the results of this book, there remain a number of questions left open by the present thesis, the answers to which, however, are beyond its scope. For one, there is the question of practical relevance: economic valuation does not happen in a 'political vacuum', its ultimate goal is to inform decision-making processes at various levels of societal organisation. What would be the added value of demonstrating the economic value of biodiversity in a given ecosystem from a political perspective? Does it go beyond the general added value of more precise and detailed information on economic values of ecosystems? Other than strengthening the case for sustainable use of natural systems by adding a further argument in its favour, would knowledge of the economic value of biodiversity change anything? One possible suggestion of relevance is that conceptual contributions such as the present book's can influence the definition of standards formulated by public agencies, such as, for example, the *Methodenkonvention* of the German Federal Environment Agency (Umweltbundesamt), in which standard economic values (or 'standard cost units') for different environmental goods and services are identified to be used in cost–benefit analyses of environmentally relevant projects and in policy appraisal (Förster et al., 2017). Furthermore, the case study discussed in Chapter 5 offered at least some tentative suggestions regarding policy-relevant questions, in that it showed that stakeholders might reject the trade-off, implicit for example in the German idea of national parks, between biodiversity protection and the use of ecosystems. They accepted that biodiversity is valuable and embraced its protection, but they also expressed serious doubts that it is necessary, sensible or justified to completely set aside areas to achieve that goal. This is an avenue that should be pursued further – in fact, there already exist economic valuation studies suggesting that it is not only the policy goal itself that is relevant to stakeholders, but also the way by which it is achieved (e.g. Czajkowski et al., 2009). Also, outside of economics, there are a number of arguments in favour of sustainable use and community-based conservation as an alternative to the 'traditional' mode of setting areas aside (e.g. Stoll-Kleemann et al., 2010). But the 'mode' of conservation can also be understood at a lower level of abstraction and be directly linked to biodiversity: for instance, when targeting option value, is it necessary to conserve biodiversity *in situ* or are *ex situ* approaches such as gene banks sufficient? In other words, is it 'a difference whether genetic diversity is preserved in a genetic library or within its natural or human influenced habitats' (Jax and Heink, 2015, p. 203)? These are highly relevant questions that the present book cannot answer. But it offers some hints as to which particular issues deserve more research attention.

Even if we leave aside the question of *in situ* vs *ex situ* and focus on biodiversity in natural and semi-natural ecosystems, there is the question of how the conceptual framework developed here applies to other ecosystems. It was developed mainly with terrestrial ecosystems in mind and should also be applicable to agricultural and urban ecosystems, as it does not depend on 'naturalness' (cf. Box E.1). Of course, in non-natural ecosystems the relative importance of different value categories should be expected to be different – for instance, in agricultural ecosystems the option value of biodiversity is likely rather low (quite in contrast to the option value of natural biodiversity *for* agriculture), while in urban ecosystems stability (insurance value) is less central, since their importance to human well-being is mostly restricted to recreational and aesthetic factors (although ecosystem services such as micro-climate regulation, provision of clean air and, increasingly, food provision,[4] also play a role and are 'insurable'). It would be particularly interesting to investigate the applicability of the conceptual framework to aquatic ecosystems – both marine and fresh-water. The argument that biodiversity provides economic insurance was made in marine contexts (Fung et al., 2015) and there is no obvious reason to expect that aquatic ecosystems are not potential providers of future options; also, migratory life cycles, which are the basis of the spill-over value of biodiversity, are quite common in marine and fresh-water ecosystems. Aesthetics seems less important because most marine ecosystems are not seen regularly by anyone, but even here, biodiversity can be valuable in coastal areas (Polak and Shashar, 2013). However, these arguments are only based on plausibility considerations and should be investigated more rigorously in the future. Furthermore, they only suggest that the value categories identified in the conceptual framework can be found elsewhere – it would be another question whether, for instance, aquatic biodiversity is valuable in additional ways and through other channels.

To summarise, there are quite a few questions left open (or created) by the present book. Of course, this is the quintessence of every scientific endeavour, as science is a dynamic process, leading from one question to another, to myriad others, and so on. These open questions can and should be understood as indications of future avenues of research.

Final remarks

Finally, there is no avoiding the question, 'what should I value?' if we are to see ourselves living through time, rather than in time. It is, for example, a mistake to try to justify [...] the preservation of ecological diversity solely on instrumental grounds; on the grounds that we know they are useful to us, or that they may prove useful to our descendants. Such arguments have a role, but they are not all. Nor can the argument rely on the 'welfare' of the members of such species (it does not account for the special role species preservation plays in the argument); or, indeed, on the 'rights' of animals. A full justification must base itself as well on how we see ourselves, on what kind of people we ought try to be, on what our rational desires are. In examining our values, and thus our lives, we should ask if the destruction of an entire species-habitat for some immediate gratification is something we can live with comfortably.

(Dasgupta, 1998, p. 151)

Economic valuation of the environment is not a panacea for the manifold environmental problems we face. And it is not an overly precise enterprise – too much depends on knowledge limitations, psychological biases, uncertainties, imperfect methods, structural inertia in society and markets. And yet, economic valuation has a message to convey: it can illuminate what people value about the natural world, how much they value particular items compared to others and, at least in some cases, why they do so. This can then be the starting point of and support for a societal debate about how we want to interact with the natural environment.

Economic valuation of biodiversity is not different in this respect. Even if the conceptual perspective developed here will be taken up and applied in actual valuation studies, this will not by itself stop biodiversity loss. But it might inform our individual and collective choices by showing why biodiversity is valuable, how important uncertainty in general and uncertainty-reducing properties of ecosystems in particular can be, how biodiversity could be protected and which ways of protection are too costly (in a broad sense).

This book provides much of this information: it shows on an abstract level why biodiversity is valuable from an economic point of view; how its economic value can be identified in practice; and the case study offers some insights into acceptable means of biodiversity-friendly ecosystem management. Applying the conceptual framework in valuation studies would further enrich this information, especially by making it more context-specific. But the main message was already voiced: biodiversity is valuable, especially in the uncertain world we live in.

Notes

1 Regarding influence on decision-making processes, see the publications of the TEEB initiative, both its international (ten Brink, 2011; Wittmer and Gundimeda, 2012) and national stages (e.g. www.naturkapital-teeb.de/aktuelles.html). On potential conflicts between 'economic' and other arguments for/against conservation, see, for instance, Rode et al. (2015) and Eser et al. (2014).
2 This and similar remarks in the discussion should not be understood as relativist or an epistemological 'anything goes' (Feyerabend, 1999). They are meant to stress the fuzziness of boundaries in (social) science, i.e. the impossibility of differentiating in a clear-cut way between what is scientifically the 'right choice' in a given situation (e.g. when evaluation criteria are chosen) and what is not: while it is easy to include/exclude some choices, others are much more ambiguous. This is unavoidable in social science and the best coping strategy is transparency, a standard to which this book adheres.
3 Democratisation of economic valuation has been a theme for quite a few decades (Sagoff, 1988). For a more recent debate, see Schläpfer (2016), Bartkowski and Lienhoop (2017) and Meinard et al. (2017).
4 In 'Western' cities, urban gardening and similar practices, undertaken both individually and collectively, have become an important ingredient of a sustainable lifestyle.

References

Bakhtiari, F., Jacobsen, J.B., Strange, N., Helles, F., 2014. Revealing lay people's perceptions of forest biodiversity value components and their application in valuation method. Glob. Ecol. Conserv. 1, 27–42.

Bartkowski, B., Lienhoop, N., 2017. Democracy and valuation: A reply to Schläpfer (2016). Ecol. Econ. 131, 557–560.

Bartkowski, B., Lienhoop, N., Hansjürgens, B., 2015. Capturing the complexity of biodiversity: A critical review of economic valuation studies of biological diversity. Ecol. Econ. 113, 1–14.

Cardinale, B.J., Duffy, J.E., Gonzalez, A., Hooper, D.U., Perrings, C., Venail, P., Narwani, A., Mace, G.M., Tilman, D., Wardle, D.A., Kinzig, A.P., Daily, G.C., Loreau, M., Grace, J.B., Larigauderie, A., Srivastava, D.S., Naeem, S., 2012. Biodiversity loss and its impact on humanity. Nature 486, 59–67.

Chan, K.M.A., Guerry, A.D., Balvanera, P., Klain, S., Satterfield, T., Basurto, X., Bostrom, A., Chuenpagdee, R., Gould, R., Halpern, B.S., Hannahs, N., Levine, J., Norton, B., Ruckelshaus, M., Russell, R., Tam, J., Woodside, U., 2012. Where are cultural and social in ecosystem services? A framework for constructive engagement. BioScience 62, 744–756.

Christie, M., Hanley, N., Warren, J., Murphy, K., Wright, R., Hyde, T., 2006. Valuing the diversity of biodiversity. Ecol. Econ. 58, 304–317.

Czajkowski, M., Buszko-Briggs, M., Hanley, N., 2009. Valuing changes in forest biodiversity. Ecol. Econ. 68, 2910–2917.

Dasgupta, P., 1998. Population, consumption and resources: Ethical issues. Ecol. Econ. 24, 139–152.

Eser, U., Neureuther, A.-K., Seyfang, H., Müller, A., 2014. Prudence, justice and the good life: a typology of ethical reasoning in selected European national biodiversity strategies. Bundesamt für Naturschutz, Bonn.

Farnsworth, K.D., Adenuga, A.H., de Groot, R.S., 2015. The complexity of biodiversity: A biological perspective on economic valuation. Ecol. Econ. 120, 350–354.

Feyerabend, P., 1999. Theses on anarchism. In: Motterlini, M. (Ed.), For and against Method: Including Lakatos's Lectures on Scientific Method and the Lakatos-Feyerabend Correspondence. University of Chicago Press, Chicago, pp. 113–119.

Förster, J., Schmidt, S., Bartkowski, B., Lienhoop, N., Albert, C., Wittmer, H., 2017. Schätzung der Umweltkosten infolge Schädigung oder Zerstörung von Ökosystemen und Biodiversitätsverlust, Methodenkonvention 3.0: Weiterentwicklung und Erweiterung der Methodenkonvention zur Schätzung von Umweltkosten. Umweltbundesamt, Dessau.

Fung, T., Farnsworth, K.D., Reid, D.G., Rossberg, A.G., 2015. Impact of biodiversity loss on production in complex marine food webs mitigated by prey-release. Nat. Commun. 6.

Hansjürgens, B., Schröter-Schlaack, C., Berghöfer, A., Lienhoop, N., 2017. Justifying social values of nature: Economic reasoning beyond self-interested preferences. Ecosyst. Serv. 23, 9–17.

Isbell, F., Craven, D., Connolly, J., Loreau, M., Schmid, B., Beierkuhnlein, C., Bezemer, T.M., Bonin, C., Bruelheide, H., de Luca, E., Ebeling, A., Griffin, J.N., Guo, Q., Hautier, Y., Hector, A., Jentsch, A., Kreyling, J., Lanta, V., Manning, P., Meyer, S.T., Mori, A.S., Naeem, S., Niklaus, P.A., Polley, H.W., Reich, P.B., Roscher, C., Seabloom, E.W., Smith, M.D., Thakur, M.P., Tilman, D., Tracy, B.F., van der Putten, W.H., van Ruijven, J., Weigelt, A., Weisser, W.W., Wilsey, B., Eisenhauer, N., 2015. Biodiversity increases the resistance of ecosystem productivity to climate extremes. Nature 526, 574–577.

Jax, K., 2010. Ecosystem functioning. Cambridge University Press, Cambridge; New York.

Jax, K., Heink, U., 2015. Searching for the place of biodiversity in the ecosystem services discourse. Biol. Conserv. 191, 198–205.

Kenter, J.O., 2016. Editorial: Shared, plural and cultural values. Ecosyst. Serv.

Kenter, J.O., O'Brien, L., Hockley, N., Ravenscroft, N., Fazey, I., Irvine, K.N., Reed, M.S., Christie, M., Brady, E., Bryce, R., Church, A., Cooper, N., Davies, A., Evely, A., Everard, M., Fish, R., Fisher, J.A., Jobstvogt, N., Molloy, C., Orchard-Webb, J., Ranger, S., Ryan, M., Watson, V., Williams, S., 2015. What are shared and social values of ecosystems? Ecol. Econ. 111, 86–99.

Lienhoop, N., Völker, M., 2016. Preference refinement in deliberative choice experiments. Land Econ. 92, 555–557. doi:10.3368/le.92.3.555.

Lo, A.Y., Spash, C.L., 2013. Deliberative Monetary Valuation: In search of a democratic and value plural approach to environmental policy. J. Econ. Surv. 27, 768–789.

MacMillan, D.C., Hanley, N., Lienhoop, N., 2006. Contingent valuation: Environmental polling or preference engine? Ecol. Econ. 60, 299–307.

Meinard, Y., Grill, P., 2011. The economic valuation of biodiversity as an abstract good. Ecol. Econ. 70, 1707–1714.

Meinard, Y., Remy, A., Schmid, B., 2017. Measuring impartial preference for biodiversity. Ecol. Econ. 132, 45–54.

Nijkamp, P., Vindigni, G., Nunes, P.A.L.D., 2008. Economic valuation of biodiversity: A comparative study. Ecol. Econ. 67, 217–231.

Paracchini, M.L., Zulian, G., Kopperoinen, L., Maes, J., Schägner, J.P., Termansen, M., Zandersen, M., Perez-Soba, M., Scholefield, P.A., Bidoglio, G., 2014. Mapping cultural ecosystem services: A framework to assess the potential for outdoor recreation across the EU. Ecol. Indic. 45, 371–385.

Polak, O., Shashar, N., 2013. Economic value of biological attributes of artificial coral reefs. ICES J. Mar. Sci. 70, 904–912.

Potthast, T., 2014. The values of biodiversity: Philosophical considerations connecting theory and practice. In: Lanzerath, D., Friele, M. (Eds), Concepts and values in biodiversity. Routledge, London; New York, pp. 132–146.

Rode, J., Gómez-Baggethun, E., Krause, T., 2015. Motivation crowding by economic incentives in conservation policy: A review of the empirical evidence. Ecol. Econ. 117, 270–282.

Sagoff, M., 1988. The economy of the earth: Philosophy, law, and the environment. Cambridge University Press, Cambridge; New York.

Schläpfer, F., 2016. Democratic valuation (DV): Using majority voting principles to value public services. Ecol. Econ. 122, 36–42.

Stoll-Kleemann, S., De La Vega-Leinert, A.C., Schultz, L., 2010. The role of community participation in the effectiveness of UNESCO Biosphere Reserve management: Evidence and reflections from two parallel global surveys. Environ. Conserv. 37, 227–238.

ten Brink, P. (Ed.), 2011. The economics of ecosystems and biodiversity in national and international policy making. Earthscan, London; Washington, DC.

Winthrop, R.H., 2014. The strange case of cultural services: Limits of the ecosystem services paradigm. Ecol. Econ. 108, 208–214.

Wittmer, H., Gundimeda, H. (Eds), 2012. The economics of ecosystems and biodiversity in local and regional policy and management, TEEB: The economics of ecosystems and biodiversity. Earthscan, London; New York.

Index

Page numbers in *italics* denote tables, those in **bold** denote figures.

market failure *see* externalities
Marshallian welfare measures 14, 25
McShane, Katie 54, 57, 58, 59n3, 60n4
Meinard, Yves 1, 38–40, 47n4, 91, 120,
    139, 147, 149, 172, 175n3
micro-habitats *see* spill-over value
migrating species *see* spill-over value
Mill, John Stuart 140
Millennium Ecosystem Assessment
    (MEA) 1, 20–2, 38, 43, **69**, 73, 106, 113
monocultures 85, 127, 132–4
moral community *see* demarcation
    problem

National Strategy on Biological Diversity
    121, 128, 133, 154n9
nativeness *see* alien species
natural capital 17, 115, 150; critical natural
    capital (CNC) 115, 150
naturalness *see* alien species
neoclassical economics 13, 53, 149, 154n5
Nijkamp, Peter 4, 6, 82, 166, 169
Noah's Ark 7, 80, 81, 83, 87, 90, 92, 104,
    110, 166
Nominal Group Technique (NGT) 123,
    124, 128
Nunes, Paolo A.L.D. 5, 41, 65, 66, 82, 83

objectivity 57, 84, 89, 107, 148, 150, 166,
    169
option value 3, 24–6, **24**, 55, 65, 76, 81,
    85, 86, 88, 90–2, 106, 107, **107**, *109*,
    110, 112, 114–19, **116**, 127, 128, 132,
    134, 137, 138, 151–3, 154n5, 167, 170,
    171, 173

participation 121, 140
Pascual, Unai 3, 15, 16, 24–6, **24**, **26**, 28,
    82, 84, 89, 90, 93n10, 109, 115, 116
Pearce, David W. 5, 13, 17, 27, 65, 67, 69,
    69
planetary boundaries 2
pollination *see* Californian almond
    orchards
portfolio 83, 86, 88, 90, 92, 93, 102, 166,
    167
preferences: collective 3, 13, 142, 155n14,
    174; elicitation of 24, 29, 55, 59n1, 66,
    73, 75, 123, 139, 141, 142, 145–8,
    155n14, 155n20, 171; formation of 141,
    145–7, 149, 155n14, 155n16, 171; and
    motivations 13, 54, 128, 153; predefined
    139, 149
public consultation *see* participation

public goods 13, 17, 24, 25, 29, 55, 79,
    103, 142, 145, 147, 149, 168, 169

qualitative social research 7, 118, 120,
    168, 170, 172; *see also* focus groups;
    Nominal Group Technique
quasi-option value 25, 93n8

rare species *see* endangered species
Rawls, John 140
redundancy hypothesis 45, 80, 89, 108,
    170
resilience 2, 26, 75, *78*, 82, 84, 86, 91,
    93n13, 108, 115, *119*, 137
revealed preferences 13, 27, 28, 68, 87,
    106, 136, *136*, 137, 139, 142; *see also*
    hedonic pricing
risk-aversion 25, 45, 84, 89, 108–10, 115
rivet hypothesis 45, 81
Rosen, Walter 37

Schmiedefeld 123, *124*, 125, *125*, 128–33
Sen, Amartya 25, 30n1, 53, 59n2, 60n5,
    88, 93n15, 109, 140, 146, 149, 155n15
shadow prices 4, 9n4, 13, 15
Spash, Clive L. 13, 30n7, 53–5, 141, 142,
    145, 146, 149, 155n15, 171
spatial interconnections *see* spill-over
    value
species abundance 38, 42, 65, 81, 104, 138
species richness 8, 38, 40, 42–4, *65*, 74,
    78, 104, 106, 151, 152
spill-over value 23, 78, 86, 92, 93n6, 102,
    106, **107**, 108, *109*, 110–12, 115, **116**,
    127, 128, 134, 141, 151, 153, 154n6,
    167, 170, 173
spruce (*Picea abies*) 121, 127, 131, 133, 134
stakeholders 7, 8, 17, 21, 103, 104, 112,
    133, 135, 137, 141, 146, 153, 167, 170,
    172, 173; laypeople 7, 59n3, 75, 87,
    106, 107, 118–20, 122, 123, 134, 135,
    145, 150, 153, 168, 170, 172
stated preferences 13, 24, 27–9, 65, 68, 69,
    71, **71**, 73–5, 79, 87, 91, 106, 118,
    136–42, *136*, 145–51, 171; *see also*
    contingent valuation; discrete choice
    experiments
Stirling, Andy 38, 40–2, 94n16, 104, 109
strategic behaviour 145, 147
subjectivity 13, 84, 87, 89, 90, 107, 110,
    135–8, *136*, 142, 154n3
substitutability 13, 17, 40, 108, 113, 115;
    see also natural capital, critical natural
    capital

For Product Safety Concerns and Information please contact our
EU representative GPSR@taylorandfrancis.com Taylor & Francis
Verlag GmbH, Kaufingerstraße 24, 80331 München, Germany